Anita R. Brown-Graham

# Affordable Housing and North Carolina Local Governments

**UNC**
SCHOOL OF GOVERNMENT

THE UNIVERSITY
*of* NORTH CAROLINA
*at* CHAPEL HILL

*School of Government*, UNC Chapel Hill

Established in 1931, the Institute of Government provides training, advisory, and research services to public officials and others interested in the operation of state and local government in North Carolina. The Institute and the university's Master of Public Administration Program are the core activities of the School of Government at The University of North Carolina at Chapel Hill.

Each year approximately 14,000 public officials and others attend one or more of the more than 200 classes, seminars, and conferences offered by the Institute. Faculty members annually publish up to fifty books, bulletins, and other reference works related to state and local government. Each day that the General Assembly is in session, the Institute's *Daily Bulletin*, available in electronic format, reports on the day's activities for members of the legislature and others who need to follow the course of legislation. An extensive Web site (www.sog.unc.edu) provides access to publications and faculty research, course listings, program and service information, and links to other useful sites related to government.

Operating support for the School of Government's programs and activities comes from many sources, including state appropriations, local government membership dues, private contributions, publication sales, course fees, and service contracts. For more information about the School, the Institute, and the MPA program, visit the Web site or call (919) 966-5381.

Michael R. Smith, DEAN
Thomas H. Thornburg, SENIOR ASSOCIATE DEAN
Patricia A. Langelier, ASSOCIATE DEAN FOR OPERATIONS
Ann Cary Simpson, ASSOCIATE DEAN FOR DEVELOPMENT AND COMMUNICATIONS
Bradley G. Volk, ASSOCIATE DEAN FOR FINANCE AND BUSINESS TECHNOLOGY

FACULTY

Gregory S. Allison
Stephen Allred (on leave)
David N. Ammons
A. Fleming Bell, II
Maureen M. Berner
Frayda S. Bluestein
Mark F. Botts
Joan G. Brannon
Mary Maureen Brown
Anita R. Brown-Graham
Shea Riggsbee Denning
James C. Drennan
Richard D. Ducker
Robert L. Farb
Joseph S. Ferrell
Milton S. Heath Jr.
Cheryl Daniels Howell
Joseph E. Hunt
Willow S. Jacobson
Robert P. Joyce
Diane M. Juffras
David M. Lawrence
Janet Mason
Laurie L. Mesibov
Kara Millonzi
Jill D. Moore
Jonathan Q. Morgan
David W. Owens
William C. Rivenbark
John Rubin
John L. Saxon
Jessica Smith
Carl W. Stenberg III
John B. Stephens
Charles A. Szypszak
Vaughn Upshaw
A. John Vogt
Gary A. Wagner
Aimee N. Wall
W. Mark C. Weidemaier
Richard B. Whisnant
Gordon P. Whitaker

Printed in the United States of America

21 20 19 18 17  2 3 4 5 6

ISBN 1-56011-445-1

# Contents

# Foreword

Two decades ago *New York Times* reporter Jason DeParle wrote: "Experts dicker over the details, but the housing problem[s] of . . . [America] have grown so severe that they lie almost beyond the realm of controversy, with virtually everyone agreeing that the problem is vast and that near-term solutions are so expensive they are politically unimaginable."[1] Deparle was focused on the need for affordable housing nationally. This publication focuses on the same issue in North Carolina. It examines the actual and possible efforts on the part of local governments within the state to create affordable housing opportunities for low- and moderate-income residents, and it describes the laws that enable those efforts.

---

1. Jason DeParle, *A Growing Choice: Housing or Food?* N.Y. Times, Dec. 12, 1991, at A22.

# Preface

Families facing affordable housing challenges in North Carolina live in diverse circumstances requiring diverse solutions. In some fast-growing communities, teachers, firefighters, and others in young families may lack the income or savings to buy, or sometimes even to rent, a home. These families often need only one-time or short-term housing subsidies. Other lower-income households require longer-term subsidy assistance to supplement their inadequate incomes. In some localities in North Carolina, families might need a broad range of housing choices, including mobile and manufactured housing. For other families, the eradication of discrimination in the private market would make available a host of housing opportunities.

Local governments possess no inherent powers to respond to these various circumstances. Whatever powers they possess must be granted to them by the state, even when all of the funds to support the housing activity come from the federal government. And because the enabling state statutes have been enacted at different times and in response to different federal programs, local governments' authority to undertake affordable housing activities is not laid out neatly in one place. This publication identifies the most important grants of affordable housing authority the state has given to local governments, organizing them by function. This book should make it easier for local governments to determine which activities they have statutory authority to perform as they respond to the affordable housing crisis growing in many parts of the state.

Turning to factors that limit authority, the book examines those local government activities that have significant effects on housing markets and sets forth some important statutory and constitutional limitations on such activities. It also looks at the ways local governments organize themselves to engage in housing activities, and it points out particular legal issues associated with these organizational schemes.

The final chapter reports on housing conditions and needs in North Carolina as evidenced by the 2000 census, and it reports some local strategies to address those needs as documented in a 2004 survey of North Carolina local governments.

To illustrate the general principles discussed, each chapter presents a "case in point" that seeks to apply the principles to a particular housing problem as addressed by the United States Supreme Court or by a programmatic measure.

The appendixes include definitions of terms used throughout the book, a list of federal laws that have had a significant effect on the development of local government housing activity, a list of common affordable housing funding sources, and the text of certain state statutes related to affordable housing.

# Acknowledgments

Much has been written on the law of affordable housing. However, most existing publications focus on the laws and the regulations governing federal funding programs. The value of this book is its emphasis on those matters of North Carolina law and affordable housing activity not typically treated elsewhere.

I have been aided in this work by my interactions over the years with many government officials and employees. It is impossible to pay adequate tribute to all of those persons. I must, however, acknowledge a few specific contributions. First, I am indebted to the hundreds of public servants who responded to the School of Government's survey on community development in 2004. Those responses shaped the topics covered in this book. Second, I must acknowledge the North Carolina Housing Finance Agency (NCHFA) for so freely sharing its research on housing conditions and needs in the state. Much of that data, and the benefit of NCHFA's analyses, have made it into this book. In addition, Mark Shelburne, counsel and policy coordinator at NCHFA, reviewed the entire book and provided valuable feedback. Third, a group of affordable housing practitioners willingly agreed to serve as an advisory committee on this effort. The committee provided invaluable feedback to the survey instrument, and some of the members reviewed drafts of chapters of this book. The members of the committee were Cathy Alston-Kearny, executive director, Warren Family Institute, Inc.; Mark Dorosin, interim director, University of North Carolina at Chapel Hill School of Law Community Development Clinic; David Harris, president, RSM Harris and Associates; M. Todd Hefner, community development director, City of Hickory; Bill McNeil, former director of the Division of Community Assistance, North Carolina Department of Commerce; Bill Rowe, general counsel, the North Carolina Justice Center; and Andrew Scott, director of housing and community development, City of Greensboro.

Others contributed to the substance of this effort, including many past and present colleagues at the School of Government who are experts in related areas. I have relied on the works of Frayda Bluestein, Joan Brannon, Phillip Green Jr., Kurt Jenne, David Lawrence, Ben Loeb, and David Owens to complete this book. I have also relied on the work of able research assistants, including Chloe Brooke, Hunter Schofield, Emily Williamson, and Alan Windsor.

Notwithstanding the many sources of support, errors in this book are solely the fault of the author. I welcome any feedback about the book's scope, organization, and content. I can be contacted by mail at the School of Government, CB# 3330 Knapp-Sanders Building, The University of North Carolina at Chapel Hill, Chapel Hill, NC 27599-3330; or by e-mail at brgraham@sog.unc.edu.

# 1 | Local Governments' Authority to Engage in Affordable Housing Activities

## The Emergence of Affordable Housing as a Local Function

Housing is a complicated concept that is best described in terms of a collection of attributes that come bundled together. These attributes include a physical structure, neighbors and neighborhoods, accessibility to work and other amenities, private and public rights, income, and investment opportunities. Although housing prices, household incomes, and household preferences are major determinants of housing allocation, housing experts recognize that the actual distribution of households is also influenced largely by the behaviors of housing market participants, including builders and developers, real estate agents, and financial institutions, each imposing its own political, institutional, and cultural framework and interests on the others.

While these private-market institutions and procedures are usually sufficient for the allocation of households that can afford market prices, public sector interventions must either regulate or complement them in order to assist those whose incomes are inadequate or who may be subject to discriminatory treatment. These interventions might include creative financing, waivers of land use or other regulatory requirements to reduce costs, construction of smaller "starter" homes, financial allowances from public sources, and vigorous enforcement of antidiscrimination laws.

## Evolution of Public Sector Housing Activity

In the United States housing has been viewed historically as a function solely for the private sector.[1] Thus, local governments in North Carolina and, indeed, throughout the country, have had relatively little history with housing programs. Not until the economic and social disturbances of the Great Depression did the federal government intervene to provide resources that strengthened and facilitated the private sector's efforts to make housing opportunities available to those otherwise unable to afford housing. Although the debates regarding government intervention in the private markets were bitter, America finally rallied around housing as a legitimate government function in order to confront two uncomfortable phenomena: the unprecedented numbers of families losing their homes and a housing industry in a serious slump.

The rally resulted in passage of the National Industrial Recovery Act of 1933 (NIRA) and the National Housing Act of 1934. The NIRA provided for both federal and local development, ownership, and operation of public housing. The National Housing Act of 1934 established the Federal Housing Administration, which would provide insurance for private residential mortgages, and created a secondary market for mortgages through various national mortgage associations.[2]

While Congress and the federal executive branch of government may have finally reached consensus on the appropriate role for the federal government in the housing market, the courts did not concur. Almost immediately after Congress passed the NIRA, the courts began to strike down the authorization for federal public housing activity on the ground that some of the activities exceeded the power of the federal government. The courts were particularly troubled by the federal government's role in condemning local property in order to build federally owned and operated public housing. In the courts' view, that activity did not further a legitimate federal purpose.[3]

Congress responded by passing the United States Housing Act of 1937, which authorized the federal government to enter into partnerships with state and local governments to create "low rent" housing for poor families. In drafting the act, Congress was very careful to craft the federal role in public housing primarily as a funder.[4] While the initiative for publicly sponsored affordable housing remained federal, the delivery mechanisms became local. Similarly, the Housing Act of 1949, which sought to provide a decent home for every American,[5] had a decidedly local delivery system.

Appendix 2 provides a list of significant federal legislation that has spurred the expansion of local housing functions.

## The North Carolina Response to the Changing Public Sector Role

Wanting to encourage localities to take advantage of federal funding, the North Carolina General Assembly historically has responded to federal housing programs by providing the legislation that would enable local governments to participate.[6] These responsive state statutes are actually more significant to North Carolina local governments than the federal laws creating the funding programs. Since local governments have no inherent powers, without a grant of state authority they could not participate in a federally funded program. To do so would subject them to a charge of ultra vires activity—activity that exceeds the scope of the powers delegated by the state.[7] Local governments in North Carolina may exert only those powers that are either expressly granted by the state or implied. Implied powers are those that are "additional and supplementary" and "reasonably necessary or expedient" to carry out an expressly delegated authority.[8]

The enabling statutes granting housing powers were enacted at different times and in response to different federal housing programs, so a local government's expressed and implied authority to undertake affordable housing activities is not laid out neatly in one place. Despite the disarray of the statutes, they collectively provide considerable authority for local governments to undertake a wide variety of affordable housing projects.[9] The most important of these statutes is the Housing Authorities Law, set forth in Chapter 157 of the North Carolina General Statutes (hereinafter G.S.).

## Authority to Engage in Affordable Local Housing Projects

### What Local Governments Can Do

North Carolina's local governments are authorized under the Housing Authorities Law, G.S. 157-1 through -70, to engage in housing projects. The term "housing project" is defined broadly to include planning for buildings and improvements, demolition of existing structures, construction, reconstruction, alteration, and repair of the improvements and all other work connected to affordable housing.[10] The enabled affordable housing–project activities may be viewed as supply-oriented and demand-oriented. Supply-oriented programs are designed to increase the supply of housing directly, through government or government-induced (that is, subsidized) building. Demand-oriented programs indirectly increase the housing supply by providing housing assistance funds to home seekers who stimulate demand through their purchasing power.

Specific housing activities include

1. Demolition of existing unsanitary or unsafe housing
2. Direct ownership and operation of housing for low- and moderate-income persons
3. Rent subsidies to low-income persons
4. Financial assistance to low- and moderate-income persons to own or rehabilitate their homes
5. Financial assistance to public or private developers of housing for low- and moderate-income persons
6. The acquisition and disposition of property[11]
7. Displacement and relocation activity under separate authority[12]

In addition to the more direct housing-project activities, local governments are authorized to provide other related housing production assistance as they "prepare, carry out, and operate housing projects" (G.S. 157-9). Related assistance often includes improvements that must be made to the neighborhoods where the housing will be located, such as water and sewer service, open spaces, and parks.[13]

Local governments are also authorized to engage in activities that affect housing markets. They enforce comprehensive building codes and regulate land use through zoning and other measures. Such activities may significantly affect the availability and quality of affordable housing.

### The Definition of Affordable Housing under North Carolina Law

Many people are understandably confused by the term "affordable housing." The term is probably best defined as physically adequate housing that is made available to those who, without some special intervention by government or the providers of housing, could not afford to pay the rent or the mortgage that would be available ordinarily in the private marketplace.[14] While it is undeniable that with the rising costs of housing, many upper-income persons may struggle to afford the housing they desire, affordable housing programs are those that are typically targeted to persons of low and moderate income.

North Carolina law, for purposes of affordable housing programs, defines these groups as follows: Persons of "low income" are those persons in households with annual incomes, adjusted for family size, of 60 percent or less of the local area median family income as determined by the United States Department of Housing and Urban Development (HUD),[15] and persons of "moderate income" are those deemed to require assistance because of insufficient personal or family income. In determining a person's moderate-income status, a locality is authorized to consider, among other factors it deems appropriate,

1. the amount of the person's total income that is available for housing needs;
2. the size of the person's family;
3. the cost and condition of housing facilities available; and
4. the person's eligibility for federal housing assistance that is predicated on a moderate- or low-income basis.[16]

Affordable housing in Cary, North Carolina, funded, in part, by local bond funds.

Based on the fourth of these considerations a person's moderate-income status under North Carolina law may, in effect, be predetermined by federal program guidelines.[17]

The notion of affordability has its definition in federal law. It involves normative judgments about the proportion of income that a family should pay for housing and is expressed in the housing affordability standard. The standard defines affordable units as "units for which a family . . . would pay no more than 30 percent of their income for rent and no more than 2.5 times their annual income to purchase."[18] This federal standard for affordability has changed over time. In 1969, the housing affordability standard was set at 25 percent of income. It was raised to 30 percent in 1981.

*Authority to Finance Affordable Housing Projects*

Just as the General Assembly has enacted state statutes to allow local governments to receive and expend federal dollars for affordable housing projects, it has also authorized local governments to spend local dollars on such projects, including local tax revenues and funds generated through the sale of general obligation bonds. While cities have long enjoyed the authority to spend local tax dollars on affordable housing projects, counties were not so enabled in the area of affordable housing until 1999.[19] Before then, counties—except those with populations in excess of 400,000 according to the most recent census—had to seek voter approval to use local tax revenues to support housing rehabilitation activities.

In addition to their authorization to use local tax revenues, counties are authorized under G.S.159-48(c)(6) to borrow money and to issue general obligation bonds for

> [p]roviding housing projects for persons of low or moderate income, including construction

or acquisition of projects to be owned by a county, redevelopment commission, or housing authority and the provision of loans, grants, interest supplements, and other programs of financial assistance to such persons. A housing project may provide housing for persons of other than low or moderate income if at least forty percent (40%) of the units in the project are exclusively reserved for persons of low or moderate income. No rent subsidy may be paid from bond proceeds.

Cities are authorized to borrow money and issue general obligation bonds under G.S. 159-48(d)(7) for

> [p]roviding housing projects for the benefit of persons of low income, or moderate income, or low and moderate income, including without limitation (i) construction or acquisition of projects to be owned by a city, redevelopment commission or housing authority, and (ii) loans, grants, interest supplements and other programs of financial assistance to persons of low income, or moderate income, or low and moderate income, and developers of housing for persons of low income, or moderate income, or low and moderate income. A housing project may provide housing for persons of other than low or moderate income, as long as at least twenty percent (20%) of the units in the project are set aside for housing for the exclusive use of persons of low income. No rent subsidy may be paid from bond proceeds.

Many of North Carolina's local governments have used general obligation bonds to fund myriad affordable housing projects. In 2003, for example, the residents of the city of Charlotte passed a $20 million affordable housing bond to support a mixture of new construction, housing rehabilitation, special needs housing, and land acquisition for future construction of affordable units.

## Direct Ownership and Operation of Housing for Low-Income Households through Public Housing Agencies and Authorities

Public housing agencies and authorities (PHAs) are created under state law, financed under federal law, and regulated under both state and federal law.[20] Despite this tripartite funding and regulatory structure, PHAs' basic legal authority is found in the state statute enabling their formation. The state enabling legislation specifies PHAs' powers, composition, mode of operation, and limitations.

## North Carolina Delegations and Limitations of Powers

The fact that a significant majority of PHAs in North Carolina manage public housing units is not surprising. The construction and operation of subsidized public housing are the earliest form of involvement in housing by local governments in the state. In fact, until recently G.S. 157-9, which is the housing authorities law, was used primarily to build, operate, and maintain multi-family rental housing for low-income persons who were trying to get a foothold on the first rung of the economic ladder.[21] In this setting, the role of the city or county in providing assisted housing was limited to working with the PHA in approving the project for federal assistance and site location, providing the municipal services spelled out in the cooperation agreement with the PHA,[22] and providing an exemption to the PHA from local real estate taxes.[23]

In no other affordable housing program described in this book does a lower-income person enter into a landlord–tenant relationship with the government. It is important to note that public housing—with the government serving as landlord—carries unique implications. Those PHAs engaged in operating public housing units should be aware that federal housing laws, including those governing PHAs, do not always preempt state housing laws.[24] For example, in 1985 the North Carolina General Assembly passed an act establishing criminal penalties for recipients who obtain housing assistance through fraudulent misrepresentation. This housing fraud provision subjects to a criminal offense any person who (1) "willingly and knowingly and with intent to deceive makes a false statement or misrepresentation or who willfully and knowingly and with intent to deceive fails to disclose a material fact," and (2) as a result of these actions obtains or attempts to obtain housing assistance. Receipt of or an attempt to receive less than $400 worth of housing assistance fraudulently is a misdemeanor; and receipt of over $400 worth of housing assistance fraudulently is a Class I felony.[25] These penalties apply even if the federal government provides its own penalties for fraudulent conduct in connection with public housing.

On the other hand, local governments and their public housing authorities should also be aware that, under federal law, the operation of public housing may sometimes be governed by different—and more stringent—rules than those affecting private landlords, particularly those private landlords who do not accept tenants who are recipients of federal housing assistance. For example, most private landlords do not have to give rejected applicants a formal or informal hearing or even reasons for the rejection. However, public landlords (and those private landlords who participate in housing certificate or housing voucher programs)[26] must give rejected applicants these protections. Similarly, owners of government-assisted housing must take certain procedural steps before evicting tenants to ensure that the tenants' "constitutionally protected expectation" of remaining in the house is not violated.[27]

## Federal Funding and Regulations

Under its public housing program, HUD gives grants to PHAs to finance the development of public housing, including capital costs of construction, rehabilitation, or acquisition. HUD also pays operating subsidies to most PHAs to cover the shortfall between tenant rents and operating expenses.[28] For the most part, the federally constructed units are low-rent public housing projects.[29] In 2004 HUD reported that of the 128 PHAs in North Carolina, 99 managed public housing units.[30]

In order to protect the national interests of the public housing program, Congress has given HUD authority to regulate PHAs. For example, HUD may establish procedures and requirements to assure sound management practices in such areas as tenant selection criteria, rent collections, tenant evictions, and security, among others. Failure to comply with these regulations may subject PHAs to adverse action from HUD and may also be the basis for legal action by tenants.[31]

## Special Legal Issues for Public Housing Authorities

*Powers of a Public Housing Authority*

PHAs are recognized by law to be municipal corporations with all the powers of a public body.[32] This includes the power to sue and be sued, to incur indebtedness, to make and execute contracts, to issue subpoenas for witnesses and the production of documents, to conduct examinations and investigations, and to hear testimony and take proof under oath at public and private hearings on any matter material to its operation.

*Tort Liability Issues for Public Housing Authorities*

Under North Carolina law, certain municipal corporations, such as cities and counties, may not be held liable for damages in tort caused while engaged in a governmental activity unless they waive their immunity by purchasing liability insurance.[33] There is no immunity for harm caused while engaged in a proprietary act. PHAs facing legal challenges grounded in tort law should be aware that their activities are deemed to be proprietary rather than governmental.

While governmental activities are those that are "discretionary, political, legislative or public in nature and performed for the public good in behalf of the State,"[34] proprietary activities, for which there is no immunity, are "commercial or chiefly for the private advantage of the compact community . . . ."[35] Courts consistently have found public housing activities to be proprietary activities.[36] For example, the court imposed liability against a PHA in a case in which a tenant died because the housing authority failed to exercise due care in preventing a heating flue from becoming clogged by dead birds and other debris.[37] In finding housing to be a proprietary activity, the court relied on a prior case in which the court looked to the substantial rental and other benefits that localities receive for operating federal public housing.

*Application of Planning, Zoning, and Building Regulations*
All housing projects of a PHA must comply with the planning, zoning, sanitary, and building laws and the ordinances and regulations applicable in the local jurisdiction in which the housing project is situated.[38]

*Exemption from Real Estate Licensure*
The PHA and its regular salaried employees are exempt from the real estate licensure requirements of G.S. 93A-2(c)(8).[39]

*Bidding Procedures*
The legislature has exempted housing authorities from those laws regarding the acquisition, operation, and disposition of property that affect other public bodies unless the law specifically indicates its applicability. Thus under G.S. 157-9(a) housing authorities are exempt from state bidding procedures.

*Taxation*
The property acquired by a housing authority through the construction, ownership, and rental of apartments and dwellings is exempt from state, county, and municipal taxation since the property is held for a public purpose.[40]

# Dealing with Existing Unsanitary or Unsafe Housing

Dilapidated and vacant buildings can haunt neighborhoods, blighting the city landscape, lowering surrounding property values, increasing crime and the risk of fire, and posing health and safety hazards to children.[41] Sociologists James Wilson and George Kelling have described the problem of untended property as the Broken Windows Syndrome. Under their theory, one broken window left in disrepair will actually lead people to break more windows.[42] On a larger scale, local government leaders are aware that the physical breakdown in a neighborhood's appearance can indicate to both community residents and outsiders that no one is in control, thus giving free license to those engaged in destructive behavior.[43]

Given the possible risks of a local government's failure to intervene, the North Carolina General Assembly has armed local governments with a number of tools to combat the physical decay of housing and neighborhoods. This section addresses those tools that local governments most frequently use to conserve existing housing and prevent blight in neighborhoods.[44]

## Police Powers Generally

The underlying grant of authority to regulate the use of land and the condition of existing housing comes from the police powers granted to local governments. This delegation of authority grants local governments the power to, by ordinance, "define, regulate or abate . . . conditions detrimental to health, safety or welfare of citizens."[45]

Local governments often use their police powers to produce and conserve housing by exercising their authority to abate nuisances, enforce health and sanitation regulations, enforce safety regulations, regulate use and occupancy, condemn buildings and land, zone for the uses of land, and eliminate urban blight.[46] If there is a rational relationship between the regulation and a legitimate public purpose,[47] courts will not interfere with a local government's authority unless it clearly is unreasonable.[48] However, the regulation must be reasonably calculated, under existing conditions and surrounding circumstances, to accomplish a legitimate purpose without creating an undue burden.[49]

Although the courts have found police power to be an independent authority for land use regulations,[50] the General Assembly often makes more specific grants of authority through legislation. Some examples of such legislation are discussed below.

## Minimum Housing Ordinances

North Carolina local governments often use housing codes, more commonly known as minimum housing ordinances, to combat blight in existing neighborhoods. The tool allows a local government to require that a property owner rehabilitate his or her property without the benefit of any public financing.

Although the general police power itself provides a basis for enacting a local housing code, the General Assembly has limited local governments' activity in this arena. In order to enact such a code, a city or county must rely upon the authority granted by the General Assembly, which enables them to adopt "housing ordinances" that establish the minimum standards a dwelling must meet in order to be judged fit for human habitation.[51]

Under the authority granted by G.S. 160A-441, minimum housing ordinances may address issues relating to

- Structural dilapidation and defects
- General disrepair
- Lighting
- Sanitary facilities
- Fire hazards
- Ventilation
- General cleanliness

Enforcement options under the statute vary according to the classification and size of the city or county and the extent of structural disrepair of the property in question.

*History of Minimum Housing Codes*

The first housing codes in the country were enacted in the mid-nineteenth century by northeastern states, such as New York, as a response to the large concentrations of immigrant poor living within their communities.[52] Housing codes did not become commonplace, however, until they were firmly entrenched in federal policy and funding opportunities. Examples of early federal support for housing codes include the Housing Act of 1949, which established and made funding available for urban renewal, and the Housing and Development Act of 1965,[53] which stipulated that in order to be eligible for federal housing subsidies, municipalities had to adopt a "workable plan" that included rehabilitation and conservation. As a justification for requiring the enactment of codes, federal agents made clear their belief that

> [s]lums and blight are brought about by owners of property who are unable or unwilling to maintain or improve their property at decent levels, by unconscionable, profiteering landlords squeezing bootleg profit out of wretched housing, and occasionally by tenants who are indifferent to their squalid environments. But . . . the ultimate causation factor is the local government itself [that fails] to enforce effectively . . . adequate police power measures to control bad housing, improper environments and overcrowding.[54]

The Housing and Development Act of 1965 also embodied the belief that housing code enforcement could reduce blight in deteriorating neighborhoods. To this end the act authorized funding to local governments to adopt housing codes and enforcement programs.

*Scope of North Carolina Minimum Housing Codes*

As a result of federal law and funding, local standards in North Carolina are designed not only to ensure safety for specific occupants but also to encourage communities to maintain their affordable housing stock and improve their properties and neighborhoods. Illustrating this point, G.S. 160A-441 includes a finding that dwellings unfit for human habitation stand as a threat to the health and welfare of the state's residents—not just those persons occupying or in proximity to those dwellings. Based on this finding, the statute authorizes cities and counties to exercise their police powers to repair, close, or demolish any such dwellings that exist within their jurisdictions. The statute also authorizes cities to provide for the repair, closing, or demolition of abandoned structures that pose a health or safety hazard.

*Enforcement of a Minimum Standard Housing Ordinance*

G.S. 160A-441, as it authorizes local governments to adopt and enforce minimum housing ordinances, comtemplates a mechanism for enforcement. G.S. 160A-443 provides the enforcement mechanism, which includes a designated public officer and processes for serving complaints and orders.

**Initiating an Action.** Under this statute a local government's ordinance must designate a public officer who will exercise its prescribed powers. The public officer is charged with issuing and serving complaints against owners and other persons having an interest of record in a property. This action is called for when a preliminary investigation discloses some basis for a petition that has been filed by

1. a housing authority or any officer who is in charge of a department or branch of government relating to health, fire, building regulations, or other activities concerning dwellings;
2. at least five residents of the jurisdiction; or
3. the public officer on his or her own motion because it appears that the property is unfit for human habitation.

Such complaints must contain a statement of the charge that the dwelling is unfit for human habitation and a notice that a hearing will be held by the public officer or a designated agent not less than ten days nor more than thirty days after the complaint is served. The complaint must be served on the property's owners and any parties of interest, all of whom must be given the right to file an answer and give testimony at the hearing. If the public officer fails to provide an opportunity for the owners and parties of interest to be heard on the question of whether the property is fit for human habitation, any finding and resulting orders will be invalidated by the courts.[55]

**Serving Complaints.** Complaints should be served either personally or by registered or certified mail.[56] When service is made by registered or certified mail, it will be deemed sufficient if the mail is unclaimed or refused but a copy of the notice that was sent by regular mail is not returned by the post office within ten days of mailing. If service of the complaint depends on regular mail, a notice of the pending proceedings should also be posted in a conspicuous place on the property that is the subject of the proceedings.

If the identities of the owners or their whereabouts are unknown and cannot be determined by the public officer, or if the owners are known but they refuse to accept service by registered or certified mail, the public officer can swear to these facts under oath and then effectuate service through publication in a newspaper of general circulation in the area. When service is made by publication, a notice of the pending proceedings must be posted in a conspicuous place on the premises.[57] As a way of dealing with absentee property owners, several jurisdictions, including Winston-Salem, Gastonia, Durham, and Cumberland County, have sought and received special authority from the General Assembly to require nonresident owners of rental property to designate a local resident to serve as agent for receipt of notice of housing code violations.

For purposes of determining who is entitled to be heard on these issues, the statute defines owners as both the holder of title in fee simple and every mortgagee of record.[58] Parties of interest are defined as all individuals, associations, and corporations that have an interest of record in the dwelling, such as the holder of a mortgage or those in possession of the dwelling, including tenants.[59]

**Serving Orders.** If the public officer determines after the notice and hearing that the dwelling is unfit for human habitation, he or she must state in writing the findings of fact in support of that determination and serve the owner with an order. The public officer has two options for the order: The owner may be ordered to repair, alter, or improve the dwelling within a specified time frame or, if the owner is unable to make the dwelling fit for human habitation within that time frame, the building must be vacated and closed. An order to repair, alter, or improve is issued when the changes can be made at a reasonable cost in relation to the value of the property.[60] If the repair, alterations, or improvements cannot be made at a cost that represents a reasonable percentage of the value of the dwelling, the owner may be required to remove or demolish the dwelling within a specified time. However, if the building is located in a historic district and the Historic District Commission determines that the dwelling is of particular significance to maintaining the character of the historic district, the public officer cannot require that the building be removed or demolished. In this case the public officer's only option is to require that the dwelling be vacated and closed while the historic commission negotiates with the owner to find a means of preserving the building under G.S. 160A-400.1(a), which governs delays in demolitions of landmarks and buildings within historic districts.

*Minimum Housing Standards and Uncooperative Property Owners*
Too often, owners fail to comply with a public officer's initial order. At that point, the public officer may be authorized by the governing board to take additional action. Authority for such action must be set out in an ordinance specific to the particular property or properties at issue.

**Authorization for Additional Action.** If the initial order was to repair, alter, or improve the dwelling, the governing board's ordinance may authorize the public officer to take the necessary steps. The ordinance may also allow the public officer to take steps to vacate and close the dwelling. After the building has been closed, the public officer may place a placard on the dwelling that reads "This building is unfit for human habitation; the use or occupation of the building for human habitation is prohibited and unlawful." Occupation of a building after this placard has been posted is a Class 1 misdemeanor. The courts have held that the notice is valid even if there are minor variations in the wording.[61]

If the owner fails to comply with an order to remove or demolish the dwelling, the public officer may by authority of the ordinance cause the dwelling to be removed or demolished. However, G.S. 160A-443 makes clear that an ordinance authorizing removal or demolition of property may not be adopted until the owner has been given a reasonable opportunity to bring the dwelling into conformity with the housing code. An ordinance authorizing removal or demolition of a building must be recorded in the office of the register of deeds in the county where the property or properties are located and must be indexed in the name of the property owner in the grantor index.

**Converting an Order to Repair into an Order to Demolish.** A local government may find that property subject to an order to repair has deteriorated sufficiently during the owner's period of noncompliance that an order to demolish is warranted. The question that then arises is whether the local government may simply notify the owner and parties of interest that the order to repair has been converted into an order to demolish.

The case law suggests that the local government may not convert the order without first providing for a new hearing. The reasoning of the courts has been based in the different criteria for repair orders and demolition orders: A local government may issue an order to repair only after it determines that repairs can be made at a reasonable cost in relation to the value of the dwelling; and further, it may issue an order to demolish only after making an entirely different determination—namely, that the repairs cannot be made at a reasonable cost in relation to the value of the dwelling. Therefore, in a case in which a city's demolition order was issued almost three years after it had held a hearing and issued its order to repair, the court held that the owner was entitled to another hearing on the issue of demolition.[62]

*Minimum Housing Codes and the Less Than Vigilant Local Government*
Questions often arise as to whether a local government that has failed to cite violations of its housing code of which it was aware may later cite the same ongoing violation as a basis for unfavorable findings and an order.[63] The answer is usually yes. While the legal doctrine of estoppel usually operates to prevent a person from raising an issue that should have been raised earlier, it is generally recognized in North Carolina that the doctrine of estoppel will not be applied against a local government.[64] Thus local governments do not waive the right to cite violations simply because they failed to or chose not to cite them earlier.

*Minimum Housing Codes and the Overly Vigilant Local Government*
From time to time a city may seek to avoid the notice and hearing requirements of the minimum housing ordinance statute by resorting to G.S. 160A-193, which

gives authority to cities to "summarily remove, abate, or remedy everything in the city limits, or one mile thereof, that is dangerous or prejudicial to the public health or public safety." By its terms, G.S. 160A-193 may apply to buildings also subject to the provisions of G.S. 160A-443. However, G.S. 160A-193 has been interpreted by the courts as permitting summary demolition of a dwelling only in the very narrow circumstances in which the owner cannot be provided with notice and a hearing because the "building constitutes an imminent danger to the public health or safety, creating an emergency necessitating the building's immediate demolition."[65] One court noted that such emergency conditions might exist if "the building were in such a ruinous state that it was on the verge of falling onto a sidewalk frequented by pedestrians or in a situation where the destruction of the building is necessary to stop or control a large destructive fire."[66] That court was not persuaded that an emergency existed simply because the building would have been dangerous to anyone who occupied it due to a caving roof and heavy water infiltration. The building in question had been boarded up for several years, and there was no evidence that anyone had entered the property during that time.

The local government may be prohibited from demolishing a building outside of the procedures prescribed by G.S. 160A-443. However, in some jurisdictions, including the cities of Clinton, Durham, Fayetteville, Goldsboro, High Point, and Lumberton and the towns of Garner, Franklin, Hope Mills, and Spring Lake, an inspector has additional authority under G.S. 160A-425.1 to affix a notice of the dangerous character of a building to a conspicuous place on the exterior wall of the building.

*Appeals*

The governing board may provide for the creation and organization of a housing appeals board to which appeals may be taken from any decision of the public officer; or it may provide for such appeals to be heard and determined by the zoning board of adjustment. If a housing appeals board is created, it must have five members who serve for three-year staggered terms.

An appeal from a decision or order of the public officer must be made within ten days from the rendering of the decision or the service of the order. The appeals board must hear the appeal within a reasonable time. Thereafter, its decision is subject to review by a superior court. If the person aggrieved by the officer's or board's decision seeks review by the court, the court must hear the matter within twenty days and must give it preference over other matters on the court's calendar.

## Nuisance Ordinances

Many local governments rely upon their police powers to enact nuisance ordinances that prevent one person's use of their land from harming neighbors. For example, nuisance lot ordinances typically set minimum standards to prevent lots from becoming overgrown or becoming repositories for unsightly and unhealthy collections of refuse. Similarly, junk car and abandoned car ordinances limit keeping inoperable vehicles on a site.

## Urban Homesteading

North Carolina law authorizes local governments to attempt housing rehabilitation and neighborhood conservation through locally initiated homesteading programs. Properties of little or no value that the locality acquires through abandonment, tax delinquency foreclosures, dedication, gift, or purchase may be conveyed to eligible families at nominal cost.[67] The families must then commit themselves to making the major repairs and to living in the dwelling for a specified number of years. They must rehabilitate the property so that it meets or exceeds minimum code standards and maintain property insurance on the property.

Urban homesteading programs are premised on the theory that previously unattractive units can be made available to qualified owners for little or no initial cost, with the result that parcels that have not been economically viable can come back on the market simply for the cost of rehabilitation borne by the new owners. One advantage of such programs is that the city avoids the time-consuming and expensive processes of either rehabilitating the building itself or forcing the property owner to do so.

In many large cities across the country, a variety of urban homesteading programs are becoming increasingly popular tools. For example, disturbed by the significant number of tax-delinquent, distressed properties, the New York City Council enacted an ordinance in 1996 to transfer dilapidated property with outstanding bills to successful for-profit and nonprofit housing operators to correct the code violations and hazardous housing conditions for the benefit of low- and moderate-income persons.

While the laws regarding the disposition of property, which are discussed in detail beginning on page 12 of this book, authorize local governments to convey dilapidated property to nonprofits for less than fair market value, the North Carolina homesteading statute authorizes a program that is different in two respects from the type enacted in New York and elsewhere. First, the North Carolina program anticipates that the property will be given directly to the person who will use it as their principal residence rather than to a housing developer. Second, the North Carolina law does not appear to require that the program be reserved for low- or moderate-income persons, although local governments are certainly not prohibited from including income eligibility restrictions in their programs.

## Redevelopment

Rather than focusing on individual housing, local governments sometimes seek to redevelop an entire neighborhood or area. They may accomplish this objective through the state's Urban Redevelopment Law.[68] Under this law "redevelopment" is defined as the acquisition, replanning, clearance, rehabilitation, or rebuilding of an area for residential, recreational, commercial, industrial, or other purposes, including the provision of streets, utilities, parks, recreational areas, and other open spaces.

Specific redevelopment projects may include efforts to

1. acquire blighted or nonresidential redevelopment areas or portions thereof, or individual tracts in rehabilitation, conservation, and reconditioning areas, including lands, structures, or improvements, the acquisition of which is necessary or incidental to the proper clearance, development, or redevelopment of such areas or to the prevention of the spread or recurrence of conditions of blight;
2. clear any such areas by demolition or removal of existing buildings, structures, streets, utilities, or other improvements thereon, and to install, construct, or reconstruct streets, utilities, and site improvements essential to the preparation of sites for uses in accordance with the redevelopment plan;
3. sell land in such areas for residential, recreational, commercial, industrial, or other use, or for the public use, to the highest bidder as herein set out or to retain such land for public use, in accordance with the redevelopment plan;
4. carry out plans for a program of voluntary or compulsory repair, rehabilitation, or reconditioning of buildings or other improvements in such areas, including the making of loans; and
5. engage in programs of assistance and financing, including the making of loans, for rehabilitation, repair, construction, acquisition, or reconditioning of residential units and commercial and industrial facilities in a redevelopment area.[69]

Specific activities may also include preparation of a redevelopment plan; planning, surveying, and other work incidental to a redevelopment project; and the preparation of all plans and arrangements for carrying out a redevelopment project.[70]

While the scope of redevelopment projects is broad, the actual authority to carry out such projects is limited by geography and process. In order for a locality to engage in redevelopment under the statute, the target area must be designated as

1. a blighted area;
2. a nonresidential redevelopment area; or
3. a rehabilitation, conservation, and reconditioning area.

Blighted areas are either residential in character or have a predominance of buildings or improvements that, by reason of

1. dilapidation, deterioration, age, or obsolescence;
2. inadequate provision for ventilation, light, air, sanitation, or open spaces;
3. high density of population and overcrowding;
4. unsanitary or unsafe conditions;
5. the existence of conditions that endanger life or property by fire and other causes; or
6. any combination of these factors

substantially impair the sound growth of the community; are conducive to ill health, transmission of disease, infant mortality, juvenile delinquency, and crime; and are detrimental to the public health, safety, morals, or welfare.[71] Moreover, a residential area may not be considered blighted unless at least two-thirds of the number of buildings within the area are blighted, and those buildings must contribute substantially to the conditions that make the entire area blighted.

A nonresidential redevelopment area is one in which there is a predominance of buildings or improvements (that is, it cannot be predominantly vacant or agricultural land), and those buildings must, for essentially the reasons enumerated for blight,

1. substantially impair the sound growth of the community;
2. seriously and adversely affect surrounding development; and
3. pose a detriment to the public health, safety, morals, or welfare.

In a nonresidential redevelopment area, at least one-half of the number of buildings within the area must be blighted and substantially contribute to the conditions making the area a nonresidential redevelopment area.[72]

Finally, a rehabilitation, conservation, and reconditioning area is one that the planning commission finds presents a clear and present danger and that, in the absence of governmental action, will become a blighted area or a nonresidential redevelopment area.[73]

The process for determining a redevelopment area is a laborious one. First, the planning commission makes the initial finding that an area is appropriate for redevelopment. After that, the planning commission or local redevelopment commission, if one is appointed, must prepare a redevelopment plan before any action is taken. The authority of the redevelopment commission is both derived from and created by the adoption of this redevelopment plan.[74]

Next, there are a number of procedural steps required before the redevelopment plan can be finalized. The redevelopment commission must hold a public hearing before sending the plan forward for approval.[75] Then the plan should be submitted for review by the local planning commission,[76] which may approve, reject, or modify it. Within forty-five days the planning commission must certify to the redevelopment commission its recommendations on the redevelopment plan.[77]

Next the city council becomes involved. The plan must be submitted to them with any recommendations, and they must also hold a public hearing to allow public discussion of the plan. Notice of the meeting must be made in a manner designed to be understandable by the general public.[78] At the hearing the governing body must give all interested persons or agencies an opportunity to be heard, and it must receive, make known, and consider any recommendations received in writing regarding the redevelopment plan. The governing board may then approve, amend, or reject the redevelopment plan as submitted.[79]

Once the plan has been approved, areas that are blighted may not be enlarged to include areas that are not blighted. As one court put it, the legislature never intended to permit a planning commission or a redevelopment commission to include within the boundaries of a "blighted area" an area not meeting the statutory definition.[80]

If a citizen challenges the redevelopment commission's determination that an area is blighted, the court looks at the condition of the condemned property at the time the governing board approved the redevelopment plan rather than the condition of the property on the date of the filing of the condemnation complaint. For the court to do otherwise would mean that one property owner's renovation of property prior to the actual condemnation, but after the plan's approval, could thwart a redevelopment commission's extensive plans for the community.[81]

## Rehabilitation Assistance to Owners of Housing for Low- and Moderate-Income Persons

In addition to efforts to force existing owners or encourage new ones to rehabilitate substandard properties, public investment in rehabilitating older homes comprises a significant amount of affordable housing activity in North Carolina. This is done in the hope of arresting some decay and inducing the myriad private decisions that ultimately determine whether an area will be upgraded over time. As we have seen, local governments sometimes directly rehabilitate deteriorated housing by doing the work for the owner using outside contractors or the government's own work crews; or by acquiring, repairing, and disposing of the property; or by giving a grant, loan, or loan subsidy to the property owner. They may also do any of these things through a contract with the housing authority, the

redevelopment authority, or a responsible private not-for-profit organization. (See Chapter 4 for a more extensive discussion of how local governments are organized to deliver housing services.)

State authorization for local governments to conserve existing neighborhoods through rehabilitation of deteriorated housing is found in the housing authorities law, G.S. 157-9, which gives local governments significant discretion to engage in housing projects. Projects might include substantial rehabilitation of units that are in such disrepair that they are no longer considered part of the housing stock, less substantial rehabilitation to preserve housing beginning to fall into disrepair, and other light rehabilitation such as weatherization assistance.

Rehabilitation activity is also authorized under the redevelopment law (G.S. 160A-512) and under the newer community development law (G.S. 153A-376, 377; 160A-456, 457). Under each of these laws, local governments may underwrite the costs of rehabilitating both owner- and renter-occupied houses so long as the principal beneficiaries are low- and moderate-income persons. Some local governments limit their programs to owner-occupied houses, however, because the governing board finds an apparent subsidy to landlords to be politically unacceptable.

## Direct Assistance to Low- and Moderate-Income Renters and Home Owners
### Rent Subsidies to Low-Income Persons

Many public housing authorities in North Carolina administer federal rental certificate and voucher programs,[82] and under the Housing Authorities Law local governments are authorized to use local funds to provide similar rental supplements. These kinds of direct assistance are sometimes collectively referred to as housing allowances.

Housing allowances are forms of economic assistance to low-income households who require help to pay rent for a dwelling unit that meets certain minimum physical standards. The most important advantage of housing vouchers and certificates is that they give a recipient household the freedom to choose the kind of housing and the location that best meets its needs. This freedom of choice often results in less segregation of the beneficiaries of affordable housing than do other more supply-driven programs. In fact research analyzing the distribution of federal voucher recipients in the nation's fifty largest metropolitan areas concluded that virtually every census tract in these areas contained some voucher recipients.[83] That is not to say, however, that rental voucher and certificate programs are without problems. Some families who receive a voucher may not be able to find a landlord willing to accept it. This is especially true in tight housing markets.

Countywide Community Development Corporation, a nonprofit organization in Brunswick County, rehabilitates a bathroom. *Left*, before; *right*, after.

There are some limits on local governments' authority to fund rental payments in the form of two important exceptions imposed by North Carolina state law. First, if the local government is the owner or operator of a housing project that includes units for persons of other than low or moderate income, no rent subsidy may be provided to any tenant who is not a person of low income and no rent subsidy may be paid from bond proceeds. The operating expense of that project must be met entirely from rents for the project together with any rent subsidies provided to low-income tenants in the project.[84]

Second, while they may fund housing allowances, local governments may not rely on the Housing Authorities Law as a basis for making income payments. A housing allowance is solely a remedy for a rent gap. While it can be paid either directly to the landlord or to the program participant, it should be directed to shelter affordability gaps rather than more general income deficits.

### Mortgage Assistance to Persons of Low and Moderate Income

Home ownership has long been a cherished part of the American housing ideal. Local governments often seek to facilitate residents' access to this ideal by providing down payment assistance or second mortgages. Some local governments, such as Cary, reserve these programs for local government employees who otherwise could not afford to own a home in the jurisdiction. Others make the program available to any lower-income person seeking to buy a home in the jurisdiction.

Authority for such activity is found in the Housing Authorities Law, G.S. 157-9.2, which authorizes local governments in larger jurisdictions (cities in counties with populations of more than 100,000 and an area of more than 250 square miles), as part of housing projects, to make certain kinds of housing loans when they are not otherwise available from public or private lenders with equivalent

terms and conditions. These include mortgage loans to sponsors of residential housing, direct loans to persons and families of lower and moderate income for residential housing, and mortgage loans to mortgage lenders on terms and conditions that require the proceeds to be used to originate new mortgage loans on behalf of persons and families of low and moderate income. The statute also allows local governments to collect and pay reasonable fees and charges in connection with making, purchasing, and servicing its loans, notes, bonds, commitments, and other evidences of indebtedness.

While it is generally illegal for any person in North Carolina to make mortgages without first obtaining a license from the commissioner of banks,[85] local governments are expressly exempt from these licensure requirements when acting under the authority of a specific statute.[86]

### Displacement and Relocation

Efforts to improve the quality of the existing affordable housing stock can sometimes yield unexpected consequences. Indeed, there are times when the intended beneficiary—the low-income household—can lose out and direct assistance programs can become important in addressing the resulting situations. Such conditions may exist when extensive rehabilitation is under way or when a house that is beyond repair is to be demolished and residents have to be temporarily or permanently relocated. Also, a landlord forced to make improvements under a minimum housing ordinance may seek to protect his or her investment and to maintain an adequate return by demanding more rent from the low-income tenant or by seeking another tenant for the upgraded house. In either case the low-income renter may be forced to look for other housing that, unless he or she has rental assistance, will be as substandard as the former unit.

In some cases, displacement has been widespread. The tale is well recounted of the federal urban renewal program begun in the 1940s underwriting the widespread exercise of eminent domain (discussed on pages 13–17) by local governments to condemn blighted areas, resulting in wholesale destruction of entire neighborhoods. In the quest to eliminate blight, urban renewal projects razed homes and displaced hundreds of thousands of families and tens of thousands of businesses. Several hundred thousand more families and businesses were displaced during the same period to make way for the interstate highway system.[87] Long-term studies of these urban renewal projects found not only economic loss, they found that the forced displacement destroyed the social fabric and support systems of many close-knit communities.[88]

To remedy at least the economic inequities of involuntary displacement that occur as a direct result of government-initiated projects, a community may want to provide relocation assistance to the affected individual owners and renters. Local governments are authorized to deal with such problems in G.S. 133-5 through -18 —a statute originally enacted in 1971 in accord with the federal Uniform Relocation Assistance and Real Property Acquisition Policies Act of 1970.[89] Both the state and federal laws allow the local government to help relocated residents with moving expenses, temporary or permanent rental payments, a down payment on the purchase of a house, or a lump sum to buy another house if the permanently displaced family owns the house to be demolished.

While the use of local funds for displacement and relocation activity is an option under G.S. 133-5 through -18, the federal Uniform Relocation Assistance Act *requires* all "programs or projects undertaken by a Federal agency or with Federal financial assistance" to adopt a "relocation assistance advisory program." That program must, among other things, assure that a person[90] shall not be required to move from a dwelling unless the person has had a reasonable opportunity to relocate to a comparable replacement dwelling, except in cases of

1. a major disaster,
2. a national emergency declared by the President, or
3. any other emergency that requires the person to move immediately from the dwelling because continued occupancy would constitute a substantial danger to the health or safety of the person.[91]

The law also contains procedural requirements that give reasonable protection to a displaced person or family, including timely notices, expeditious processing of claims and payments, and an administrative appeal process.

Housing with ongoing rental subsidies: Creekridge Apartments, Middlesex, North Carolina.

## Acquisition and Disposition of Property

In order to carry out affordable housing projects, local governments must both acquire and dispose of real and personal property. However, the acquisition and disposition of property is legal only when the local government

1. is granted statutory authorization for the transaction (as discussed below);
2. satisfies the public purpose requirement of the state constitution (as discussed in Chapter 2); and
3. does not violate any provision of state law, including any legal procedures that are prescribed.[92]

## General Statutory Authority for Acquiring and Disposing of Housing-Related Property

The Housing Authorities Law, G.S. 157-1 through -70, contains a number of provisions regarding the acquisition and disposition of property related to affordable housing projects. G.S. 157-9 makes clear that housing authorities may purchase, lease, obtain options on, or acquire by gift, grant, bequest, devise, or otherwise any property real or personal; may acquire by eminent domain any real property, including improvements and fixtures; and may sell, exchange, transfer, assign, or pledge any real or personal property. In addition, G.S. 157-12 authorizes a housing authority to acquire by purchase or eminent domain any property for any housing project that is constructed or operated by a government. This statute also authorizes a housing authority to convey title or deliver possession of real or personal property to a government for use in connection with a housing project. As noted in Chapter 4, G.S. 160A-456 authorizes a city council to "exercise directly those powers granted by law to . . . housing authorities." G.S. 153A-376 grants the same authority to boards of county commissioners. Therefore a city or county may undertake any of these acquisition- and disposition-of-property activities that may be undertaken by a housing authority.

There are additional laws authorizing cities and counties to deal with property associated with affordable housing projects. G.S. 160A-457 and 153A-377, among other provisions, authorize local governments to acquire real property used in affordable housing projects through voluntary purchase from an owner or owners and to dispose of property acquired for public purposes through sale, lease, or other method to any person, firm, corporation, or governmental unit. G.S. 160A-457 further authorizes cities to sell, exchange, or otherwise transfer real property or any interest therein in a community development project area to any redeveloper at private sale for residential, recreational, commercial, industrial, or other uses or for public use in accordance with the community development plan. The statute does not define "community development plan" or "community development project area." As those terms are understood in community development generally and the Community Development Block Grant program in particular, however, a housing project should be designed to benefit at least in part low- and moderate-income persons in order to take advantage of the authority granted under G.S. 160A-457 or 153A-377.

For a discussion on whether state bidding procedures apply to affordable housing contracts, see page 44–45.

## Authority to Dispose of Property at Less than Fair Market Value

Local governments may convey property related to housing projects at less than fair market value in exchange for a promise that the property will be used for affordable housing. Pursuant to this authorization, counties may convey residential property by private sale directly to persons of low or moderate income, with the board of commissioners attaching any terms and conditions it deems appropriate to the conveyance.[93] The same statute authorizes counties to convey property by private sale to any public or private entity that provides affordable housing to persons of low or moderate income. The only procedural requirement on the county is that it include, as part of the conveyance conditions, assurance that the property will be developed to benefit low- and moderate-income persons.[94]

Under G.S. 160A-279, a city or a county may convey property, including redevelopment property, to any entity that carries out a public purpose for which a local government has authority to appropriate funds. Conveyances under this statute must be approved by the governing board. Notice of the proposed action must be advertised, and the unit must wait ten days after the notice is published before completing the transaction. The statute also requires that the local government place conditions on the conveyance to ensure that the property will be put to a public use. In the case of real property, the condition could be embodied in a deed limitation providing reversion of the property to the government if it ceases to be used for a public purpose. For personal property the condition would likely take the form of a contractual agreement with the recipient, who promises to return or pay fair value for the goods if the use changes. Property acquired through the exercise of eminent domain may not be conveyed under this statute.

Similarly, G.S. 160A-278 permits a city to lease land to any person, firm, or corporation that will use the land to construct housing for the benefit of low- or moderate-income persons. A lease so authorized may be made by private negotiation and may extend for longer than ten years. However, such property may be leased only pursuant to a resolution of the council authorizing the lease. The resolution must be adopted at a regular council meeting upon ten days' public notice. The notice must be given by publication describing the property to be leased, stating the value of the property, stating the proposed payment or other consideration for the lease, and stating the council's intention to authorize the lease.

## Eminent Domain

In addition to the voluntary acquisition authority outlined in the preceding section, North Carolina law allows cities and counties, their public housing authorities,[95] and their redevelopment commissions[96] to acquire (or damage) property for public use or benefit through the use of eminent domain,[97] which is "an involuntary transfer of property on payment of just compensation." G.S. 40A-2 defines property as "any right, title, or interest in land, including leases and options to buy or sell." Rights of access, rights-of-way, easements, water rights, and air rights are also considered elements of property as defined by the statute.

Each entity authorized to exercise the power of eminent domain is limited to the specific purposes set forth in the enabling legislation. All are limited by the North Carolina and federal constitutions' requirements that the purpose satisfy the public use or benefit test. Whether a condemnor's intended use of property is for public use or benefit is a question of law for the courts. However, courts grant great deference to policy makers and they recognize that the concept must be flexible and adaptable to changes in society and governmental duties. As a practical matter, courts equate "public benefit" with "public interest" even in cases where the property taken is transferred to a private entity.[98] Thus, eminent domain takings for the benefit of affordable housing projects will likely be upheld by the courts as meeting the public-purpose requirement even if the government is not the ultimate developer for the project.[99]

### A Case in Point: HOPE VI

Launched in 1992, the $5 billion HOPE VI program is one of the most ambitious urban redevelopment efforts in the nation's history and represents a dramatic turnaround in public housing policy. The HUD-administered program provides funding for PHAs to replace severely distressed public housing that is occupied exclusively by poor families with redesigned mixed-income housing, and it provides housing vouchers to enable some of the original residents to rent apartments in the private market. While the future of HOPE VI is uncertain, even ardent critics of the program respect the program's attempt to combine strategies for redevelopment, new construction, displacement, and relocation. In North Carolina HOPE VI has been used in Charlotte, Durham, Greensboro, High Point, Raleigh, Winston-Salem, and Wilmington to transform public housing.

HOPE VI grew out of the work of the 1992 National Commission on Severely Distressed Public Housing that Congress established, charging it with identifying "severely distressed" public housing developments, assessing strategies to improve conditions in these developments, and preparing a national action plan for dealing with the problem. Based on its investigation, the commission concluded that roughly 86,000 of the 1.3 million public housing units nationwide qualified as severely distressed and that a new and comprehensive approach would be required to address the range of problems identified.

In response to these findings, Congress enacted the HOPE VI program as a combination of grants for physical revitalization and funding for management improvements and supportive services to promote resident self-sufficiency. The program operated as a demonstration from 1993 to 1998. Congress authorized HOPE VI as a permanent program in 1998 as part of the Quality Housing and Work Responsibility Act. The Act aimed to lessen public housing authorities' dependence on a federal subsidy, provide market practices, and integrate public housing within communities.

Today HOPE VI grants are awarded in the pursuit of five major objectives:

1. Improving public housing through the demolition of severely distressed public housing projects, replacing concentrated, close-quarter housing with townhouses or garden-style apartments that are visually pleasing to the surrounding community
2. Reducing the concentration of poverty through the encouragement of mixed-income housing
3. Providing public services such as education and training programs, childcare services, and job counseling to assist residents in securing and maintaining employment
4. Establishing and enforcing high standards of personal and community responsibility through expressed requirements
5. Forging partnerships that include residents, state and local government officials, nonprofit groups, and the private sector in planning and developing communities

The HOPE VI program offers funding for two categories of community development:

1. Revitalization grants: These grants may include costs associated with major rehabilitation, new construction, demolition of severely distressed public housing, acquisition of sites for off-site construction, and community support programs.
2. Demolition grants: These grants may be used to fund demolition of severely distressed public housing, resident relocation necessitated by such demolition, and supportive services for relocated residents.

The focus in most judicial reviews of eminent domain cases is the government's means rather than the end it seeks to achieve. A taking by eminent domain or condemnation will not be upheld by the courts, however, if it is done in an arbitrary and capricious manner or if it constitutes an abuse of discretion. The words "arbitrary" and "capricious" have similar meanings, generally referring to acts done without reason or in disregard of the facts.[100] For a condemnation to have been arbitrary and capricious or for it to have constituted an abuse of discretion, a court must find as a matter of law that the acts were done without reason or in disregard to the facts. Even where less intrusive means of accomplishing the public purpose exist, a condemnation will not be invalidated when the taking is not arbitrary and capricious and is necessary to accomplish the purpose.[101] Indeed,

> where the general power to condemn exists, the right of selection as to route, quantity, etc., is left largely to the discretion of the . . . [condemnor] and does not become the subject of judicial inquiry except on allegations of fact tending to show bad faith . . . or an oppressive and manifest abuse of the discretion conferred . . . by law.[102]

Between 1992 and 2002, HUD awarded 446 HOPE VI grants in 166 cities. As a result, 63,100 severely distressed units were demolished and another 20,300 units were slated for redevelopment. As of the end of 2002, 15 of 165 funded HOPE VI programs were fully complete. The billions of federal dollars allocated for HOPE VI have leveraged billions of dollars more in other public, private, and philanthropic investments.

**The Effects of HOPE VI.** Perceptions about the impact of HOPE VI vary widely. Some people view it as a dramatic success; others as a profound failure.

There is no question that the program has had some notable accomplishments. Hundreds of severely distressed developments have been targeted for demolition, and many of them have been replaced with well-designed, high-quality housing serving a mix of income levels. Indeed, some projects have helped to turn around conditions in the surrounding neighborhoods and have contributed to the revitalization of whole inner-city communities. Along the way HOPE VI has been an incubator for innovations in project financing, management, and service delivery. But HOPE VI implementation also has encountered significant challenges. Some HOPE VI projects have been stalled by ineffective implementation on the part of the housing authority or by conflict with city government. In others, developments were simply rehabilitated or rebuilt in the same distressed communities, with little thought to innovative design, effective services, or neighborhood revitalization.

Most seriously, there is substantial evidence that the original residents of HOPE VI projects have not always benefitted from redevelopment, even in some sites that were otherwise successful. This may be attributed in part to a lack of meaningful resident participation in planning as well as insufficient attention to relocation strategies and services. As a consequence, some of the original residents of these developments may live in equally or even more precarious circumstances today.[a]

---

a. *See* Susan J. Popken, Bruce Katz, Mary Cunningham, Karen D. Brown, Margery Austin Turner, *A Decade of HOPE VI: Research Findings and Policy Challenges*, Urban Institute (May 18, 2004), http://www.urban.org/Uploadedpdf/411002_HOPEVI.pdf.

Under this standard, a court held that a redevelopment commission is not required to articulate its reasons for condemning some, but not all, of the property located within a blighted redevelopment area.[103]

Localities exercising eminent domain takings related to housing projects are governed by regulations and restrictions outlined in G.S. 40A covering right of entry, complaint, just compensation, memorandum of action, dispute process, and costs.[104] The steps outlined[105] are as follows:

1. **Prior Offer and Right of Entry.** A condemning locality may enter lands, but not structures, identified for condemnation without having filed a complaint, deposited any funds for just compensation, or taken any other action except for serving the property owner and person in possession of the land with notice at least thirty days in advance.[106] The locality may enter the property to conduct surveys, borings, examinations, or appraisals. Entrance for these activities is not a trespass or taking, but the local government must make reimbursement for any damages that result from its activities on the land. Contrary to widespread belief, a locality exercising eminent

domain power is not required to have first tried to acquire the property through gift or purchase prior to the condemnation proceedings.

2. **Complaint, Declaration of Taking, and Notice of Deposit.** At least thirty days prior to filing a complaint, the condemning locality must serve a notice to the owners of a property to be condemned. This notice must identify and describe the property to be condemned, and must include an estimated value for just compensation. The notice must also state the purpose for which the property is being condemned and the date—at least 30 days hence—that the locality intends to file the complaint in court. Property owners have 120 days from the date of receipt of the notice to answer.[107]

3. **Just Compensation.** An amount equal to the estimated just-compensation value of the property must be deposited with the court upon filing the complaint. A summons (with a copy of the complaint) is then served on the property owner. If during the 120 days following receipt of the notice the owner does not answer, the amount deposited by the condemning locality is established as just compensation, and the owner loses any right to further proceedings on the issue of just compensation.

   To determine the amount of just compensation, the value of the property immediately prior to condemnation is used. Just compensation is equal to the property's fair market value, unless only a portion of the property is to be condemned.[108] If only a portion of the property is to be condemned, then just compensation is determined by the greater of either (1) the amount by which the fair market value of the entire tract immediately before the taking exceeds the fair market value of the remainder immediately following condemnation, or (2) the fair market value of the property taken.[109]

4. **Memorandum of Action.** Along with the complaint and estimated just-compensation deposit, the condemning locality files a Memorandum of Action. This Memorandum of Action must be recorded with the register of deeds in all counties in which the land involved is located.[110] The memorandum must include the names of the property owners and other parties to the action, a description of the property, a statement that the property is being taken for public use, and the date and county in which the complaint is filed.

5. **Handling Disputes: Appointment and Duties of Commissioners.** If there is no dispute over the title of the property, the owners of the property (those identified in the complaint) may apply for the disbursement of the deposited amount. However, should a dispute arise over the issue of just compensation (articulated in the owner's answer), the owner may request that the clerk of the superior court appoint a three-member commission to address the dispute. The members of this commission must be "competent, disinterested persons who reside in the county." The commissioners may inspect the property, hold hearings, swear witnesses, and take evidence. Following the completion of these tasks the commission files a final report with the superior court.

Each party to the condemnation proceeding receives a copy of the commission's report from the clerk of the superior court. A party wishing to contest the report and request a jury trial on the issue of compensation must file exceptions to the report within 30 days of its mailing. If no exceptions are filed, the superior court judge enters a just-compensation judgment based upon the findings of the commission's report.

Based on standing conferred in G.S. 40A-28(c), any party to such dispute proceedings may file an exception to the clerk's final determination and may seek to have the matter heard by a jury.

Questions often arise regarding who has standing to challenge a condemnation proceeding, including on the issue of just compensation. G.S. 40A defines "owner" as any person having an interest or estate in the property."[111] Usually, a lessee has standing to litigate its portion of the total award upon condemnation. In addition, the North Carolina Supreme Court has determined that a lessee might also have standing to challenge the condemnation proceeding itself.[112]

6. **Costs And Interest.** The condemning locality pays all court costs. The court may also award to the owner of the property reimbursement for charges paid to appraisers and engineers.

### Eminent Domain under the Redevelopment Statutes

Pursuant to the Urban Redevelopment Law, a redevelopment commission may acquire property, execute contracts for clearance and preparation of the land for resale, and take other actions necessary to carry out a redevelopment plan. Such actions include the acquisition of property by condemnation if the property is located in an area designated as a "blighted area,"[113] a "nonresidential redevelopment area,"[114] or a "rehabilitation, conservation, and reconditioning area,"[115] as well as conveyance of the cleared property to private developers to redevelop the area in compliance with the redevelopment plan.

Some portions of an area to be redeveloped under redevelopment laws may be vacant lands or may contain structures that themselves are not blighted, but this does not always affect the ability of the redevelopment commission to designate the area as blighted or to take property by eminent domain.[116] However, a "blighted area" cannot be subjected to the power of eminent domain unless it is determined by the planning commission that at least two-thirds of the number of buildings within the area are blighted and substantially contribute to the conditions creating the blight.[117] In a nonresidential redevelopment area, at least half of the properties must substantially contribute to the conditions creating blight before eminent domain may be exercised.[118] The standard is more stringent in rehabilitation, conservation, and reconditioning areas, where no individual tract, building, or improvement may be subjected to eminent domain unless that particular structure is blighted.[119]

## Notes

1. "The United States, among all western democracies, relies most heavily on market forces to house its population." John Atlas and Ellen Shoshkes, *Saving Affordable Housing: What Community Groups Can Do and What Government Should Do*, National Housing Institute, Orange, N.J. (1997), *at* http://www.nhi.org/online/issues/90/success.html

2. The federal government established six major housing-related organizations between 1932 and 1947: the Federal Home Loan Bank Board (FHLBB), the Federal Savings and Loan Insurance Corporation (FSLIC), the Federal Housing Administration (FHA), the Federal National Mortgage Association (FNMA), the home financing division of the Veterans Administration, and the Housing Home Finance Agency (HHFA). These organizations have provided enormous impetus to the large-scale production of housing—particularly single family housing—by exercising vast influence over the housing credit markets and housing insurance. The FHA, for example, through the provision of mortgage insurance, made low down payments and long-term fully amortized mortgage loans feasible. *See* HOUSING FOR ALL UNDER THE LAW: NEW DIRECTIONS IN HOUSING, LAND USE AND PLANNING LAW 17 (Richard P. Fishman, ed., A.B.A. Advisory Commission on Housing and Urban Growth, Ballinger Publishing Company, 1978).

3. *See* United States v. Certain Lands in Louisville, Jefferson County, Ky., 78 F.2d 684 (6th Cir. 1935) ("In the exercise of its police power a state may do those things which benefit the health, morals, and welfare of its people. The federal government has no such power within the states.") (citations omitted); *see also* United States v. Certain Lands in the City of Detroit, 12 F. Supp. 345 (E.D. Mich. 1935).

4. The Declaration of Policy in the first section of the Housing Act of 1937 indicates:

It is the policy of the United States to promote the general welfare of the Nation by employing the [Nation's] funds and credit . . . to *assist States and political subdivisions* . . . remedy unsafe housing conditions and the

acute shortage of decent and safe dwellings for low income families. (Emphasis added.)

The courts supported this new role. *See, e.g.,* City of Cleveland v. United States, 323 U.S. 329 (1945) (Supreme Court holding that the Housing Act, which provided for the use of federal funds and credit to improve housing conditions, was a valid exercise of Congress's power to provide for the general welfare under the Commerce Clause). Pub. L. No. 75-412, ch. 896, 50 Stat. 888 (codified as amended at 42 U.S.C. §§ 1437, 1437z-7 (2004)).

5. The Housing Act of 1949, Pub. L. No. 81-171, ch. 338, 63 stat. 413 (codified as amended at 42 U.S.C. §§ 1441-69 (2004)) adopted the twin strategies of public housing and urban renewal.

6. For example, the Public Works Administration, created under the National Industrial Recovery Act of 1933, authorized the first federally assisted construction of low-income housing. The General Assembly responded by passing the Housing Authorities Law (1935). This law, as amended, appears as N.C. GEN. STAT. Ch. 157 (hereinafter G.S.). In 1951, responding to the broader purposes of the federal Housing Act of 1949, the General Assembly passed the Urban Redevelopment Law, which, as amended, appears as G.S. 160A, art. 22. Finally, in response to the Housing and Community Development Act of 1974, the General Assembly passed and later amended G.S. 153A-376 and 153A-377 and G.S. 160A-456 and 160A-457 to permit counties and cities to engage in Community Development Block Grant (CDBG) activities authorized by the federal act.

7. While the general legal principle—that local governments have only those powers given to them by the state—is universal, individual states may alter the state–local government relationship. Thus, local governments' autonomy varies from state to state. For example, some states grant to local governments Home Rule Authority—the power of self-government, except in subject areas over which the state legislature has exclusive control. *See, e.g.,* MD. CONST. art. XI-A, § 2. In non–home rule states such as North Carolina, however, the local government may exert only powers that are either expressly granted or implied.

8. G.S. 153A-4 and 160A-4.

9. A local government's power to regulate land and housing is not without limitations, however. Limits can be found in state and federal constitutional provisions, state and local laws, and principles of equity. As an illustration, the Fifth Amendment of the United States Constitution and the parallel provision of the North Carolina Constitution (N.C. Const. art. I, § 19) require that the government pay "just compensation" to the owner of a condemned property. If the exercise of police power is deemed a "taking," the local government must pay just compensation. However, other police power regulation, such as regulation of the condition of housing, does not require payment of just compensation. On a separate matter, the Fourteenth Amendment and a similar clause in the state constitution require procedural due process in police power regulation of buildings. Most exercises of this police power, including both condemnation by eminent domain and eviction of a tenant of public housing, require that reasonable notice and hearing opportunities—the traditional protections of procedural due process—are afforded to those adversely affected by the government's actions. Equitable principles limit police powers by requiring local governments to apply the least severe enforcement method to any particular problem. Thus, for example, a local government should not order a building demolished if its defects are easily remedied.

Demolition of the building under these circumstances could result in liability in tort for damages. A more detailed discussion of these and other limitations can be found in Chapter 3.

10. Any fiscal involvement by local governments in housing activity is predicated on satisfying the threshold constitutional test that public funds be expended for a public purpose. *See* Madison Cablevision, Inc. v. City of Morganton, 325 N.C. 634, 386 S.E.2d 200 (1989). Article V, section 2(1) of the North Carolina state constitution provides: "The power of taxation shall be exercised in a just and equitable manner, for public purposes only, and shall never be surrendered, suspended, or contracted away." Although the constitutional language speaks of the "power of taxation," the limitation has not been confined to government use of tax revenues. For further discussion of this principle see DAVID M. LAWRENCE, ECONOMIC DEVELOPMENT LAW FOR NORTH CAROLINA LOCAL GOVERNMENTS 3–6 (Chapel Hill, N.C.: Institute of Government, 2000).

*See In re* Denial of Approval to Issue $30,000,000.00 Single Family Housing Bonds and $30,000,000.00 of Multi-Family Housing Bonds for Persons of Moderate Income, 307 N.C. 52, 296 S.E.2d 281 (1982) (holding that the North Carolina Housing Finance Agency's issuance of bonds to finance single- and multi-family housing for persons of moderate income serves a public purpose); Martin v. North Carolina Hous. Corp., 277 N.C. 29, 175 S.E.2d 665 (1970) (finding a public purpose in the housing finance agency's authority to provide financing for residential housing constructions, new or rehabilitated, for sale or rental to persons and families of lower income); Wells v. Hous. Auth. of City of Wilmington, 213 N.C. 744, 197 S.E. 693 (1938) (finding the public purpose in the creation of urban housing authorities); *accord* Cox v. City of Kinston, 217 N.C. 391, 8 S.E.2d 252 (1940) (statute authorizing the rehabilitation of congested city areas through the construction, ownership, and rental of apartments and dwellings by housing authority is constitutional and constitutes a "public purpose"); Mallard v. Hous. Auth., 221 N.C. 334, 20 S.E.2d 281 (1942) (finding that a rural area housing authority was created for a public purpose).

11. G.S. 157-3(12).

12. G.S. 133-5-18.

13. Affordable housing rehabilitation, when coordinated with other community development activities, should result in improvements to not only the physical but also the economic and social fabric of the target community. If houses are rehabilitated in a concentrated area, concurrent improvements in the public facilities that serve those houses are often also made to ensure that the full value of improving the condition of a given house is realized and long-lived. Consequently, local governments undertake neighborhood public improvements to complement housing improvements in their target areas. North Carolina counties and cities tend to emphasize a balanced strategy of housing improvements supported by public facilities.

The kinds of public improvements most commonly undertaken in a target neighborhood in conjunction with affordable housing rehabilitation or construction include the following:

1. Sewer: usually installation or rehabilitation of collector lines; also, house connections or outfalls under certain circumstances
2. Water: installation or refurbishment of distribution lines and house connections
3. Open space: common areas, buffers between incompatible uses, and drainage areas

Unlike most housing activities, the kinds of improvements just listed are normal and traditional functions of local governments in North Carolina, and statutory authority to undertake any of them is clear and well understood. These activities therefore are not treated in detail anywhere in this publication.

14. *See* Charles G. Field, *Building Consensus for Affordable Housing*, 8 HOUSING POLICY DEBATE 697 (1997).

15. G.S. 157-3(15a).

16. G.S. 157-3(15b).

17. The same is not necessarily true when a local government is determining a person's low-income status. However, notwithstanding the state's definitions, local governments that administer federally funded programs must often look to federal guidelines to determine the appropriate income eligibility standards. In the Housing Act of 1937, as amended, income levels are defined as follows: middle income, 80–120 percent of median metropolitan income; low income, 50–80 percent of median metropolitan income; very low income, 30–50 percent of median metropolitan income; extremely low income, 0–30 percent of median metropolitan income. *See Fiscal Year 1990 HUD Four-Person Very Low & Lower Income Limits and Area Median Family Income*, U.S. Dep't of Housing & Urban Development (Sept. 15, 2000), *available at* http://www.huduser.org/datasets/il/fmr00/sect82.html. Note that the North Carolina definition of "low income" in nonfederally funded projects is different from and not limited by HUD's definition. G.S. 157-3(15a).

18. According to HUD, housing is affordable when all housing costs (rent or mortgage, utilities, property taxes, and insurance) do not exceed 30 percent of total household income. This standard applies to any person or household regardless of their source or level of income. *See The Widening Gap: New Findings on Housing Affordability in America*, U.S. Dep't of Housing & Urban Development (1999) *available at* http://www.huduser.org/publications/affhsg/gap.html

19. Cities may spend local tax dollars on all of the affordable housing projects contemplated by G.S. 157-3 (see G.S. 160A-209). G.S.153A-378, along with G.S. 153A-149(15b), gives counties the authority to expend funds for residential housing construction (new construction and rehabilitation) on behalf of low- and moderate-income housing programs.

20. A "public housing agency" (PHA) is any state or local government entity "authorized [under state law] to engage or assist in the development or operation of low-income housing." 24 C.F.R. § 5.100 (1996).

21. Although local PHAs built their own developments in the beginning of the program, since the mid-1960s the main format for housing productions has been the turnkey format through which a PHA contracts with a private developer for the construction of the project. HUD agrees to buy the finished product, including land and buildings, from a private developer, who "turns the keys" over to the PHA.

22. A PHA and the local jurisdiction sign what is known as a Cooperative Agreement in which the local jurisdiction waives normal real estate taxes, but requires the authority to make payment in lieu of taxes in an amount equal to 10 percent of the annual rentals received. 42 U.S.C. § 1437d(d). The Cooperative Agreement typically obligates the locality to provide usual municipal services such as police and fire protection as well as utilities such as water and sewer to the public housing development on the same basis as it provides them to private users.

23. G.S. 157-26 makes clear that a PHA is a local government agency and is exempt from taxations to the same

extent as a unit of local government. *See also* Wells v. Hous. Auth., 213 N.C. 744, 197 S.E. 693 (1938); *but see* Hous. Auth. v. Johnson, 261 N.C. 76, 134 S.E.2d 121 (1964) (neither the state constitution nor any federal laws prohibit the collection of a sales tax on the purchases of tangible property made by a housing authority. While a housing authority is a municipal corporation, it is not an incorporated county or town and is therefore not entitled to the refund of sales taxes paid on purchases of tangible personal property pursuant to G.S. 105-164.14(c)).

24. The basic law governing landlord-tenant disputes in North Carolina is found in G.S. Ch. 42, art. 3, 7. A comprehensive review of these laws is beyond the scope of this publication, but suffice it to say that local governments should be aware of these provisions if (1) they act as landlords in the operation of rental housing or (2) they provide rental assistance to lower-income persons.

25. G.S. 157-29.1.

26. *See supra* pp. 10–11 for further discussion of certificate and voucher programs.

27. *See* Thorpe v. Hous. Auth. of Durham, 386 U.S. 670 (1967) (Public Housing); Swann v. Gastonia Hous. Auth., 675 F.2d 1342 (4th Cir. 1982) (Section 8 rent supplements). While tenants in public housing are entitled to fairly formal due process hearings prior to eviction, tenants in privately owned, federally assisted housing generally are not entitled to pre-eviction hearings as long as the state landlord–tenant law will provide the tenants with a post-eviction due process type of hearing. *See* Joy v. Daniels, 479 F.2d 1236 (4th Cir. 1973). Under federal law a tenant who lives in publicly assisted housing may not be evicted except for "good cause," *id.* at 1241; *and see* Caulder v. Durham Hous. Auth., 433 F.2d 998 (4th Cir. 1970). This means that a landlord cannot evict a tenant from publicly assisted housing unless the landlord can prove

1. a serious or repeated violation of a material term of the rental agreement or other good cause (*see* Maxton Hous. Auth. v. McLean, 313 N.C. 277, 328 S.E.2d 290 (1985);
2. criminal activity that threatens the health, safety, or right to peaceful enjoyment of the premises by other tenants (*see* 42 U.S.C.A. § 1437d(1), (4), (5) (West 1995)); or
3. any drug-related criminal activity.

"Good cause" has been held to mean that public landlords cannot evict for arbitrary, discriminatory, or otherwise manifestly improper reasons. Bogan v. New London Hous. Auth., 366 F. Supp. 861 (D. Conn. 1973). Interestingly, the North Carolina General Assembly appears to have departed from federal law and overruled the North Carolina Supreme Court in its 1985 amendment to the Housing Authorities Law. In *Maxton* the plaintiff, Maxton Housing Authority, sought to evict a tenant for nonpayment of rent from an apartment it owned. The court ruled that the tenant could not be evicted under the facts of the case. Specifically, the court held that "in order to evict a tenant occupying public housing for failure to pay rent as called for in the lease, there must be a finding of fault on the part of the tenant in failing to make a rental payment." The court emphasized that its holding applied only to leases between PHAs and their tenants. However, the holding made landlords across the state nervous. PHAs in particular lobbied the General Assembly, arguing that the decision undermined their fiscal stability. The General Assembly nullified the need to find fault on the part of the tenant in G.S. 157-29(c).

28. Indian housing authorities previously were eligible to receive funds under this program. In 1998, the Indian component of the Public and Indian Housing program was removed and folded into the Native American Housing Block Grant program.

29. In 1998, Congress substantially revised the public housing program, placing greater emphasis on property and asset management and encouraging local public housing authorities to enter into public–private partnerships to transform public housing into mixed-income communities. Quality Housing and Work Responsibility Act of 1998, Title V, Department of Veterans Affairs and Housing and Urban Development, and Independent Agencies Appropriations Act, Pub. L. No. 105-276, § 112 Stat. 2518 (1998).

30. There were twenty-nine PHAs that administered Section 8 Housing Choice Vouchers (HUD provides funds for certificate and voucher programs) but that did not operate public housing units. Voucher and certificate programs are rental assistance programs in which tenants lease property from private landlords with their rent being subsidized by HUD.

31. *See* Wright v. City of Roanoke Redevelopment & Hous. Auth., 479 U.S. 418 (1987) (allowing tenants to bring a civil rights action under section 1983 against the housing authority for violations of the federal statute).

32. G.S. 157-9. *See* Cox v. City of Kinston, 217 N.C. 391, 8 S.E.2d 252 (1940) (a housing authority is a municipal corporation entitled to incur indebtedness without the approval of voters).

33. *See e.g.,* G.S. 153A-435(a) (counties) and G.S. 160A-485(c) (cities).

34. Millar v. Town of Wilson, 222 N.C. 340, 341, 23 S.E.2d 42, 44 (1942).

35. *Id.*

36. *See, e.g.,* Carter v. City of Greensboro, 249 N.C. 328, 106 S.E.2d 564 (1959) (liability for igniting and abandoning trash on premises).

37. Jackson v. Hous. Auth. of City of High Point, 73 N.C. App. 363, 326 S.E.2d 295 (1985), *aff'd,* 316 N.C. 259, 341 S.E.2d 523 (1986).

38. G.S. 157-13.

39. G.S. 157-26.1.

40. Wells v. Hous. Auth. of City of Wilmington, 213 N.C. 744, 197 S.E. 693 (1938).

41. *See* David T. Kraut, *Hanging Out the No Vacancy Sign: Eliminating the Blight of Vacant Buildings from Urban Areas,* 74 N.Y.U. L. Rev. 1139 (1999).

42. *See id.* (citing James Q. Wilson & George L. Kelling, *Broken Windows,* Atlantic Monthly, March 1982, at 29).

43. *See* Catherine E. Ross & John Mirowsky, *Disorder and Decay: The Concept and Measurement of Perceived Neighborhood Disorder,* 34 Urb. Aff. Rev. 412, 413 (1999) (finding a positive correlation between crime rates and the decay and disorder of neighborhoods).

44. Sometimes significant public investment in a lower-income neighborhood makes the area so attractive to private investments that it results in the overall gentrification of the area. Gentrification is the process by which neighborhoods that have undergone disinvestment and economic decline experience a reversal, reinvestment, and the in-migration of a relatively well-off, middle- and upper-middle-class population. While gentrification is a highly contested phenomenon, and data on the number of people evicted and displaced is limited, there is little doubt that gentrification may exacerbate an already severe housing shortage. Local governments' authority to deal with displacement problems

that might arise as part of their housing community development activities is found in G.S. 133-5 through -18 and discussed on pages 51–66.

45. G.S. 153A-121 & 160A-174.

46. *See* 7A. E. McQuillin, Municipal Corporations § 24.558 (3d ed. Rev. 1981 & Supp. 1988).

47. State v. Scoggins, 236 N.C. 1, 72 S.E.2d 97 (1952).

48. Sykes v. Belk, 278 N.C. 106, 179 S.E.2d 439 (1971).

49. GI Surplus Store Inc. v. Hunter, 257 N.C. 206, 125 S.E.2d 764 (1962).

50. Summey Outdoor Advertising, Inc. v. County of Henderson, 96 N.C. App. 533, 386 S.E.2d 439 (1989), *review denied*, 326 N.C. 486, 392 S.E.2d 101 (1990).

51. G.S. 160A-441.

52. See Serena D. Madar, *Mandatory Rent Escrow: A Bill Relative to Rent Withholding*, 36 New Eng. L. Rev. 283 (2001) ("New York's tenement house law of 1867 was mainly enacted in response to the large concentration of immigrant poor who were living in deplorable conditions, and in response to the fear that these conditions were responsible for the widespread cholera epidemics which affected the poor and rich." (p. 299)) ("The migration of lower income African Americans and Whites to the urban centers of the United States after World War II was a principal impetus in the enactment of the Housing Act of 1949. 'Implicit in this legislation . . . was the belief that a housing code, properly drafted and effectively enforced, would be a significant weapon in the fight against spreading "blight"—the phenomenon of undermaintenance.'" (footnote omitted)).

53. Housing and Development Act of 1965, Pub. L. No. 89-117, 79 Stat. 451.

54. *Id.* (citing Samuel Bassett Abott, *Housing Policy, Housing Codes and Tenant Remedies: An Integration*, 5b B.U.C. Rev. 1, 44 (1976)).

55. Dale v. City of Morganton, 270 N.C. 567, 576, 155 S.E.2d 136, 144 (1967).

56. G.S. 160A-445.

57. *Id.*

58. G.S. 160A-442(4).

59. G.S. 160A-442(5).

60. The ordinance sets out what is a presumptively reasonable percentage of a dwelling's value for orders to repair, alter, or improve.

61. *Dale*, 270 N.C. at 576, 155 S.E.2d at 144. The variation was not material between the notice prescribed by the statute and the wording of a posted notice reading "This Building Is Unsafe, And Its Use for Occupancy has Been Prohibited By the Building Official."

62. Newton v. City of Winston-Salem, 92 N.C. App. 446, 374 S.E, 2d 488 (1988).

63. Carolina Holdings, Inc. v. Hous. Appeals Bd. of the City of Charlotte, 149 N.C. App. 579, 561 S.E.2d 541 (2002).

64. *Sykes*, 278 N.C. at 121, 179 S.E.2d at 701.

65. Monroe v. City of New Bern, 158 N.C. App. 275, 278–79, 580 S.E. 2d 372, 374–75 (2003).

66. *Id.* at 278, 580, S.E.2d at 375.

67. Residential property is considered to be of little or no value if the cost of bringing the property into compliance with the city's housing code exceeds 60 percent of the property's appraised value on the county tax records. *See* G.S. 160A-457.2; *see also* Note, *Homesteading Urban America After Moore v. Detroit: The Constitutionality of Detroit's Nuisance Abatement Plan and Its Implications for Urban Homesteading Legislation*, 34 Wayne L. Rev. 1609 (1988).

68. G.S. 160A-500 through -526.

69. G.S. 160A-503(19).

70. *Id.*

71. G.S. 160A-503(2).

72. G.S. 160A-503(10).

73. G.S. 160A-503(21).

74. Redevelopment Comm'n v. Hagins, 258 N.C. 220, 224, 128 S.E.2d 391, 394 (1962) ("[T]he adoption of the plan is equivalent to a cease and desist order preventing any development, rental, or sale of the property within the area.")

75. G.S. 160A-513(e).

76. G.S. 160A-513(f).

77. *Id.*

78. G.S. 160A-513(g)&(h).

79. G.S. 160A-513(i).

80. Horton v. Redevelopment Comm'n of High Point, 264 N.C. 1, 140 S.E.2d 728 (1965).

81. Redevelopment Comm'n of Greensboro v. Agapion, 129 N.C. App. 346, 499 S.E.2d 474 (1998).

82. Under the federal rental assistance programs, vouchers were originally distinguishable from certificates in that there was no maximum amount above the subsidy that landlords could charge. Thus, in the certificate program, the tenant had to find a landlord willing to rent a dwelling unit at a gross rent that did not exceed the applicable fair market rent, whereas in the voucher program, the family was not required to find a unit that rented within any rent limitations. Legislation enacted in October 1998 established a single tenant-based rental-assistance program with a uniform rent payment standard of between 90 and 110 percent of local fair market rents. Act of Oct. 21, 1998, Pub. L. No. 105-276, 545, 112 Stat. 2596 (amending 41 U.S.C. § 1437 f(o)). See Chapter 5 for further discussion of rental supplement programs in North Carolina.

83. Deborah J Devine et al., U.S. Dep't of Hous. & Urban Dev., Housing Choice Voucher Location Patterns: Implications for Participant and Neighborhood Welfare (2003).

84. G.S. 157-9.3.

85. G.S. 53-243.02.

86. *See* G.S. 53-243.01(8)a.

87. *See generally* Urban Renewal, The Record and the Controversy (James Q. Wilson ed., 1966); *see also* Jon C. Teaford, The Rough Road to Renaissance: Urban Revitalization in America, 1940–1985, at 44–80 (1990); Michael R. Klein, *Eminent Domain: Judicial Response to the Human Disruption*, 46 Urb. Law. 1, 7–8 (1968).

88. Bernard J. Frieden & Lynne B. Sagalyn, Downtown, Inc.: How America Rebuilds Cities 15–37 (1989).

89. 42 U.S.C. § 4601–4655. In addition, section 104(d) of the Housing and Community Development Act of 1974, as amended (42 U.S.C. § 5304, which is the 1988 amendment "Conserving Neighborhood and Housing by Prohibiting Displacement," commonly known as the "Barney Frank Amendment") applies to the displacement of "low and moderate income persons" as a direct result of an assisted-development project with certain types of HUD funds, such as CDBG, HOME, UDAG, or Section 108 Loan Guarantee Program funds. Such displacement must meet the Fair Housing Act (42 U.S.C. § 3601-20) requirements that each displaced resident must move to a community that is not racially impacted.

90. In order to qualify, the person must have been an owner or occupant who meets specific length-of-occupancy requirements

(at least 90 days for occupants or renters and 180 days for home owners). 49 C.F.R. § 24.401-02.

91. 42 U.S.C. § 4625 (Supp. V. 1987).

92. *See generally* Frayda Bluestein & Anita R. Brown-Graham, *Local Government Contracts with Nonprofit Organizations*, POPULAR GOVERNMENT, Fall 2001, at 32. A discussion of the third criterion, regarding provisions and procedures of state law, would require a thorough examination of all local government acquisition- and disposition-of-property laws, which is beyond the scope of this book. For a comprehensive discussion of the topic, see DAVID M. LAWRENCE, LOCAL GOVERNMENT PROPERTY TRANSACTIONS IN NORTH CAROLINA, (Chapel Hill, N.C.: Institute of Government, 2000).

93. G.S. 153A-378(4).

94. G.S. 153A-378(3).

95. A PHA may acquire by purchase or through exercising the power of eminent domain any property for any project being constructed or operated by any government. G.S. 157-12. The Housing Authorities Law also provides that corporations as defined in G.S.157-50 have the power of eminent domain.

96. G.S. 160A-512(6) and 160A-515.

97. *See* G.S. 40A-3(c).

98. For United States Supreme Court cases upholding this principle, see *Berman v. Parker*, 348 U.S. 26 (1954); *Hawaii Hous. Auth. v. Midkiff*, 467 U.S. 229 (1984).

99. See the discussion on public purpose, page 35.

100. *In re* Hous. Auth. of Salisbury, 235 N.C. 463, 70 S.E.2d 500 (1952), *aff'd as modified*, 318 N.C. 686, 351 S.E.2d 289 (1987).

101. Transcon. Gas Pipe Line Corp. v. Calco Enters., 132 N.C. App. 237, 511 S.E.2d 671 (1999).

102. Redevelopment Comm'n v. Grimes, 277 N.C. 634, 641, 178 S.E.2d 345, 349 (1971) (citations omitted).

103. Redevelopment Comm'n of Greensboro v. Johnson, 129 N.C. App. 630, 500 S.E.2d 118 (1998).

104. The General Assembly has passed a number of local modifications to G.S. 40A. Particular jurisdictions may be subject to additional procedures or may be able to use eminent domain for additional purposes. For example, the Town of Carrboro was granted authority in 1987 to use eminent domain for bikeways, bikepaths and other facilities designed for travel by the bicycle-riding public. In addition, cities and counties may use a "quick take" procedure set forth in G.S. 40A-42(a) for a number of purposes, many of which may relate to a housing project. Under this procedure, if a city or county condemns for one of the specified purposes, the title to the property and the right to immediate possession vest in the local government when the complaint is filed and the deposit is made in accordance with G.S. 40A-41. A city may choose to use this procedure for roads, storm sewer and drainage systems, sewer systems, electric power systems, water supply systems, wastewater collection and treatment facilities, gas production and distribution systems, solid waste collection and disposal systems, and cable television systems. *See* G.S. 160A-311(a)(1), (2), (3), (4), (6), (7), and 40A-42(b)(1),(4),(7). Counties may use quick take procedures for water supply systems, solid waste collection and disposal, stormwater drainage systems and wastewater systems. *See* G.S. 40A-3(b) and 153A-27491(1), (2), (3).

105. For a comprehensive treatment of the procedures and forms to be used in eminent domain proceedings, see BEN F. LOEB, EMINENT DOMAIN PROCEDURE FOR NORTH CAROLINA LOCAL GOVERNMENTS, (Univ. of N.C. Chapel Hill, Inst. of Gov't (1997)).

106. G.S. 40A-11.

107. The contents of the answer are set forth in G.S. 40A-45.

108. The fair market value of property can be determined in any number of ways, including (1) through testimony of a witness, who need not be an expert but who must have knowledge of the value of the property gained from experience, information, and observation (Huff v. Thorton, 287 N.C. 1, 6, 213 S.E.2d 198, 202 (1975)); and (2) in an action involving a county as condemnor, through introduction by the property owner of real property valuation made for ad valorem tax purposes (Craven County v. Hall, 87 N.C. App. 256, 360 S.E.2d 479 (1987)).

109. G.S. 40A-64(b).

110. The contents of the memorandum are identified in G.S. 40A-43.

111. G.S. 40A-2(5).

112. Transcon. Gas Pipe Line Corp. v. Calco Enterprises, 132 N.C. App. 237, 511 S.E.2d 671 (1999) (the court upholds a month-to-month tenant's challenge to a private condemnation proceeding brought by a gas pipeline corporation).

113. A "blighted area" is one "in which there is a predominance of buildings or improvements (or which is predominantly residential in character), and which, by reason of dilapidation, deterioration, age or obsolescence, inadequate provision for ventilation, light, air, sanitation, or open spaces, high density of population and overcrowding, unsanitary or unsafe conditions, or the existence of conditions which endanger life or property by fire and other causes, or any combination of such factors, substantially impairs the sound growth of the community, is conducive to ill health, transmission of disease, infant mortality, juvenile delinquency and crime, and is detrimental to the public health, safety, morals or welfare." G.S. 160A-503(2).

114. "Nonresidential redevelopment area" shall mean an area in which there is a predominance of buildings or improvements, whose use is predominantly nonresidential, and which, by reason of

   a. Dilapidation, deterioration, age or obsolescence of buildings and structures,

   b. Inadequate provisions for ventilation, light, air, sanitation or open spaces,

   c. Defective or inadequate street layout,

   d. Faulty lot layout in relation to size, adequacy, accessibility, or usefulness,

   e. Tax or special assessment delinquency exceeding the fair value of the property,

   f. Unsanitary or unsafe conditions,

   g. The existence of conditions which endanger life or property by fire and other causes, or

   h. Any combination of such factors

     1. Substantially impairs the sound growth of the community,

     2. Has seriously adverse effects on surrounding development, or

     3. Is detrimental to the public health, safety, morals or welfare

115. A "rehabilitation, conservation, and reconditioning area" is an area in danger of becoming a blighted area (or a nonresidential redevelopment area) in the absence of municipal action. G.S. 160A-503(21).

116. *See Johnson, supra* note 103.

117. G.S. 160A-503(2).

118. G.S. 160A-503(10).

119. G.S. 160A-503(21).

# 2 Local Government Activity Affecting Housing Markets

## Building Codes

The first known building code—found in the Code of Hammurabi (from the sixteenth century B.C. Babylonian ruler)—specified that a builder should be slain if a house fell in and killed the head of the household. Today's builders do not have to lay their lives on the line, but they must comply with strict building construction standards intended to ensure the health and safety of occupants. These standards have evolved over time, and today building codes cover structural matters, electrical, plumbing, heating—every facet of residential, commercial, and industrial construction. While local governments are active in enforcing these comprehensive building codes, the code is actually a state regulation.

In North Carolina, cities and counties are required by state law to adopt and enforce the North Carolina State Building Code, which is uniform throughout the state. No local variations are allowed. The state also sets standards for building inspectors by which each inspector must pass the appropriate state examination to be licensed to conduct inspections.

In a discussion of housing it is important to remember that *building codes* regulate how new construction must be done, focusing on the condition of the structure (building safety and electrical, plumbing, and heating systems), and as such may be distinguished from *minimum housing codes* (discussed on pp. 6–9), which focus on the effect of a structure on its inhabitants.

## NIMBY and Exclusionary Zoning

The term NIMBY (not in my backyard) was originally used to describe local opposition to projects that would threaten the environment and public health, such as landfills and hazardous waste sites. The term is now used to describe broad-scale opposition to many changes in neighborhoods, including the provision of affordable housing. In 1991 an affordable housing advisory commission established under President George Bush described NIMBY this way:

The NIMBY syndrome is often widespread, deeply ingrained, easily translatable into political actions, and intentionally exclusionary and growth inhibiting. NIMBY sentiment can variously reflect legitimate concerns about property values, service levels, community ambience, the environment, or public health and safety. It can also reflect racial or ethnic prejudice masquerading under the guise of these legitimate concerns. It can manifest itself as opposition to specific types of housing, as general opposition to changes in the character of the community, or as opposition to any and all development.[1]

The relationship between zoning and housing is obvious but bears repeating: "Housing requires buildings and buildings require land."[2] The primary means by which local governments regulate land is zoning; thus zoning has a significant effect on housing. It is no surprise then that local governments have been accused of inappropriately using their zoning powers to respond to residents' NIMBY sentiments. This phenomenon, known as "exclusionary zoning," has been defined as zoning

whose purpose or effect is to essentially close an entire community to unwanted groups—typically people of low income who might put a heavy burden on the public fisc yet at the same time contribute little to it, resulting in increased property taxes and reduced land values throughout the community.[3]

Exclusionary zoning is not necessarily motivated by discriminatory intent. Zoning ordinances may properly restrict land use and the types, size, and density of dwelling units that may be constructed on land in accordance with a comprehensive plan. Such provisions in zoning ordinances—even those enacted for a valid, nondiscriminatory purpose—can serve to discourage affordable housing. For example, zoning for single-family residences may prevent a landowner from building more affordable apartment dwellings or converting a home to a multi-family dwelling. It may also prohibit very-low-income unrelated persons from pooling their resources to buy or rent a home which, individually, they would be unable to afford.

Courts are generally deferential to zoning ordinances, and as a result they have typically upheld even exclusionary zoning ordinances.[4] In *Village of Belle Terre v. Boras*, the United States Supreme Court articulated the basis for courts' deference, holding: "The police power is not confined to elimination of filth, stench, and unhealthy places. It is ample to lay out zones where family values, youth values, and the blessings of quiet seclusion and clean air make the areas a sanctuary for people."[5]

Judicial scrutiny of exclusionary zoning has increased in the past two decades, however.[6] This increased scrutiny on the part of the courts follows increased attention to the issue by academics and policy makers. In 1976 author Michael Danielson observed,

> Zoning regulations, building codes, and other local policies prevent construction of inexpensive housing, increase the cost of houses which are built, and otherwise severely restrict access to the metropolitan rim by lower income families. . . . [T]he exclusionary policies of local governments . . . produce far more spatial separation [among racial, ethnic, and economic groups] than would be the case if only economic and social factors influenced the distribution of people in the spreading metropolis.[7]

Danielson pointed out that in other societies where municipal governments played a minor role in regulatory land use and housing, division along social and economic lines was "far less pervasive than in the United States."[8]

More recently, in March 2004, HUD unveiled the regulations associated with its new policy of awarding priority points in its funding competitions to communities that demonstrate efforts to reduce regulatory barriers that prevent families from living in the communities where they work. According to HUD, "over the last 15 years, there has been increased recognition that unnecessary, duplicative, excessive or discriminatory public processes often significantly . . . impede the development or availability of affordable housing without providing a commensurate or demonstrable health or safety benefit."[9] The "affordable housing" to which HUD refers is "decent quality housing that low-, moderate-, and middle-income families can afford to buy or rent without spending more than 30 percent of their income." To assess an applicant community's efforts along these lines, HUD has prepared a questionnaire on regulatory barriers as part of its funding application. This questionnaire is applicable to any funding that Congress appropriates annually and for which HUD generally issues a Notice of Funding Availability. In essence, it applies to HUD's competitive grant applications.

A full listing of the programs covered and the questionnaire can be found at *Federal Register*, volume 69, number 55/Monday, March 22, 2004, or at http://www.hud.gov/offices/adm/grants/frregbarrier.pdf.[10]

## Inclusionary Zoning

In recognizing that local zoning ordinances have broad extraterritorial impact, some courts and policy makers sometimes determine that each community must provide its share of a region's affordable housing needs. This fair-share principle is often articulated as inclusionary zoning. It is, in effect, the converse of exclusionary zoning.

Inclusionary zoning and its correlative, inclusionary housing, are terms used to describe a wide variety of techniques local governments use to link the construction of low- and moderate-income affordable housing to the construction of housing for the marketplace. Under an inclusionary zoning program, affordable housing is constructed and integrated into more expensive housing developments, thereby becoming an integral part of the overall residential development of a community. Simply put, inclusionary zoning encourages or requires developers, as a condition of permit approval, to include some portion of affordable housing in new market-rate housing developments. The principal objectives of inclusionary zoning are to increase the supply of affordable housing in a community and to do so in a manner that fosters greater economic and racial integration.

The role zoning should play in the provision of affordable housing is an issue that attracts much heated debate and controversy. Even those who do not question the need to provide affordable housing for those unable to pay market prices may question whether it is proper or lawful for the planning system to become the driving force behind private production of affordable units, rather than playing its more facilitative role. Opponents of inclusionary zoning programs argue that this more direct role of government seeks to impose a positive obligation on the private sector to do something that, if left to its own devices, it might properly choose not to do.

## Types of Inclusionary Zoning Programs

There are three types of inclusionary zoning programs: mandatory, conditional, and voluntary.[11] *Mandatory* inclusionary zoning is a local government requirement on residential developers to set aside a portion of the homes in new market-rate developments as affordable for low- and moderate-income families. These programs are based largely on the design and adoption of an inclusionary zoning ordinance. The ordinance will contain both an affordable housing threshold, setting forth how many market-rate homes a development can contain before the affordable housing obligation pertains, and an affordable set-aside, establishing what percentage of total housing in the development must be affordable. Mandatory programs typically provide some alternative ways that developers can meet the affordable housing requirement. These alternatives include

1. fee-in-lieu or cash payment by the developer to a local affordable housing fund;
2. development off-site, that is, constructing the affordable homes on a site different from that of the market-rate homes; and
3. land donation.

The town of Davidson is the only local government in North Carolina to mandate that developers provide affordable housing in new residential developments. Davidson's program requires all new developments of eight or more homes to include 12.5 percent affordable housing. The affordable homes must be built on-site. Developments of fewer than eight homes are allowed a fee-in-lieu option. The affordable homes are to be targeted for purchase or rent by households earning 80 percent or less of the area median income, with 30 percent of the total affordable homes to be sold or rented to households earning below 50 percent of the area median income. No legal challenge has been made to Davidson's authority to enact this ordinance.

In the second type of inclusionary zoning—*conditional*—developers must receive approval from the local government before constructing a large residential project. The approval typically involves changing the zoning ordinance, or rezoning, to allow for higher-density development. Two types of rezoning in North Carolina, conditional and conditional-use district, allow the governing board to negotiate with the applicant regarding the specific uses and obligations of the proposed development prior to approval.[12] While the governing board cannot mandate that the applicant provide affordable housing in return for approval, it can "encourage" the applicant to support the goals of the community as listed in the local government's comprehensive plan—one such goal being the inclusion of affordable housing. Inasmuch as approval is granted solely at the discretion of the governing board, the "expectation" that the developer will align with the goals of the comprehensive plan in effect makes such alignment a quasi condition of approval, real or perceived.

The town council in Chapel Hill passed a resolution (based on an affordable housing policy in the town's comprehensive plan) that states: "it is the expectation of the Council that applicants seeking approval of rezoning applications with a residential component incorporate a 15% affordable [housing] feature into their plans."[13] Because Chapel Hill uses conditional-use district rezoning, every application is technically negotiable between the applicant and the town. However, the town's broad discretion to approve or deny the proposed development distinctly tilts the negotiation in its favor. Between 1995 and 2003, the Town of Chapel Hill's program produced sixty rental and fifty-one for-sale affordable homes, acquired 2.8 acres of land for the construction of affordable housing, and received $73,500 in contributions to the affordable housing fund. Chapel Hill has been able to lower the administrative costs of its program by partnering with a local affordable housing nonprofit organization. This nonprofit organization negotiates with each applicant about the terms of the affordable housing donation and is responsible for the long-term administration of the affordable homes.

The third type of inclusionary zoning, and a distinct alternative to the mandatory or conditional types, is *voluntary* inclusionary zoning or voluntary density bonus incentives. With this incentive, developers volunteer to construct integrated affordable housing in return for a density bonus, which results in the building of more market-rate homes in a development than allowed by right. The voluntary density bonus typically is adopted as a provision in the local zoning ordinance or other local land use regulation and is similar to but less complex than mandatory inclusionary zoning ordinances. It specifies the amount of density bonus granted to residential developers in relation to the percentage of affordable housing in their projects. It also identifies any additional requirements or incentives that apply to the developer. For example, a provision in Durham offers developers one additional market-rate home for every affordable home provided, as well as additional incentives if the affordable homes are targeted to those whose incomes are below 50 percent of area median income.

Wilmington,[14] the city of Durham and Durham County,[15] the city of Winston-Salem and Forsyth County,[16] and Orange County[17] have all received authorization to utilize voluntary density bonus programs promoting affordable housing through the same methods that might be part of an inclusionary zoning ordinance. The legislature has either amended the local government's charter or amended the application of the zoning-enabling statutes in relation to the local government. Whatever the method, the legislation allows local governments to grant density bonuses to developers in return for the provision of affordable housing or in-lieu payments to a local affordable housing fund.

That local governments have sought such special authorization does not necessarily mean that they were required to do so. There are indications that state law may already provide the authority to enact not only a voluntary inclusionary zoning ordinance but a mandatory one as well. Local governments that have sought special authorization may have chosen simply to avert a legal challenge by obtaining legislation that addresses their programs directly.

## Legal Concerns about Inclusionary Zoning

Confusion is rampant among state and local officials, constituency groups, and the general public as to whether local governments have the statutory authority to enact mandatory inclusionary zoning programs. The confusion stems from the fact that local governments derive all of their power from the state and consequently cannot carry out any act unless empowered by the state to do so.

Some local mandatory inclusionary zoning programs across the country are state-initiated—that is, the product of a state court[18] or legislative directive. Without a mandate from either the courts or the state legislature, a local government that initiates a mandatory inclusionary zoning program is subject to challenge on the ground that the program is ultra vires, meaning that it exceeds the scope of the powers delegated to the local government.

A local government could obtain express authority to enact a mandatory inclusionary zoning program by seeking passage of local legislation by the state legislature. In both the 2001–2002 and 2003–2004 sessions of the North Carolina General Assembly, bills were introduced on behalf of communities in the Research Triangle region of the state seeking such authority. None of the bills survived their respective legislative committee assignments. Such action could indicate opposition to granting the authority, or it might simply mean that the legislature believes that such authority already exists.

Surprisingly few legal cases have considered the statutory authority of local governments to initiate mandatory inclusionary zoning ordinances in the absence of an enabling state statute or a judicial mandate. In a notable exception, the Virginia Supreme Court invalidated an inclusionary zoning ordinance in 1973 on the ground that it "exceed[ed] the authority granted by the enabling act to the local governing body. . . ."[19] The court reasoned that the ordinance was socioeconomic zoning that attempted to control compensation for the use of land and any improvements to it. The court further reasoned that the Virginia legislature had authorized its local governments to regulate the physical characteristics of buildings but not the identity of housing occupants. Thus, according to the court, Virginia's local governments had no authority to enact inclusionary zoning ordinances.

The Virginia Supreme Court's reasoning is not likely to persuade a North Carolina court. For one thing, Virginia has a very conservative tradition of property rights and is a strict Dillon's Rule state, meaning that it requires courts to strictly construe local government authority as constituting only those powers expressly granted by the state legislature, those necessarily incident to the powers expressly granted, and those indispensable to the declared objects and purposes of the local government. North Carolina courts followed Dillon's Rule (named after a nineteenth-century Iowa Supreme Court Justice) until 1971, when the General Assembly obviated the need to do so by explicitly stating that grants of state power to local governments in North Carolina should be broadly construed.[20] In addition, subsequent state courts have resoundingly rejected the Virginia court's decision. The New Jersey Supreme Court, for example, held:

> "It is nonsense to single out inclusionary zoning (providing a reasonable opportunity for the construction of lower income housing) and label it 'socio-economic' if that is meant to imply that other aspects of zoning are not. . . . It would be ironic if inclusionary zoning to encourage the construction of lower income housing were ruled beyond the power of a municipality because it is 'socio-economic' when its need has arisen from the socioeconomic zoning of the past that excluded it."[21]

Finally, legal commentators have characterized the Virginia case as "almost uniquely lacking in legal reasoning or rationale."[22]

Despite the apparent broad construction to be given to state grants of local authority in North Carolina and the rejection of the Virginia Supreme Court's reasoning by other courts and commentators, significant questions remain about a local government's authority to enact a mandatory inclusionary zoning program because there is no specific statutory provision in North Carolina law expressly granting such authority. Therefore, a local government in North Carolina seeking to enact a mandatory inclusionary zoning ordinance will have to rely on its implied powers.

Two independent considerations will determine whether a court will find that a local government has implied authority to enact a mandatory inclusionary zoning ordinance. First, the court will not find implied authority if there is a statute expressly prohibiting the act. Second, the court will find implied authority only if the ordinance constitutes a reasonable means of accomplishing an expressly granted power.

North Carolina law does not expressly prohibit inclusionary zoning. On the contrary, the General Assembly has expressly recognized, as a matter of public policy, the need for local governments to increase the supply of affordable residential housing for persons of lower income. The state legislature has addressed this need specifically by, for example, establishing both public housing authorities and the Housing Finance Agency. In neither of these moves did the legislature dictate that the provided-for housing production actions were to be governments' exclusive response to the need for more affordable housing. In the absence of (1) a complete and integrated regulatory state scheme to the exclusion of local regulation, (2) language that limits local governments to any particular method of meeting the affordable housing need, or (3) a judicial finding that inclusionary zoning is contrary to state law or the public policy of the state, there should be no basis for the court to find that an inclusionary zoning ordinance is preempted by state law.

It could be argued that inclusionary zoning ordinances are a legitimate means of local governments in North Carolina carrying out those expressly delegated powers, as the General Assembly has granted local governments authority to regulate land use. For example, local governments have the authority to implement zoning,[23] approve or deny the development of subdivisions,[24] and exercise general police power.[25] Of these three, zoning authority appears to provide the strongest argument in favor of inclusionary zoning authority, but the use of inclusionary zoning programs could be seen as a reasonable means of furthering the goals of each of these expressly delegated powers.

Despite the General Assembly's directive that grants of state power to local governments should be broadly construed, recent North Carolina court opinions make it unclear whether the courts will impose a liberal or strict interpretation of the state's grant of implied authority to local governments. For instance, the North Carolina Supreme Court upheld a local ordinance enacting a set of user fees for services performed by city departments, although the fees themselves were not expressly authorized under state law.[26] The court found that the services were part of the express authority of the local government to regulate development and that the fees were reasonably necessary or expedient to the authorized goal. The court reasoned that a legislatively provided means by which to meet a goal does not expressly prohibit other means of reaching the same goal. On the other hand, the court voided an ordinance imposing a fee to cover the cost of a stormwater management system based on impervious surfaces.[27] The court found that the statute authorizing local governments to assess fees to pay for stormwater utilities clearly and unambiguously limited such fees to the costs of constructing and maintaining a stormwater and drainage system.

Despite the ambiguity in the case law, it is clear that one of the factors to which courts have looked in the past to determine how strictly to interpret a local government's delegated authority has been whether the ordinance is deemed a regulation or a tax. Courts, including those in North Carolina, usually show less deference to local government ordinances that amount to a tax.[28] Recently, for example, a court in Massachusetts invalidated a mandatory fee for low-income housing on the ground that, because it seemed to operate as a mandate to developers rather than an incentive, it constituted an unlawful exercise of the taxing power.[29] Similarly, the Washington Supreme Court invalidated an ordinance requiring developers either to pay into a trust fund or to build low-income units, declaring that the ordinance amounted to a tax because it required developers to make a significant expenditure for the public good.[30] Thus, to the extent that an inclusionary zoning

program, even one that is mandatory, offers incentives to developers, it may bolster its chances of surviving a legal challenge.

## Statutory Limitations on Local Government Authority to Regulate Housing
### Housing Discrimination

A multiplicity of actors and actions may be involved in housing discrimination. Some examples are situations in which a realtor steers clients to a particular neighborhood based solely on the client's religious background; a bank refuses to approve mortgages based on the gender of the applicant; a landlord tells an immigrant that there are no vacant units, although there are; an insurance company refuses to issue property insurance to a neighborhood based on the age of the people who live there; or a local government enacts regulations on the kinds of housing that can be built, where housing can be built, and how much of it can be built based on the race of the prospective occupants. While each of these actions is prohibited by law, this discussion focuses exclusively on local government activity that constitutes unlawful housing discrimination under state and federal statutes. Local government action that may violate constitutional provisions is treated in Chapter 3.

*Discrimination on the Basis of Race, Color, and Ethnicity*
In the wake of the Civil War, Congress enacted the Civil Rights Act of 1866. Its two main elements were (1) racial discrimination could not be a factor in decisions to engage in a contract of any sort and (2) racial discrimination could not enter into decisions concerning the acquisition and subsequent use of housing or other property. In effect, this statute was the nation's first fair housing act. Not surprisingly, its interpretation has changed over time. In 1948, the United States Supreme Court found racially restrictive covenants were enforceable under section 1982 of the act.[31] However, the statute lay mostly dormant until the 1968 case of *Jones v. Alfred H. Mayer*,[32] when the Supreme Court ruled that a developer's refusal to sell a home to a man just because he was black violated section 1982.[33] Thereafter, public housing tenants used the statute to fight racially segregated public housing.[34] Notably, while the text of section 1982 appears restricted to race and color, courts have construed "race" to cover much of what is now categorized as ethnicity. Thus Jewish, Arab, and Latino plaintiffs have successfully sued under Section 1982.[35]

Title VI of the Civil Rights Act of 1964 prohibits discrimination against persons who are eligible to participate in and receive the benefits of any program receiving federal financial assistance. However, under the affirmative mandate and expanded coverage of Title VIII of the Civil Rights Act of 1968—commonly called the Fair

Housing Act—federal activity to assure equal opportunity in housing for minorities has increased dramatically.

The Fair Housing Act expands prohibitions against housing discrimination in terms of both the kinds of transactions and the protected classes covered. Generally speaking, the act (as originally enacted) prohibits discrimination in the sale or rental of private as well as publicly assisted housing, when such discrimination is based on race, color, religion, or national origin. The North Carolina State Fair Housing Act,[36] administered by the North Carolina Human Relations Council in the Department of Administration, was enacted in response to and substantially consistent with the federal act.

The federal Fair Housing Act provides an exemption to the general prohibition of nondiscrimination under certain circumstances, including the sale or rental of a single-family home by an owner who

1. does not own interests in more than three houses at one time,
2. does not use any type of real estate broker or salesperson, and
3. does not use any type of discriminatory advertising.[37]

An owner not residing in the home may make only one such transaction every twenty-four months. In addition, the exemption applies to the rental of rooms or units in dwellings occupied by no more than four families when the owner occupies one of the units.[38]

### The Fair Housing Amendments Act of 1988

The Fair Housing Amendments Act of 1988 (FHAA) served to amend the Fair Housing Act (Title VIII of the Civil Rights Act of 1968) by extending the classifications of those protected in the provision, sale, or rental of housing.[39] The FHAA also significantly modified the range of legal and administrative options available for the government and aggrieved individuals in fair housing complaints. Since its enactment, the number of fair housing complaints and the awards under such complaints have risen dramatically, with the greatest increases focusing on discriminatory practices in advertising, leasing, lending, and insurance.

### Discrimination Based on Familial Status

By adding "familial status" to the FHAA, Congress sought to eliminate the ability of a housing provider to discriminate in the provision of housing based on the presence of children in the household. While familial status is defined as "one or more individuals under the age of eighteen living with a parent, a person having legal custody of such individual or individuals, or the designee of such parent or legal guardian," its protections also extend to individuals or families who are pregnant or expecting children and persons who expect to "secure custody of someone under the age of eighteen."[40] Familial status

protections outlaw both intentional discrimination and those housing practices that have a disproportionate impact on families with children.

A major exception to familial status protections is provided for housing targeted to senior citizens or older persons. Such housing is exempt from the provisions of the FHAA only if it falls within one or more of the following classifications:

1. Housing that receives public subsidies and is specifically intended for elderly persons
2. Housing where all residents are age 62 or older
3. Housing "intended and operated for occupancy by persons 55 years of age or older," where
   - 80 percent of units are occupied by one or more individuals 55 years of age or older
   - A clear indication is made that the housing is intended for older persons

This exception is applicable only to the specific provisions of familial status protection. It does not provide exceptions to prohibitions of discrimination on the basis of race or color, national origin, religion, sex, or disability.

### Discrimination Based on Disability

By adding persons with disabilities to the FHAA, Congress aimed to eliminate discrimination against individuals with defined disabilities and individuals associated or residing with such persons.[41] The act does so by prohibiting housing providers from refusing residency to persons with disabilities and from placing conditions on their residency. Although it does not preempt local zoning laws—that is, act to prevent a local government from passing laws affecting land use—the FHAA prohibits local governments from enacting land use policies or engaging in other actions that treat groups of persons with disabilities less favorably than groups of nondisabled persons. For example, a local government might violate the act if it enacted an ordinance that prohibited housing for persons with disabilities or a specific type of disability, such as mental illness, in a particular area but allowed other groups of unrelated individuals to live together in that area.

The FHAA definition of persons with disabilities includes

1. individuals with a physical or mental impairment that substantially limits one or more major life activities;
2. individuals who are regarded as having such an impairment; and
3. individuals with a record of such an impairment.

The term "major life activities" means those activities that are of central importance to daily life, such as hearing, walking, breathing, performing manual tasks, caring for oneself, learning, and speaking.

Northwestern Regional Housing Authority converts a historic school into affordable housing in Elk Park, North Carolina.

The disability discrimination provisions of the FHAA do not extend to persons who claim to be disabled solely on the basis of having been adjudicated a juvenile delinquent, having a criminal record, or being a sex offender. Furthermore, the act does not protect persons who currently use illegal drugs (it protects those who are recovering from substance abuse), persons who have been convicted of crimes involving the manufacture or sale of illegal drugs, or persons with or without disabilities who present a direct threat to the person or property of others.

Further addressing the specific needs of individuals with disabilities, the FHAA has three additional provisions. These provisions require that housing providers

1. Allow disabled persons to make "any reasonable modifications necessary for their full enjoyment of the premises," at their own expense[42] (including widened doorways, shower and tub handles, and lowered fixtures such as cabinets and electrical switches)
2. "Make reasonable accommodations in rules, policies, practices, or services" in order to accord disabled individuals "equal opportunity to use and enjoy a dwelling"
3. Provide specified accessibility features to all "covered multifamily dwellings" constructed after March 13, 1991—"covered multifamily dwellings" are defined as buildings "with at least one elevator that have four or more units and ground floor units in non-elevator buildings with four or more units."

### Siting of Group Homes

Some local governments in North Carolina have become concerned that particular neighborhoods have more than their fair share of group homes. One way that these governments have attempted to address the problem is by requiring that group homes be at certain minimum distances from one another. In fact, G.S. 168-22 permits a local government in North Carolina to prohibit a family care home for handicapped persons from being located within a one-half-mile radius of another family care home. The Department of Justice, HUD, and many courts that have considered the issue take the position that similar density restrictions are generally inconsistent with disability protections of the FHAA. This is especially true when the effect is to foreclose group homes from locating in entire neighborhoods. As an alternative strategy, HUD suggests that the local government offer incentives to group homes to locate in other neighborhoods in the jurisdiction.

Siting of group homes also requires local governments to make reasonable accommodations in their rules and policies. Thus, even though a zoning ordinance imposes on group homes the same restrictions it imposes on other groups of unrelated persons, a local government may be required, in individual cases and when requested to do so, to grant a reasonable accommodation to a group home for a person with disabilities. It may be a reasonable accommodation to waive a setback requirement so that a paved path of travel can be provided to residents who have mobility impairments, for example. In making the determination of whether a requested modification is reasonable, a local government must ask whether the request imposes an undue burden or expense and whether it creates a fundamental alteration in the zoning scheme.

In determining whether a group home's request for an accommodation is required under the FHAA, a local government must look at the composition of the residents. Although the term "group home" is often used loosely to refer to any group of unrelated persons who live together in a dwelling—such as a group of students who voluntarily agree to share the rent on a house—the act does not affect local governments' ability to subject such renters to nondiscriminatory land use regulations. For the FHAA to apply, the residents must be disabled as defined by the act.

### Housing Discrimination Complaints

The FHAA gives HUD the power to receive and investigate complaints of discrimination, including complaints that a local government has discriminated in exercising its land use and zoning powers. The statute of limitations for complaints under the FHAA is two years.

Under the act, FHAA complaints received by HUD from complainants are often referred to a state's "substantially equivalent" agency, if there is one. For North Carolina, these are referred to the North Carolina Human Relations Commission. Other substantially equivalent jurisdictions that may handle fair housing complaints within their jurisdiction include the Human Relations Commissions of Asheville–Buncombe, Charlotte–Mecklenburg, Durham, Greensboro, New Hanover, and

An assisted living care facility in Gastonia, North Carolina.

## A Case in Point: *City of Edmonds v. Oxford House, Inc.*

In a 6 to 3 decision resolving a dispute over the application of the FHAA, the United States Supreme Court held that communities may set occupancy limits, space requirements, and other restrictions on houses occupied by unrelated people, like group homes, but only if the restrictions also apply to everyone else living in the area.[a]

The case involved the following facts: A national organization called Oxford House rented a house in the City of Edmonds, Washington, and opened a group home for ten to twelve recovering alcoholics and addicts. The city cited the operator of the Oxford House group home for violating the city's zoning code, which provided that the occupants of single-family dwellings must compose a "family," defined as "persons [without regard to number] related by genetics, adoption, or marriage, or a group of five or fewer [unrelated] persons." The group home acknowledged that it was in violation of the ordinance but claimed that it was entitled to be in the neighborhood because the FHAA required the city to "make reasonable accommodations in rules, policies, practices, or services, when such accommodations may be necessary to afford [handicapped] person[s] equal opportunity to use and enjoy a dwelling."[b] The city responded that it was not required to accommodate a group home because the FHAA exempts from its coverage "any reasonable, local, State, or Federal restriction regarding the maximum number of occupants permitted to occupy a dwelling."[c]

---

Winston-Salem. Those complaints that are retained by HUD may be resolved in one of three ways:

1. **Conciliation.** This path of resolution does not involve a formal determination of discrimination.
2. **Election of Trial in Federal District Court.** Should one party to the complaint elect to proceed to federal district court with the complaint, the case is handled by a HUD prosecutor, and the aggrieved individual may seek equitable relief, actual damages, and attorneys' fees.
3. **HUD Administrative Hearing.** All complaints not handled by conciliation or federal district court are resolved in a HUD administrative hearing. The hearing is prosecuted by a HUD lawyer and decided by a law judge appointed by HUD. The administrative judge may award actual damages to the aggrieved individual, a civil penalty of up to $50,000, injunctive relief, and attorneys' fees.

In matters involving zoning and land use, HUD does not issue a charge of discrimination. Instead, HUD refers matters it believes may be meritorious to the Department of Justice, which, in its discretion, may decide to bring a suit against the local government. The Department of Justice may also bring a suit in a case that has not been the subject of a HUD complaint by exercising its power to initiate litigation alleging a pattern or practice of discrimination or denial of rights to a group of persons protected by the act.

*Affirmatively Furthering Fair Housing*

It is important to note that section 3608(e)(5) of the FHAA and several HUD regulations articulate a duty to localities receiving federal funds to affirmatively further fair housing. Local governments receiving funds under the Community Development Block Grant program, for example, are required to conduct an analysis of the impediments to fair housing in their communities and to take action to eradicate those impediments. A federal district court

The Court found that, although rules designed to prevent overcrowding by capping the total number of occupants allowed in a dwelling clearly fall within the exemption from the FHAA, rules designed to preserve the family character of a neighborhood by focusing on the composition of households rather than on the total number of occupants living in a dwelling do not.[d] The Court found that the city code provisions were classic examples of use restrictions and complementing family composition rules, which do not cap the number of people who may live in a dwelling but direct that dwellings be used to house families.[e]

The Court held that zoning ordinances that fail to impose uniform conditions on all residences may be challenged under the FHAA for, by its very terms, discriminating prima facie against group homes.[f] The several lower courts that have considered the issue since the *Oxford House* decision have split on whether non-uniform conditions and other non-uniform requirements imposed on group homes for the handicapped violate the FHAA.[g]

---

a. City of Edmonds v. Oxford House, Inc., 514 U.S. 725 (1995).

b. 42 U.S.C. § 3604(f)(3)(B).

c. *Id.* at 3607(b)(1).

d. The Court held that the city's zoning code definition of "family" is not a maximum-occupancy restriction exempt from the Fair Housing Amendments Act (FHAA), 42 U.S.C. § 3607(b)(1).

e. Justice Thomas, joined by Justice Scalia and Justice Kennedy, dissented, arguing that in order to take advantage of the exemption from the FHAA, zoning laws need not impose restrictions establishing an absolute maximum number of occupants but rather need only impose a restriction "regarding" the maximum number of occupants.

f. The Court was careful to note that it was not deciding this issue. In footnote 4, it stated, "We do not decide whether Edmonds' Zoning Code provisions defining 'family' as the City would apply it against Oxford House, violates the FHAA's prohibitions against discrimination set out in 42 U.S. Code, § 3604 et seq." The Court sent the case back to the lower courts to determine whether (1) the ordinance unlawfully discriminated against handicapped individuals and (2) the city's refusal to grant the group home an exemption from the ordinance as a "reasonable accommodation" deprived these handicapped individuals of their "equal opportunity to use and enjoy a dwelling." *City of Edmonds,* 514 U.S. at 742.

g. In *Oxford House-C v. City of St. Louis,* for example, the Eighth Circuit held that an ordinance that limited the number of group home occupants to eight residents did not by its terms discriminate prima facie against the handicapped because the ordinance also capped other types of housing for unrelated individuals and was therefore neutral with regard to handicap. 77 F.3d 249, 251–52 (8th Cir. 1996). On the other hand, in *Larkin v. Dep't of Soc. Servs.,* the Sixth Circuit addressed a state licensing requirement that group homes for the handicapped not locate within a 1,500-foot radius of other such group homes and must notify the communities in which the group homes are to be located. 89 F.3d 285 (6th Cir. 1996). The court ruled that these spacing and notification requirements discriminated against group homes. The court based its ruling on the finding that the statutes singled out group homes for the handicapped for regulation.

---

recently held that plaintiffs may bring a civil rights claim against a local government to "combat a violation of section 3608(e)(5)."[43]

## Rent Control

G.S. 42-14.1 provides that no county or city may enact any form of rent control unless the county or city owns the property, or has entered into an agreement with the owner for the control of subsidized rental property, or has assisted in the construction of the property with Community Development Block Grant funds. Given this law, a local government can provide rent control restrictions on privately owned property only if the owner or developer receives some public subsidy and agrees to control of the rents.

Local governments might question whether, despite the state's prohibition on the control of rents, the same objective could be accomplished through inclusionary zon-

ing (discussed on pages 24–27 ). Both inclusionary zoning and rent-control ordinances involve a situation in which the landowner retains ownership of a housing property but is restricted as to the economic return that may be realized. Despite this similarity, there are a number of arguments that have been advanced to distinguish inclusionary zoning ordinances from traditional rent control.

First, it has been argued that inclusionary zoning is a remedial response to the effects of exclusionary zoning. Second, advocates point out that inclusionary zoning applies to new developments and not to existing dwellings. Third, an inclusionary zoning ordinance can include both rental and home-ownership programs. Fourth, unlike most rent-control programs, inclusionary zoning screens owners and tenants to ensure that the program helps lower-income households.

These distinguishing arguments are unlikely to prevail in court.[44] In fact, at least one other state court has struck down an inclusionary zoning ordinance as violating a statutory prohibition against rent control. In rejecting the distinctions between inclusionary zoning and rent control, the Colorado Supreme Court invalidated a local inclusionary zoning ordinance that set a base rent and effectively limited any rental rate increase. The court held that the "scheme as a whole operated to suppress rental values below their market values"[45] in contravention of the state's prohibition against rent control.

Moreover, a North Carolina appellate court has determined that if a particular use of land is permitted, it is beyond the power of a local government to regulate the manner of ownership of that land.[46] Thus, if the land is zoned residential, a local government may not limit its residents to renters.

## Manufactured Housing

Commonly referred to as trailers or mobile homes, manufactured housing has become a relatively low-cost alternative to conventional stick-built housing. It increasingly plays a major role in providing safe, affordable, and adequate housing not only for lower-income home buyers and renters, but also for those of higher economic status. While negative images may continue to be the stereotype of the typical trailer or mobile home resident,[47] the reality is that twenty-two million Americans live in manufactured housing, and new owners represent all age groups and every economic status and lifestyle.[48]

*Manufactured housing* refers to a specific type of factory-built housing that has been constructed and manufactured in compliance with U.S. Housing and Urban Development Construction and Safety Standards.[49] Modular housing and other types of industrialized housing that are also factory-built do not comply with the HUD codes but must comply with state building codes. Often community residents confuse the two or continue to base perceptions of manufactured housing on earlier, less attractive, and structurally inadequate generations of mobile homes and those mobile home parks that are poorly maintained. Local government regulations may support these stereotypes by enacting local land use regulations that reject manufactured housing as an acceptable option for residential use, exclude it from most residential districts, or confine it to mobile-home parks or small-lot subdivisions.

The North Carolina General Assembly has recognized manufactured housing as a legitimate strategy to increase the housing supply and decrease housing costs. Also recognizing that some local governments had adopted zoning regulations that severely restricted the placement of manufactured homes, in 1987 the legislature enacted G.S. 160A-383.1, which prohibited a city from adopting or enforcing zoning regulations or other provisions that have the effect of excluding manufactured homes from the entire zoning jurisdiction. Permissible restrictions include

1. standards on location, such as allowing manufactured housing only in certain zoning districts or in mobile home parks;
2. dimensional requirements, such as allowing only double-wide units in certain zoning districts; and
3. appearance standards, such as requiring that skirting be installed or requiring units to have pitched roofs.[50]

These requirements apply only to units defined as manufactured homes. A few zoning ordinances apply similar location and appearance standards to modular homes. Most ordinances, however, treat modular homes the same as conventional site-built housing.[51]

### The Legal Status of Manufactured Homes

The manufactured home is a hybrid between vehicle and house and, as such, it presents considerable ambiguity regarding its proper legal treatment for purposes of taxation, financing, and tenant's rights. In taxation, for instance, some states treat manufactured housing as personal property while others treat it as real property or land. The trend is to treat these homes like real property, which includes any other home permanently affixed to a privately owned site. Many states, including North Carolina, compromise by treating these homes as either personal or real property, depending on how the unit is affixed to its site.[52]

Similarly, manufactured home loans traditionally have been treated like automobile loans rather than home mortgages, even when the home was permanently affixed to an owner-occupied site. Consequently, the interest charged was higher than that available to buyers of conventional home loans, and the interest paid on the loan was not tax-deductible. In North Carolina, the General Assembly passed legislation in 2003 to make it easier for owners of manufactured homes that are permanently affixed to land and subject to a land-lease of at least twenty years to gain access to loan products similar to those available to owners of site-built homes.[53]

## Historic Districts and Landmarks

Historic landmark regulations protect individual buildings. Historic district regulations, on the other hand, protect entire areas of aesthetic, architectural, or historic significance. Each can act to restrict development. A certificate of appropriateness must be secured for any new construction, for any alteration of the exteriors of existing buildings, and for any demolition or removal of a structure.[54]

## Notes

1. Advisory Comm'n on Regulatory Barriers to Affordable Housing, U.S. Dep't of Hous. & Urban Dev., 1-1. Not in My Back Yard: Removing Barriers to Affordable Housing (1991) (report to President Bush and Secretary Kemp).

2. Lynn E. Cunningham, *A Structural Analysis of Housing Subsidy Delivery Systems: Public Housing Authorities' Part in Solving the Housing Crisis,* 13 Fall J. Affordable Hous. & Cmty. Dev. L. 95, 101 (2003).

3. Jesse Dukeminer & James E. Krier, Property 1226 (2d ed. 1988).

4. *See, e.g.,* County Comm'rs v. Miles, 246 Md. 355, 228 A.2d 450 (1967) (five-acre zoning); Golden v. Planning Bd. of Town of Remapo, 30 N.Y.2d 359, 285 N.E.2d 291, 334 N.Y.S.2d 138 (1972) (phased zoning); Valley View Village, Inc. v. Proffett, 221 F.2d 412 (6th Cir. 1955) (zoning entire community for single-family use); Flora Realty & Inv. Co. v. City of Ladue, 362 Mo. 1025, 246 S.W.2d 771 (1952) (*en banc*) (three-acre zoning).

5. 416 U.S. 1, 9 (1974).

6. *See, e.g.,* Metropolitan Hous. Dev. Corp. v. Village of Arlington Heights, 558 F.2d 1283 (7th Cir. 1977) (municipality had obligation under Fair Housing Act "to refrain from zoning policies that effectively foreclose the construction of any low-cost housing within its corporate boundaries"), *on remand from* 429 U.S. 252 (1977), *cert. denied,* 434 U.S. 1025 (1978); Dailey v. City of Lawton, 425 F.2d 1037 (10th Circ. 1970) (actions of planning commission and city council in denying building permit and zoning change to low-income housing project found to be racially motivated, arbitrary, and unreasonable); Kennedy Park Homes Ass'n v. City of Lackawanna, 318 F. Supp. 669 (D.C.N.Y. 1970) (city council's actions in amending zoning ordinance to prevent construction of low-income housing subdivision violated Fair Housing Act and Equal Protection Clause), *aff'd,* 436 F.2d 108 (2d Cir. 1970), *cert. denied,* 401 U.S. 1010 (1971). Cases invalidating exclusionary zoning practices usually are brought under the Fair Housing Act, 42 U.S.C. §§ 3601–3619 (1982), which is intended to protect individuals from private discrimination and to free the housing market from regulations that perpetuate segregated housing patterns.

7. Michael Danielson, The Politics of Exclusion 23 (1976).

8. *Id.*

9. http://www.hud.gov/offices/adm/grants/frregbarrier. pdf. Last visited June 30, 2004.

10. *Id.*

11. J. Hunter Schofield, *Types of Inclusionary Zoning Programs,* in Locally Initiated Inclusionary Zoning Programs: A Guide for Local Governments in North Carolina and Beyond (Anita R. Brown-Graham, ed., Chapel Hill, N.C.: Institute of Government, 2004).

12. In North Carolina, a rezoning can be one of three types: conventional, conditional, and conditional-use district. *See* David Owens, Introduction to Zoning, 47–50 (2d ed., Chapel Hill, N.C.: Institute of Government, 2001).

13. *See* Schofield, *supra* note 11.

14. *See* An Act Amending the Charter of the City of Wilmington to Authorize Zoning Density Bonuses in Projects Containing Specified Amounts of Low and Moderate Income Housing, 1991 N.C. Sess. Laws ch. 119.

15. *See* An Act to Authorize the City and County of Durham to Allow Zoning Density Bonuses in Projects Containing Specified Amounts of Low and Moderate Income Housing, 1975 N.C. Sess. Laws ch. 671.

16. *See* An Act Concerning Zoning by the City of Winston-Salem and Forsyth County, 1993 N.C. Sess. Laws ch. 588.

17. *See* An Act to Make Various Amendments to Laws Applicable to Orange and Chatham Counties,1991 N.C. Sess. Laws ch. 246 .

18. State courts in New Jersey, New York, and Pennsylvania, relying on state constitutional provisions, require municipal land use regulations to promote the "general welfare, which they have defined as the welfare of the entire region. *See* Southern Burlington County NAACP v. Township of Mount Laurel, 67 N.J. 151, 336 A.2d 713, (1975), *appeal dismissed,* 423 U.S. 808 (1975) (commonly known as *Mount Laurel I* ); Southern Burlington County NAACP v. Township of Mount Laurel, 92 N.J. 158, 456 A.2d 390 (1983) (commonly known as *Mount Laurel II*); Berenson v. Town of New Castle, 38 N.Y.2d 102, 341 N.E.2d 236, 378 N.Y.S.2d 672 (1975); Surrick v. Zoning Hearing Bd., 476 Pa. 182, 382 A.2d 105 (1977) (ordinance unconstitutionally excluded multi-family dwellings); *In re* Girsh, 437 Pa. 237, 263 A.2d 395 (1970) (failure of ordinance to provide for apartments was unconstitutional); Camp Hill Dev. Co. v. Zoning Bd. of Adjustment, 13 Pa. Commw. 519, 319 A.2d 197 (1974) (failure of ordinance to provide for townhouses was unconstitutional).

19. Board of Supervisors v. DeGroff Enters., 214 Va. 235, 238, 198 S.E.2d 600, 602 (1973) (the court also found that the ordinance constituted an unconstitutional taking because it required the developer to sell or rent dwelling units to lower-income households "at rental or sales prices not fixed by a free market"); *see also* Middlesex v. Alderman of Newton, 371 Mass. 849, 359 N.E.2d 1279 (1977) (invalidating 10 percent set-aside requirement absent express authority in zoning legislation); *compare* Iodice v. City of Newton, 397 Mass. 329, 491 N.E.2d 618 (1986) (upholding the imposition of set-aside requirements for special-use permits).

20. David W. Owens, *Local Government Authority to Implement Smart Growth Programs: Dillon's Rule, Legislative Reform, and the Current State of Affairs in North Carolina,* 35 Wake Forest L. Rev. 671, 694 (2000) (citing N.C. Gen. Stat. 160A-4 (hereinafter G.S.)).

21. *Mount Laurel II,* 456 A.2d at 449; *but see* Town of Telluride v. Lot Thirty-Four Venture, L.L.C., 3 P.3d 30 (Colo. 2000) (distinguishing a rent-control measure in an inclusionary zoning ordinance from ordinary zoning provisions on the ground that it operated as economic legislation).

22. 3 Norman Williams, American Land Planning Law 77 (1975).

23. G.S. 153A-340 and 160A-381 (2003).

24. G.S. 153A-331 and 160A-372 (2003).

25. G.S. 153A-121 and 160A-174 (2003).

26. Homebuilders Ass'n of Charlotte v. City of Charlotte, 336 N.C. 37, 442 S.E.2d 45 (1994).

27. Smith Chapel Baptist Church v. City of Durham, 350 N.C. 805, 517 S.E.2d 874 (1999).

28. *See id.*

29. David J. Barron, *Reclaiming Home Rule,* 116 Harv. L. Rev. 2255, 2361 (2003) (citing Dacey v. Town of Barnstable, No. 00-53 (Barnstable Super. Ct. Oct 23, 2000), *available at* http://www.mhp.net/termsheets/dacey_vs_barnstable.pdf).

30. *Id.* (citing San Telmo Assocs. v. City of Seattle, 735 P.2d 673, 674–75 (Wash. 1987)).

31. Shelley v. Kraemer, 334 U.S. 1, 22 (1948).

32. 392 U.S. 409, 449 (1968).

33. Previously, section 1982 had been generally held to bar discrimination only in state actions.

34. In 1969, a federal district court granted summary judgment in favor of the plaintiffs, finding that the Chicago Housing Authority violated the Civil Rights Act of 1866 (and the Equal Protection Clause of the Fourteenth Amendment) by building public housing and discriminatorily assigning tenants to the developments based on their race. The court based its ruling on uncontested evidence that showed that the public housing system was racially segregated. Specifically, the court noted that four projects with an overwhelmingly white resident population were located in white neighborhoods, while the rest of the family units (over 99 percent) were located in black neighborhoods and housed nearly all black tenants (99 percent). Gautreaux v. Chicago Hous. Auth., 296 F. Supp. 907, 911–14 (N.D. Ill. 1969).

35. Section 1982 is also considered expansive because it covers discrimination related to any "real or personal property," not just dwellings.

36. G.S. 41A-1 through -10.

37. *See* 42 U.S.C. § 3603(b).

38. *See id.*

39. Important qualifications to the application of the FHAA to local land use regulations include (1) a statement that the amendments are not intended to invalidate or limit any law that "requires dwellings to be designed and constructed in a manner that affords handicapped persons greater access than is required by" the act and (2) a provision that dwellings do not have to be made available to individuals "whose tenancy would constitute a direct threat to the health and safety of other individuals or whose tenancy would result in substantial physical damage to the property of others." The amendments also exempt from coverage "any reasonable local, State, or Federal restrictions regarding the maximum number of occupants permitted to occupy a dwelling." In addition, the amendments exempt housing for older persons from the familial status discrimination prohibitions. *See* 42 U.S.C. § 3604(f)(8), (f)(9), (1995), 42 U.S.C. § 3607(b)(1), (2) (1995).

40. 42 U.S.C. § 3602(k).

41. The FHAA uses the term "handicap" instead of "disability." Both terms have the same legal meaning. *See* Bragdon v. Abbott, 524 U.S. 624, 631 (1998) (noting that the definition of "disability" in the Americans with Disabilities Act is drawn almost verbatim "from the definition of 'handicap' contained in the Fair Housing Amendments Act of 1988"). Disability or handicapped protection is specifically defined to include all individuals "with physical or mental impairment that substantially limits one or more of such person's major life activities," all individuals "with

a record of such impairment," and all individuals "regarded as having such an impairment." This provision also prohibits discrimination against non-disabled persons "associated or residing with disabled persons." 42 U.S.C. § 3602(h).

42. Housing providers that receive federal financial assistance are also subject to the requirements of Section 504 of the Rehabilitation Act of 1973. 29 U.S.C. § 794. Section 504 imposes greater obligations than the FHAA, such as providing and paying for reasonable accommodations that involve structural modifications to units or to public and common areas.

43. Wallace v. Chicago Hous. Auth. 298, F. Supp. 2d 710 (N.D. Ill. 2003).

44. *See* Barbara Ehrlich Kautz, *In Defense of Inclusionary Zoning: Successfully Creating Affordable Housing*, 36 U.S.F.L. Rev. 971, 1016 (2002) at 1016.

45. Town of Telluride v. Lot Thirty-Four Venture L.L.C., 3 P.3d 30, 35 (Colo. 2000).

46. Graham Court Associates v. Town Council of Chapel Hill, 53 N.C. App. 543, 281 S.E.2d 418 (1981).

47. The literature identifies negative attitudes about manufactured housing that often center on two issues: the economic impact that manufactured home communities have on a neighborhood and the types of people who live in them. Concerns about the neighborhood effects of manufactured housing are usually articulated as issues of safety, quality, appearance, and appreciation of value, and the impact these factors have on neighboring property values. For a review of the literature, see Julia O. Beamish et al., *Not a Trailer Anymore: Perceptions of Manufactured Housing*, Housing Policy Debate, vol. 12, iss. 2, 2001.

48. In a 2002 nationwide survey of manufactured housing residents, affordability, pride of ownership, low maintenance costs, and less upkeep were cited as the major advantages of living in this type of housing. Foremost Insurance Group, *2002 Manufactured Homes: The Market Facts* (Grand Rapids, Mich., *at* http://cp.foremost.com/market_facts_2002/).

49. Federal law sets construction standards for manufactured housing, and a city or county may not impose additional building or safety standards. This limited federal preemption does not prohibit local government regulation of the appearance of manufactured housing.

50. Owens, *supra* note 12, at 92.

51. *See* Owens, *supra* note 12, at 92.

52. *See* G.S. 20-50; G.S. 47-20b; G.S. 47-20.7; *see also* 105-164.3.

53. G.S. 47-20.b; *see also* G.S. § 70-288.

54. *See* Owens, *supra* note 12, at 78.

# 3  Constitutional Limitations on Local Government Housing Activities

While local governments have significant discretion in their affordable housing activities, they are required to operate within the confines of the federal and state constitutions. This section singles out some of the constitutional provisions that are most likely to be implicated by a local government's affordable housing actions.

## Public Purpose

The North Carolina Constitution, article V, section 2(1) provides: "The power of taxation shall be exercised in a just and equitable manner, for public purposes only, and shall never be surrendered, suspended, or contracted away." This provision has been interpreted to mean that any fiscal expenditure by a local government, including that involving housing activity, must be predicated on satisfying the threshold constitutional requirement that public funds be expended for a public purpose.[1] Thus, although the constitutional language speaks of the "power of taxation," the limitation has not been confined to government use of tax revenues but extended to the appropriation and spending powers of local governments.

Courts have recognized that what constitutes a "public purpose" is not fixed in time but shifts as governments adapt their activities to changes in the population, the economy, and other conditions. In the 1996 case of *Maready v. City of Winston-Salem*,[2] the North Carolina Supreme Court upheld a local government's payments and other assistance to a private business for economic development on the ground that an "expenditure does not lose its public purpose merely because it involves a private actor. Generally, if an act will promote the welfare of a state or a local government and its citizens, it is for a public purpose." The *Maready* court found that even though a private business would receive funds and other direct benefits, these were incidental to the primary public goal (economic development) of the appropriation. In other words, a private individual or business may directly benefit from a public purpose contract or an appropriation.[3]

Based on similar reasoning, North Carolina Courts have held the public purpose requirement is met by affordable housing programs, including the issuance of bonds to finance the construction or rehabilitation of housing for low- and moderate-income persons, public ownership and management of rental units for low-income persons, and the creation of housing authorities for urban or rural areas.[4]

## Equal Protection
### Defining Equal Protection Claims

The right to "equal protection of the laws" is included in the Fourteenth Amendment of the United States Constitution and in the North Carolina Constitution, article I, section 19.[5] Equal protection means that people have a right not to be treated differently from other "similarly situated" persons or groups.[6] Thus laws may usually not discriminate between two persons in the same situation.[7] A law that treats two individuals differently "must be 'reasonable, not arbitrary, and must rest upon some ground of difference having a fair and substantial relation to the object of the legislation.'"[8]

The Equal Protection Clause has evolved over the history of this nation to reflect evolving standards of civil rights. While the clause is today considered by the courts to prohibit governmental housing discrimination based on race, this was not always the case. When public housing was initiated in the 1930s, the separate-but-equal doctrine of *Plessy v. Ferguson*[9] was the law, and local housing authorities regularly selected separate locations for units to be occupied by white and minority families. "If the tenants were to be poor blacks, the project was located where poor blacks already lived; if the tenants were to be poor whites, the projects were located where poor whites already lived."[10] The *Brown v. Board of Education*[11] decision struck down the separate-but-equal doctrine in 1954.[12]

## Evaluating Equal Protection Claims

Depending on the nature of the law being challenged, courts evaluate an equal protection claim using one of two standards of review: *rational basis scrutiny* or *strict scrutiny*. Both involve the same two general components: whether the law serves a government purpose and then whether any differences in treatment of similarly situated individuals are justified to further the legitimate government objective.[13]

Of the two, strict scrutiny is a much more difficult standard for a government to overcome. The burden of strict scrutiny is especially difficult because it requires a government to demonstrate that the challenged law furthers a *compelling* governmental interest and is narrowly drawn to do so.[14] In contrast, rational basis scrutiny requires only that the law serve a *legitimate* governmental purpose and that any distinction it makes between groups be justified. Thus, assuming a finding of a legitimate government purpose, the analysis revolves around whether there is a sound basis for any distinction that the law makes.[15]

Although the standards of review are relatively similar in method, their results vary considerably in practice. Whereas the outcome under strict scrutiny is most likely to be a finding that a government action is unconstitutional, in a rational basis scrutiny review that is rarely the outcome. Under the rational basis standard, courts show extreme deference toward the governing body's decision regarding the policy goal and the means of achieving it; but under strict scrutiny, courts behave in virtually the opposite way. A court will take the strict scrutiny approach if the law either involves a *suspect classification* or restricts certain *fundamental interests*.

The classic example of a suspect classification is race, which, because of the immutable characteristics involved and the likelihood that these characteristics provide no sensible ground for differential treatment,[16] merits a more difficult standard. A court will review any express classification in an ordinance to determine if it is suspect, and it will consider evidence that an ordinance, though neutral, is being enforced through the use of a classification.[17]

Fundamental interests are those interests which a court has found to be constitutionally significant[18] to an individual's liberty such that they require greater protection (freedom of speech, freedom of association, and so on). While there are many activities that are regarded as fundamental to life, courts generally refuse to classify an interest as "fundamental" for the purposes of equal protection unless they can find constitutional support for that interest.[19] Thus, an equal protection claim that a statute affects a fundamental interest must have a basis in some other part of the United States Constitution.

City of Raleigh spending public dollars for a public purpose: Affordable housing in Meadowcreek Subdivision.

## Due Process

The Fourteenth Amendment to the United States Constitution provides, in part, that "no state shall make or enforce any law which shall deprive any person of life, liberty, or property, without due process of law." Known as the Due Process Clause, this provision may be the basis of claims of both procedural and substantive due process violations.

### Defining Procedural Due Process

Procedural due process requires that a party receive notice and an opportunity to be heard prior to being deprived of a significant interest involving life, liberty, or property In order to state a valid procedural due process claim, the plaintiff must demonstrate that

1. there existed a property interest,[20] which
2. the local government intruded upon,
3. without due process of law.[21]

Local governments are required to provide sufficient procedures to guarantee constitutional protections before acting to terminate a property interest. However, a person must already enjoy a constitutionally protected benefit in order to assert a procedural due process right in the denial of that benefit.[22] Thus a court's first task when considering a due process claim is to determine whether the governmental action intruded upon a constitutionally protected interest. Protected interests in affordable housing include, for example, a public housing tenant's continued expectation of housing during the term of the lease.

Second, the court must determine whether sufficient procedures are available to challenge the government's action. Except in emergencies, procedural due process generally requires that a hearing be held before the government takes away the protected interest.[23] Thus, while housing tenants of privately owned housing generally are not entitled to pre-eviction hearings as long as the state landlord-tenant law will provide the tenants with a post-eviction due process type hearing,[24] public housing tenants are entitled to fairly formal due process hearings prior to eviction because the courts have held that they have a property interest in the expectation of continued housing. Other affordable housing strategies, including both condemnation by eminent domain and application of a minimum housing ordinance, require that reasonable notice and hearing opportunities—the traditional protections of procedural due process—be afforded to those adversely affected by the government's actions before the government acts.

In the above examples, local governments face the most stringent due process requirements because the decisions being made are considered quasi-judicial.[25] Quasi-judicial decisions involve efforts to "investigate facts, or ascertain the existence of facts, hold hearings, weigh evidence, and draw conclusions from them, as a basis for their official action, and to exercise discretion of a judicial nature."[26] Examples of other quasi-judicial decisions include zoning variances, special- and conditional-use permits, and appeals of administrative determinations in public housing and relocation assistance cases. These quasi-judicial decisions require fair trial standards, which include "an evidentiary hearing with the right of the parties to offer evidence; cross-examine adverse witnesses; inspect documents; have sworn testimony; and have written findings of fact supported by competent, substantial, and material evidence."[27]

### Defining Substantive Due Process

The doctrine of substantive due process is concerned with whether a particular action to regulate an individual's interest is justified. Substantive due process covers the protections of most of the Bill of Rights (the first ten amendments to the United States Constitution) and provides more general protections against certain arbitrary, wrongful government actions regardless of the fairness of the procedures used to implement them.[28]

To prevail on a claim of a substantive due process violation, plaintiffs must demonstrate: "(1) that they had property or a property interest; (2) that the state deprived them of this property or property interest; and (3) that the state's action fell so far beyond the outer limits of legitimate governmental action that no process could cure the deficiency."[29]

In examining a governmental action for due process violations, the judiciary applies a two-prong test. The court first determines whether the government's action furthers a legitimate governmental interest. Upon finding a legitimate interest, the court then looks to see whether there is a reasonable relationship between the burden imposed by

the government and the benefits conferred to the public and the affected party. Whether substantive due process is violated is a question of both degree and reasonableness in relationship to the public good that is likely to result from the requirements of an ordinance. The court will invalidate a government's actions only where the record shows the action had no foundation in reason and bears no substantial relation to public health, morals, safety, or welfare in its proper sense.[30]

### Takings

The Fifth Amendment to the United States Constitution was designed "to bar Government from forcing some people alone to bear public burdens which, in all fairness and justice, should be borne by the public as a whole."[31] As such, the amendment prevents governments from taking private property for public use without just compensation. The North Carolina Constitution does not contain an express provision prohibiting the taking of private property for public use without payment of just compensation. However, the North Carolina Supreme Court has inferred such a provision as a fundamental right integral to the "law of the land" clause in article I, section 19 of the state constitution.[32] Although not necessarily controlling, federal court decisions interpreting the construction and effect of this fundamental right under the United States Constitution are persuasive authority in interpreting the "law of the land" clause.[33]

A government program is sometimes challenged as constituting a *taking on its face*—that is, as invalid in any and every application. Even when a program is not an unconstitutional taking on its face, it may be challenged as being a taking in the way it is applied to a particular person.[34]

Takings challenges can arise in affordable housing in a number of contexts. For example, where a local government demolishes a substandard house under its minimum housing ordinance or exercises its power of eminent domain to take property as part of a redevelopment plan, the owner may well bring a takings challenge. Similarly, a developer could argue that a mandatory inclusionary zoning program, or a required public dedication of part of the property to be used as a park in exchange for zoning approval on the proposed development, results in an unlawful taking because it deprives the developer of the full economic benefit of his or her property.

### Evaluating a Takings Claim under Federal Law

There are differing standards for determining whether a local government's action has resulted in an unconstitutional taking. The examples cited earlier provide

## A Case in Point: *Cuyahoga Falls v. Buckeye Community Hope Foundation*

In the case of *Cuyahoga Falls v. Buckeye Community Hope Foundation*,[a] the Supreme Court confronted a classic case of NIMBYism (not in my backyard) in opposition to an affordable housing development. The city council of Cuyahoga Falls, Ohio, passed a site plan ordinance authorizing the construction of a multi-family, low-income housing complex by Buckeye Community Hope Foundation. Responding to immediate opposition on the part of city residents, Buckeye agreed to various conditions, including the construction, on one side of the complex, of an earthen wall surrounded by a fence. The city's planning commission then unanimously approved the site plan and submitted it to the council for final authorization.

Opposition to the plan resurfaced during the final approval process. Citizens, including the mayor, voiced concerns that African American families with children would move into the development and that crime and drug activity would escalate. Despite the opposition, the city council approved the plan.

A group of citizens filed a formal petition with the city requesting that the ordinance be repealed or submitted to a popular vote. Pursuant to the city charter, the petition stayed implementation of the plan. Buckeye responded by seeking an injunction in state court to force the city to move forward with the plan. Although the state court denied the injunction, Buckeye requested building permits from the city to begin construction. The city engineer rejected the request after being advised by the city attorney that the site plan ordinance could not take effect while the petition was still pending. The voters of Cuyahoga Falls later passed the referendum, thus repealing the site plan ordinance. However, the Ohio Supreme Court invalidated the referendum, holding that the state constitution did not authorize referendums related to administrative acts. The referendum having been declared unconstitutional, the city issued the building permits and Buckeye began construction.

Buckeye and others (collectively, "Buckeye") filed a federal suit alleging violations of the Fourteenth Amendment of the United States Constitution. Specifically, Buckeye contended that the city and its officials had violated the Equal Protection and Due Process Clauses of the amendment by (1) submitting the petition to the voters and (2) refusing to issue any building permits during the time the petition was pending. As discussed earlier in this chapter, the Equal Protection Clause provides that no government "shall make or enforce any law which shall . . . deny to any person within its jurisdiction the equal protection of the laws." At the heart of this clause is the principle that, without a compelling reason, governments should refrain from intentionally distributing differing levels of public benefits to persons on the basis of race, religion, sex, or national origin. The substantive Due Process Clause, which prohibits governments from making or enforcing "any law which shall deprive any person of life, liberty, or property, without due process of law," protects persons from arbitrary, wrongful government action.

---

a good basis for examining the range of possible takings cases.

First, in most cases, the plaintiff who challenges the condemnation of a substandard building will not succeed on a takings claim in court as the police power includes the power to condemn unsafe buildings. When a building is condemned under legitimate exercise of the police power, the owner is not compensated. Instead, the local government may require the owner to demolish the building at the owner's expense or to reimburse the government for its demolition expenses. There are limits to this power, however.[35]

Second, in the case of eminent domain, the applicable state statutes themselves require that just compensation be provided to the owner of the condemned property. While courts are generally deferential to a government's determination that a taking is necessary to meet a public purpose, they will intervene to resolve disputes regarding just compensation to ensure that the government does not violate the rights of the property owner as provided for in the Constitution.[36]

Finally, courts are likely to be the least deferential in those cases that do implicate the takings clause but do not involve eminent domain and its requirement that just compensation be granted to the property owner. Even within this set of cases, however, courts apply differing standards. Where the taking is a physical one—for example, the imposed dedication of a portion of a developer's land—courts consider the taking to be an exaction and apply the more stringent *exaction standard*. Courts apply the less stringent standard to land use control measures, which are regulatory takings. The *land use control* standard usually results in a finding that the governmental action is permissible; the exaction standard is more likely to result in a finding that the action constitutes an unconstitutional taking.

General zoning ordinances are typically categorized as land use controls and not exactions. Land use controls

In reviewing the city's petition process, the Court concluded that there was no violation of the Equal Protection Clause because there was no evidence of racially discriminatory intent or purpose on the part of the city. The city's charter set out a petitioning procedure that respected the First Amendment rights of speech and petition for all residents and did not appear to be discriminatory against any group of people. Moreover, according to the Court, the city could not be said to have given effect to any voter's discriminatory motives for supporting the petition simply by placing the referendum on the ballot, pursuant to the charter.

Buckeye had also argued that city officials, including the mayor, acted in partnership with private citizens to prevent the project from being built because of the race and family status of its likely residents. The Court was unpersuaded by Buckeye's allegations that the city attorney had prompted disgruntled voters to file the petition, that the city council had intentionally delayed its deliberations to thwart the development, and that the mayor had stoked the public opposition. Finding that the city officials did not appear to have impelled the voters' decisions during the petition drive, the Court found no basis for a violation of the Equal Protection Clause based on the petition itself. Similarly, the court determined that the city engineer, in refusing to issue the building permit while the referendum was pending, could not be said to have been motivated by discriminatory intent in violation of the Equal Protection Clause. In the Court's view, he was merely carrying out his duties in the way he had been instructed.

The Court also rejected the bases advanced by Buckeye to support the substantive due-process claim. First, Buckeye had argued that because the city engineer had refused to issue the building permits, it had been arbitrarily deprived of its legitimate property interest. The Court did not address the issue of whether Buckeye had a legitimate claim of entitlement in the building permits. Instead, it summarily determined that, in light of the charter provisions, the city attorney's advice to the engineer not to issue the building permit while the petition was pending was "an eminently rational directive." Second, Buckeye contended that submitting an administrative decision to the referendum procedures provided for in the charter was in and of itself arbitrary conduct. The Court rejected as a matter of federal constitutional law the distinction that the Ohio Supreme Court had made, under state law, between administrative and legislative referendums. Though the Court pointed out that the substantive result of any referendum might be invalid if the referendum is "arbitrary and capricious," a referendum process that addresses either an administrative or a legislative decision cannot intrinsically constitute arbitrary conduct that is in violation of due process.[b]

---

a. 538 U.S. 188 (2003).

b. *See* Anita R. Brown-Graham, "Recent Supreme Court Cases Affecting Local Government," *The 2004 Municipal Lawyers Yearbook* (Washington, D.C.: International City/County Management Association, 2004).

involve what are essentially legislative determinations made at the state or local level that classify entire areas of the locality for certain uses. Intended to help localities develop in an orderly fashion, land use controls are considered to be legitimate uses of a local government's police power to protect the general welfare of the community.

To be considered a land use control, the general zoning ordinance must be generally applicable; that is, the local government must not engage in individual negotiation whereby the developer is put in a position of having to give up something in order to be allowed to develop the land.

An exaction, on the other hand, results when the local government bases development rights on the developer's making certain concessions. Zoning ordinances found to be exactions tend to involve individualized bargaining between the local government and the developer with the local government conditioning development approval on the developer's dedication of property for public use.

Property dedications result from the government's requiring a landowner to transfer title of a property to the government or to establish easements on the property. An example might involve a local government that requires, as a condition of zoning, that a developer transfer to the government part of the property to be developed as affordable housing. A takings analysis involving an exaction must be analyzed under *Nollan v. California Coastal Commission*[37] and *Dolan v. City of Tigard*,[38] both decided by the United States Supreme Court.

Under *Nollan*, there must be an "essential nexus" between the condition of approval and the impact of the project in order to meet the requirement that a governmental action "substantially advances" a legitimate state interest.[39] One way a local government could show this "essential nexus" between market-rate development and affordable housing would be by demonstrating that the construction of market-rate housing creates a need for affordable housing. A common argument, for example, is that a subdivision of luxury homes adds new consumers to a community. These consumers want to shop at nearby stores, and those stores have to hire low- and moderate-income workers. Thus, a nexus is made between the new housing construction and the local labor market needs.[40]

Under *Dolan*, there must also be a "rough proportionality" between the impact of the project and the conditions imposed by the ordinance. In order to show rough proportionality the local government must make an "individualized determination that the required dedication is related both in nature and extent to the impact of the proposed development."[41]

When analyzing a regulatory versus a physical taking (such as property dedications), all of an owner's rights in the land that is subject to the regulation must be considered together to determine whether the government has eliminated enough of the owner's rights for the courts to conclude that the government action was "tantamount to a condemnation or appropriation" of the land.[42] If not, the court will apply a three-factor balancing test laid out in the Supreme Court's decision in *Penn Central Transportation Co. v. New York City*.[43] *Penn Central* requires that a court consider

1. the economic impact of the government regulation on the landowner,
2. the extent to which the regulation interferes with investment-backed expectations of the landowner, and
3. the character of the government action.[44]

The first factor focuses on whether an "economic taking" has occurred. Under the Supreme Court's reasoning in *Lucas v. South Carolina Coastal Council*,[45] a government regulation may not deprive an owner of all economically viable uses of his or her land. Such a deprivation without just compensation is an unconstitutional taking. The second factor, which protects a landowner's investment-backed expectations, poses a more difficult hurdle. Government action need not deprive the owner of *all* economic value in the land in order for the action to be held unconstitutional;[46] the courts can invalidate the government's action if there is a significant economic impact on the land's value.[47] This is why, for example, local governments may seek to compensate for the lesser value of a development in inclusionary zoning programs by providing density bonuses, streamlined permitting, or lower site-improvement fees. The third factor of the *Penn Central* test considers whether the government action was justified.[48] Even if the local government's inclusionary zoning program avoids an economic taking, it still must be shown to substantially advance a legitimate state interest.[49]

According to the Supreme Court decision in *Agins v. City of Tiburon*,[50] a general zoning law does not result in a taking if it substantially advances the legitimate governmental purpose of providing affordable housing and does not deny developers all economically viable use of their property. Courts have defined "governmental purposes" broadly and will nullify a government taking only

in cases where the government acts in an arbitrary manner or in bad faith.[51]

The creation of affordable housing is a legitimate governmental purpose. A local government may therefore seek to create affordable housing opportunities if it can point to a shortage of such housing and also show how provisions in its responsive ordinance relate to its goal of creating affordable housing. A local government may point to these conditions even if it caused the problem it seeks to remedy.[52]

## Evaluating a Takings Claim under North Carolina Law

North Carolina courts have adopted an "ends–means" test similar to the one adopted by the federal courts.[53] When determining a regulatory taking, a North Carolina court considers whether (1) the governmental action at issue is a valid exercise of the police power by which the ends sought are related to the means used and (2) the property retains a practical use and a reasonable value.[54]

With respect to exactions, North Carolina state courts appear to have adopted a standard more stringent than the *Agins* "substantially advance" standard while stopping short of applying the *Dolan* test of "rough proportionality." While ruling on a different issue in *Batch v. Town of Chapel Hill*, the North Carolina Court of Appeals indicated that "exactions can only be imposed without compensation when the exaction condition meets a need created by the development and that as a result of the exaction there will be a commensurate benefit to the subdivision."[55]

## Notes

1. *See* Madison Cablevision, Inc. v. City of Morganton, 325 N.C. 634, 386 S.E.2d 200 (1989).

2. 342 N.C. 708, 467 S.E.2d 615 (1996).

3. For further discussion of this principle, see DAVID M. LAWRENCE, ECONOMIC DEVELOPMENT LAW FOR NORTH CAROLINA LOCAL GOVERNMENTS 3–6 (Chapel Hill, N.C.: Institute of Government, 2000).

4. *See In re* Denial of Approval to Issue $30,000,000.00 of Single Family Housing Bonds and $30,000,000.00 of Multi-Family Housing Bonds for Persons of Moderate Income, 307 N.C. 52, 296 S.E.2d 281 (1982) (holding that the North Carolina Housing Finance Agency's issuance of bonds to finance single- and multi-family housing for persons of moderate income serves a public purpose); Martin v. North Carolina Hous. Corp., 277 N.C. 29, 175 S.E.2d 665 (1970) (finding a public purpose in the Housing Finance Agency's authority to provide financing for residential housing constructions, new or rehabilitated, for sale or rental to persons and families of lower income); Wells v. Housing Authority of City of Wilmington, 213 N.C. 744, 197 S.E. 693 (1938) (finding the public purpose in the creation of urban housing authorities); *accord* Cox v. City of Kinston, 217 N.C. 391, 8 S.E.2d 252 (1940) (statute authorizing the rehabilitation of congested city areas through the construction, ownership, and rental of apartments and dwellings by housing authority as

constitutional and as comprehending a "public purpose"); Mallard v. E. Carolina Reg'l Hous. Auth., 221 N.C. 334, 20 S.E.2d 281 (1942) (finding that a rural area housing authority was created for a public purpose).

5. U.S. Const. amend. XIV, § 1 ("No State shall make or enforce any law which shall abridge the privileges or immunities of citizens of the United States; nor shall any State deprive any person of life, liberty, or property, without due process of law; nor deny to any person within its jurisdiction the equal protection of the laws"). In addition, the North Carolina Constitution states, "No person shall be denied the *equal protection of the laws.*" N.C. Const. art. 1, § 19 (emphasis added).

6. Grace Baptist Church v. City of Oxford, 320 N.C. 439, 447, 358 S.E.2d 372, 377 (1987) (quoting Maines v. City of Greensboro, 300 N.C. 126, 132, 265 S.E.2d 155, 159 (1980)).

7. For example, two owners of land of equal size with the same zoning classification and used for the same purpose should not be treated differently without clear justification. "[Any] differences must be justified by the law's purpose." Sylvia Dev. Corp. v. Calvert County, 48 F.3d 810, 818 (4th Cir. 1995).

8. *Id.* at 818 (quoting Royster Guano Co. v. Virginia, 253 U.S. 412, 415 (1920)).

9. 163 U.S. 537 (1896).

10. Housing for All Under the Law, *supra* Chapter 1, note 2, at 22.

11. 347 U.S. 483, 495 (1954).

12. Even after *Brown* struck down the separate-but-equal doctrine in 1954, publicly assisted housing programs continued to be complicit in race-conscious programming. Public housing authorities continued to make site-selection decisions based on race. *See* Comment, *The Public Housing Administration and Discrimination in Federally Assisted Low-Rent Housing,* 64 Mich. L. Rev. 871 (1966).

13. Grace Baptist Church v. City of Oxford, 320 N.C. at 446-7, 358 S.E.2d at 376-7.

14. White v. Pate, 308 N.C. 759, 766, 304 S.E.2d 199, 204 (1983).

15. Moore v. City of East Cleveland, 431 U.S. 494 (1977).

16. City of Cleburne v. Cleburne Living Center, Inc., 473 U.S. 432, 440 (1985).

17. *Id.* at 440 (the plaintiff has the burden of proving that the classification was actually utilized in the administrative action and that its use was intentional and purposeful). *See, e.g.,* Village of Arlington Heights v. Metro. Hous. Dev. Corp. 429 U.S. 252 (1977) (a predominantly white community refused to rezone an area for federally subsidized low-income housing). The Supreme Court upheld the local zoning ordinance in *Arlington Heights,* requiring the plaintiffs to prove racially motivated discriminatory intent on the part of the municipality in order to establish a violation of the Equal Protection Clause. However, on remand the Seventh Circuit in *Arlington II* held that a strong showing of discriminatory effect was enough to create a cognizable claim under Title VI. Arlington Heights II, 558 F.2d 1283, 1289-90 (1977). For a discussion of Title VI, see page 27, and Title VIII (FHA), see pages 27-31.

18. San Antonio Indep. Sch. Dist. v. Rodriguez, 411 U.S. 1 (1973).

19. *Id.* at 33.

20. For example, in order for a person to possess a property interest in a local zoning permit, it must be shown that the issuing department lacks all discretion to any issuance of the permit or to withhold its approval. No property interest exists where the local government retains discretion in awarding a permit.

21. Tri-County Paving, Inc. v. Ashe County, 281 F.3d 430, 436 (2002) (quoting Sylvia Dev. Corp. v. Calvert County, 48 F.3d 810, 826 (4th Cir. 1995)).

22. *See* Anita R. Brown-Graham, A Practical Guide To The Liability Of North Carolina Cities And Counties 7-4 (Chapel Hill, N.C.: Institute of Government, 1999) (citations omitted).

23. *See* Sinaloa Lake Owners Ass'n v. Simi Valley, 882 F.2d 1398 (9th Cir. 1989), *cert. denied,* Doody v. Sinaloa Lake Owners Ass'n., 494 U.S. 1016 (1990).

24. *See* Joy v. Daniels, 479 F.2d 1236 (4th Cir. 1973).

25. County of Lancaster v. Mecklenburg, 334 N.C. 496, 507, 434 S.E.2d 604, 612 (1993).

26. *Id.* at 508 (citing Humble Oil & Refining Co. v. Board of Aldermen I, 284 N.C. 458, 470, 202 S.E.2d 129, 137 (1974)).

27. *Id.* at 137.

28. Brown-Graham, *supra* note 22, at 7-7.

29. Sylvia Dev. Corp. v. Calvert County, 48 F.3d 810, 827 (4th Cir. 1995).

30. Graham v. City of Raleigh, 55 N.C. App. 107, 284 S.E.2d 742 (1981).

31. Armstrong v. United States, 364 U.S. 40, 49 (1960).

32. Finch v. City of Durham, 325 N.C. 352, 362-63, 384 S.E.2d 8, 14 (1989).

33. McNeill v. Harnett County, 327 N.C. 552, 563, 398 S.E.2d 475, 481 (1990).

34. Where a regulation is reasonably related to the legitimate objectives of the police power, a challenge to the facial validity of the ordinance must fail. At most, the challenge can then be considered as one to the application of the program or law. Grace Baptist Church v. City of Oxford, 320 N.C. 439, 442-43, 358 S.E.2d 372, 374-57 (1987).

35. See discussion at pages 5-8.

36. See discussion on eminent domain on pages 13-17.

37. 483 U.S. 825 (1987).

38. 512 U.S. 374 (1994).

39. 483 U.S. at 837.

40. *See* Thomas Kleven, *Inclusionary Ordinances—Policy and Legal Issues in Requiring Private Developers to Build Low Cost Housing,* 21 UCLA L. Rev. 1432, 1436 (1974).

41. 512 U.S. 374, 391.

42. Tahoe-Sierra Pres. Council v. Tahoe Reg'l Planning Agency, 535 U.S. 302, 322, n. 17 (2002).

43. 438 U.S. 104 (1978).

44. *Id.* at 124; *see* Serena M. Williams, *The Need for Affordable Housing: The Constitutional Viability of Inclusionary Zoning,* 26 J. Marshall L. Rev. 75, 89 (1992).

45. 505 U.S. 1003 (1992).

46. *Penn Central,* 438 U.S. at 130-31; *see* Williams, *supra* note 44.

47. *See* Williams, *supra* note 44.

48. *Penn Central,* 438 U.S. at 130-32.

49. Agins v. City of Tiburon, 447 U.S. 255, 260 (1980).

50. *Id.*

51. *See* Hawaii Hous. Auth. v. Midkiff, 467 U.S. 229 (1984) (finding that the government may take land in order to create a more fair distribution of property among economic classes); Berman v. Parker, 348 U.S. 26, 32-33 (1954) (allowing condemnation of blighted areas).

52. The U.S. Supreme Court has found that there is a legitimate state interest in a land use regulation even if the problem being addressed is the result of historical land use

regulations. *Penn Central*, 438 U.S. 104, 124–25 (1978) (a local government is not precluded from passing zoning ordinances meant to address problems created in part by past zoning policies).

53. *See* Webster's Real Estate Law In North Carolina § 19.2(a) (1999).

54. *Id.*

55. 92 N.C App. 601, 376 S.E.2d 22 (1989), *rev'd on other grounds*, 326 N.C. 1 (1990).

# 4 Organizing Local Governments for Affordable Housing Program Delivery

Whether a local housing program consists of only federally funded and directed activities or a broad range of federal, local, and private activities, it requires effective coordination and management. Meeting legal requirements as well as community needs and expectations to conduct an effective program requires widespread community involvement, on one hand, and concentrated executive control of a complex set of activities on the other. Neither the federal government nor the North Carolina General Statutes mandates any specific form of organization to carry out an affordable housing strategy, although there are specifications and options for the component activities discussed in previous chapters. Each local government, then, must use the options available in the General Statutes to accomplish its affordable housing objectives in a way that satisfactorily balances community involvement and executive control and best suits its local program and circumstances.

## Public Actors in Affordable Housing
### Board of County Commissioners/City or Town Council
The organizational starting points for affordable housing must be the board of county commissioners and the city or town council. Each has the authority either to undertake directly or to appoint an appropriate body to undertake on its behalf all of the local-government housing activities discussed in the earlier chapters of this guide.

## Public Housing Authorities
*Creating a City or County Public Housing Authority*
In North Carolina, the General Assembly set out the requirements by which cities with a population of more than 500 residents and counties may create public housing authorities. Under G.S. 157-4 and 157-33, any twenty-five residents of a county or twenty-five residents of a city (or its environs within ten miles) may file a petition with the clerk to the governing board declaring that there is a need for a housing authority. The clerk will then give notice of the time, place, and purposes of a public hearing at which the

governing board will determine the need for the authority. The notice must be given ten days before the hearing is to be held, and it should be published either in a newspaper of general circulation in the area or, if there is no such newspaper, by posting a notice in at least three public places in the city or county. At the hearing, the governing board must determine whether people in the jurisdiction are living in unsanitary or unsafe homes or whether there is a lack of safe or sanitary dwellings in the community.[1] If the board determines that either is true, a housing authority may be duly organized.

In cities the mayor must appoint between five and nine initial "organizing" commissioners. In counties the board of county commissioners appoints the initial commissioners for the housing authority. Those initial commissioners prepare an application to the North Carolina secretary of state. Once the secretary approves, files, and records the application, the housing authority shall constitute a public body. This status remains in effect until the secretary receives and approves a petition and resolution from the governing board and one from the authority and its members requesting a revocation or cancellation of the certificate of incorporation.

*Maintaining the Board of a City or County Housing Authority*
Once the authority has been duly organized, the mayor, in the case of a city's housing authority, may appoint between five and eleven commissioners to five-year staggered terms. In a county, the board of county commissioners may appoint between five and nine commissioners, with no requirement that the terms be staggered.[2] No city or county official may be a commissioner unless the governing board itself constitutes and acts ex officio as the authority. (This organizational scenario is discussed later in this chapter.) There is an expectation that at least one of the commissioners (but no more than one-third of all the commissioners) shall be appointed from among those directly assisted by the authority.[3] Such a commissioner is prohibited from voting on matters affecting his or her individual tenancy or official conduct. Similarly, no commissioner or employee of an authority may acquire any

direct or indirect interest in any housing project or contract associated with the housing authority without disclosure in writing to the authority. A commissioner may be removed from office by the mayor (in cities) or board of county commissioners (in counties) for inefficiency, neglect of duty, or misconduct in office. The mayor or county board must first give notice and provide a hearing.[4]

*Creating a Regional Public Housing Authority*
G.S. 157-35 provides for the creation of regional housing authorities if the boards of county commissioners of two or more contiguous counties having an aggregate population of more than 60,000 find that there is a need. The board of county commissioners of each county included in the regional housing authority is authorized to appoint only one member of the regional authority's board.[5] If there is an even number of counties represented by the authority, the governor is authorized to appoint one member to the authority's board so that the board avoids tie votes. The commissioners of the authority are then charged with selecting the other members of the authority's board.

*Alternatives to the Traditional Housing Authority*
Across the country public housing authorities (PHAs) have been at the center of significant controversy.[6] Today, under the weight of long waiting lists and fiscal impediments to the construction of new units, public housing has lost favor even among some former supporters. As a result of public displeasure, some public housing authorities are trying to reform themselves and some are being abolished by their local governments.

Even though the boards of local housing authorities are appointed by the governing board of the jurisdictions in which the authority operates, most have traditionally operated quite independently of the local government. With most of their funding (except for some rental income) coming from the federal government, PHAs have traditionally concerned themselves primarily with federal rules and policies. In recent years however, especially as federal support for housing programs has decreased, a number of local governments—primarily cities—have taken a more assertive role in the operation of their housing authorities. There are two main reasons for this change. First, the federal government has recently charged PHAs with operating complicated and comprehensive programs that require more active participation with local governments. For example the HOPE VI program, which the federal government developed to respond to the criticism that PHAs were warehousing poor people in massive high-rise projects, requires significant involvement by the local government in order to demolish and rebuild new public housing units. Second, some local governments have simply tired of what sometimes seems like the intractableness of public housing authorities' bureaucracy.

G.S. 157-4.1 and G.S. 157-4.2 offer alternative organizational arrangements to the traditional independent housing authority. First, under G.S. 157-4.2, a local government may retain a separate housing authority, but integrate that authority's budgeting and financial administration activities into its own. Under this arrangement the housing authority remains a separate organization with personnel and operating responsibilities under the control of the appointed housing authority board, and is treated like a local government department only for purposes of budgeting, accounting, and expenditure control.

Two organizational alternatives eliminate the housing authority altogether:[7] the governing board may assign the powers of the housing authority to a redevelopment commission or the local government staff may be given those powers.[8] Any designation of the local government as the housing authority should be done by passing a resolution adopted in accordance with the procedures set out in G.S. 157-4 and outlined above. In the event that an action of the housing authority requires recommendation or approval by both the housing authority and the governing board, then, under the new arrangement, action by the governing board will be deemed sufficient. Brunswick, Caswell, Columbus, Harnett, Madison, Orange, and Pender counties have all assumed direct responsibility for their public housing authorities.

## The Question of Whether State Bidding Procedures Apply to Affordable Housing Contracts

When cities or counties elect to designate the local unit of government as the housing authority, questions about the applicability of specific provisions of the Housing Authorities Law inevitably arise. For example, the Housing Authorities Law expressly exempts housing authorities from the general rules and procedures governing the acquisition and disposition of property. This exemption, presumably, covers state bidding requirements and procedures.[9] When localities choose to use local government staff to exercise directly the powers granted to housing authorities, the question that arises is whether the exception applies to the entity (the housing authority) or to the activity (the housing project).

There is no case law on the matter, and the plain text of the various statutes gives little direction on the question. However, the statutes that specifically grant to local governments exemptions from the normal rules of acquisition and disposition of property when they are engaged in affordable housing activity (such as G.S. 153A-377 and 160A-457) would be rendered superfluous if every local government could argue that they were exempted from all such rules whenever engaged in a housing project activity. A more reasonable interpretation is that local governments are entitled to the exemption only when they act as the housing authority.[10] Any designation of the local government as the housing authority should be done by passing a resolution adopted in accordance with the procedures set out in G.S. 157-4.

## Professional Staff

Many local governments are actively engaged in affordable housing activity beyond public housing authorities. Local governments that have professional affordable housing staff have organized themselves using one of three major approaches: a coordinator, a department, or a task force.

### Coordinator

Communities that need few specialized staff may use a coordinator. This one person is responsible for initiating, negotiating, monitoring, and evaluating the planning and execution of development activities by several departments—usually planning, public works, and inspection departments, and sometimes the rehabilitation staff of a redevelopment authority. Where the coordinator is placed in the administration can be an important consideration. If the person is a member of the planning staff, he or she can certainly integrate the program with other planning activities but might have little influence on operating departments that carry out the program. If the person is a member of the chief administrator's staff, he or she has more potential clout but usually has only as much actual clout as the chief administrator chooses to support.

### Department

As stated earlier, a city or county can bring its housing authority operations under the local government organization, either as a separate department or as part of a multifunctional department with broad responsibilities in community development. The multifunctional department might be formed from an existing planning department and from existing building inspection staff, housing inspection staff, engineering staff, housing and redevelopment staffs, economic development staff, or various combinations of all of these. Obviously the more functions that the department includes, the more powerful the director's influence will be over the performance of tasks that are critical to the housing program.

### Task Force

A community that takes the broadest possible view of affordable housing—as an endeavor involving many local agencies as well as private-sector organizations from time to time—might adopt a task-force approach to planning and managing its programs. Often, primary responsibility for the program goes to a deputy or assistant manager who, by his or her position, clearly and often acts with the full authority of the manager. This person organizes and supervises department and agency heads who will be responsible for various aspects of program planning and

implementation, and he or she serves as a critical link to organizations outside the government. The composition of task forces might change over time as the affordable housing program goes through different stages or changes its character. This process tends to be most successful when the manager delegates effectively and department heads and other staff are comfortable and competent in using team-management techniques.

## Citizen Boards, Commissions, and Committees

Although the governing board holds most of the ultimate authority for affordable housing activities, it can make efficient use of citizen interest and expertise by appointing a variety of citizen boards, commissions, and committees for advice or for implementation of program mandates. In fact, to help in planning and administering affordable housing activity funded by the federal Community Development Block Grant (CDBG) program, the board is required to have a citizen advisory body through which to channel public opinion.

Many local governments find these bodies to be extremely helpful. First, such a body can focus its full attention on the affordable housing strategy, whereas the board has many other responsibilities. Second, the board can effectively delegate to the advisory group the time-consuming task of gaining widespread citizen participation in planning. Third, the professional staff can secure from this body a fairly continuous flow of informal comment and information during planning. Fourth, consultants and councils of government working with the local government will look to this body to provide a meaningful frame of reference on the community to be served. Finally, the advisory body can supplement professional staff advice with a lay point of view when a program is recommended to the governing board.

Other existing boards and commissions may be useful to an affordable housing program. For example, the planning board's work with comprehensive planning and capital improvement planning can be very closely related to the formulation of the program. The governing board should consider whether to seek advice from other boards and commissions, such as parks and recreation, streets, and public works.

## Contracting with Outside Entities

A local government in North Carolina may contract for any purpose for which it may spend money if the expenditure is for a public purpose, the activity to be supported is one in which the local government has statutory authority to engage, and the expenditure is not inconsistent with the laws[11] or the constitution of the state or federal government.

Kingdom Community Development Corporation, a nonprofit organization, works closely with the city of Fayetteville to increase the availability of attractive, affordable housing through the development of the Fairley Estates subdivision.

Brick Capital Community Development Corporation, a nonprofit organization, works closely with the city of Sanford to increase attractive, affordable housing as part of a neighborhood revitalization strategy.

## Councils of Government

Local governments sometimes contract with regional councils of government for assistance in the preparation and administration of federal or state grants when there is no local government staff to carry out these functions. Councils of government are particularly active in housing programs in the western region of the state.

## Consultants

Other local governments contract with private, for-profit consultants for assistance in completing applications for and administering federal or state grants. A consultant typically works closely with a member of the local government (usually the manager, mayor, or clerk to the board) and the citizen advisory body to develop and implement the project. The board should be kept informed of important policy decisions such as program amendments to the grant because it retains ultimate responsibility for the grant. On the other hand, boards typically have little involvement with the project's day-to-day activities.

Consultants are used most often in the eastern counties of the state. A primary advantage of using consultants is that the community does not have to provide gap funding for personnel costs between grants. A disadvantage may be that consultants are less familiar with the other aspects of the government that may bear on a project.

## Nonprofit Organizations

*The Varying Roles of Nonprofit Organizations*

Nonprofit organizations have long worked with governments to respond to community needs. The resulting partnerships have been powerful, combining the flexibility and service-delivery capabilities of the nonprofit sector with the financial and direction-setting capabilities of the public sector. They have resulted in improved local services in many areas, including affordable housing.

Nonprofit involvement in affordable housing typically falls into one or more of six categories. First, an increasing number of nonprofit organizations are constructing or rehabilitating single- and multi-family dwellings either by themselves or in joint venture with real estate developers. These units are then offered for sale to low- and moderate-income families through highly leveraged financing, some of which may come from the local government. Local government contributions may include underwriting the infrastructure of the development to decrease construction costs; providing low- or no-interest second-mortgage loans to reduce the monthly payments of principal and interest home buyers are required to make; and paying general operating subsidies to nonprofit organizations to reduce their overhead costs. The nonprofits that are most likely to be involved in this specific type of affordable housing activity are classified as community development corporations.[12]

Second, nonprofits may create opportunities for home ownership by accepting "sweat equity" in lieu of cash in order to reduce the sales price of a home. Habitat for Humanity is perhaps best known for this practice. Under the Habitat model, construction materials and supplies are donated where feasible, and community volunteers, including the prospective home owners, construct or rehabilitate the

Affordable home in Pitt County constructed through a volunteer-based housing initiative with the North Carolina Baptist Men.

Housing development by Carriage Court Episcopal Housing Ministries, Rocky Mount, North Carolina.

unit under the supervision of experienced contractors and members of the building trades.

Third, nonprofits may provide first-time ownership opportunities through housing cooperatives. In a housing cooperative, the housing units actually are owned by the nonprofit, which assumes responsibility for developing, financing, and managing the housing. Low-income residents purchase a membership share in the cooperative corporation and a long-term, proprietary lease in one of the housing units owned by the cooperative corporation. Though it is not a very popular mechanism in North Carolina, in other states local public housing authorities and tenant management corporations have converted public-housing units into tenant-controlled housing cooperatives. This strategy can offer low-income persons an opportunity to gain some of the control benefits of home ownership without requiring assumption of the full financial responsibility and other responsibilities.

Fourth, nonprofits are involved in providing emergency and transitional housing opportunities for persons who have no realistic alternatives in the marketplace. These nonprofits often operate single-room housing for persons with no serious physical or mental disabilities. They also operate group homes or other forms of shared living arrangements for those with mental and physical disabilities. In shared living-space arrangements, individual privacy is preserved, but food, counseling, treatment, and other social services are provided on a regular basis.

Fifth, nonprofits are often involved in advocacy for affordable housing. Many localities in North Carolina, including Durham and Buncombe counties, have local affordable housing coalitions. These nonprofit member organizations typically include representation as diverse as developers, builders, bankers, environmentalists, public

officials, and grassroots advocates. With their strong community base and sensitivity to local concerns, these organizations can play a critical role in gaining community acceptance of low-income housing.

Finally, nonprofits in North Carolina are becoming very involved in training lower-income persons to take advantage of housing opportunities. Home ownership counseling has become particularly popular and professionalized. Many nonprofit housing counselors participate in an educational certification process that permits them to work with prospective home owners on issues such as credit repair. And further, the certification gives counselors sufficient credibility to be able to pre-certify home owners for banks.

*Special Tax Treatment for Nonprofit Organizations*
While nonprofit organizations that enter the housing business must recognize the business aspects of their work, it is not their goal to earn a profit for themselves or their members. Once nonprofits achieve what is known as 501(c)(3) status, federal and state tax policies recognize the value of their activities by allowing deductions for contributions to these organizations and by exempting their income from taxation.[13] In addition, provisions of the Tax Reform Act of 1986, which created the federal low-income tax credit and restricted the use of tax-exempt municipal bond financing, contain specific acknowledgment of and special treatment for low-income housing activities by nonprofit organizations.[14]

In addition to seeking tax-exempt status under the Internal Revenue Code, nonprofit housing organizations often seek exemptions from local property taxes. For nonprofits that develop and own rental housing units, the taxes on the value of the real property can be a significant factor in their overall ability to maintain the units at

### A Case in Point: Community Land Trusts as an Example of an Innovative Local Government and Nonprofit Affordable Housing Strategy

Several local governments in North Carolina, including the cities of Durham and Charlotte, have partnered with Community Land Trust nonprofits to deliver affordable housing opportunities. Community Land Trusts (CLTs) create affordable housing opportunities by eliminating land costs from the home ownership equation. Home owners using land trust property own only the home itself, retaining occupancy, modification, and inheritance rights for the structure, while leasing the land on which the home is situated from a community land trust organization.

Durham Community Land Trust Home.

By retaining ownership of the land itself, a CLT can create restrictive leases which regulate the terms of home resale, thus retaining the property for use as affordable housing. A CLT typically regulates eligibility for program participation through income formulas, usually based upon a percentage of the area median income.

Successful Community Land Trusts typically share several common characteristics. These trusts are

- Incorporated as nongovernmental, nonprofit 501(c)(3) organizations[a]
- Organized to work in conjunction with governmental units as well as other housing organizations
- Operated under open-membership provisions, incorporating community leaders and residents
- Governed by diverse board members, ranging from housing experts to community members
- Established by neighborhood groups or associations, local governments, community development corporations, or concerned citizens

Homeowners typically retain almost all of the rights associated with home ownership. Owners may modify their home and convey the home through inheritance. The land lease is usually ninety-nine years in length and stipulates the rights of the home owner as well as restrictions that the CLT places on occupancy and resale.

Typical land lease restrictions include a requirement of owner occupancy with subleasing only under specially outlined circumstances and with the consent of the CLT organization. This provision helps to prevent absentee landlords.

The land lease also typically requires that properties sold by CLT participants meet specified resale requirements. A typical lease may require the resale of the home to a low- to moderate-income household, as determined by the CLT. CLTs often retain "first offer" or "first refusal" rights for properties located on CLT land, helping to keep the properties

affordable rents for low-income persons. Thus, nationally, nonprofit sponsorship of housing for low- and moderate-income persons has generated significant litigation concerning the tax-exempt status of this activity. Generally, homes operated by religious organizations for low-income, aged, or disabled persons, as well as apartments for elderly persons of low and moderate income, have been accorded tax-exempt status.[15] However, housing for low- and moderate-income families that are not disabled or elderly often has been denied tax-exempt status, particularly where rents have been set at a level to amortize mortgage loans and pay operating expenses, where operating funds do not come from public or private charity, and where tenants are subject to eviction for nonpayment of rent.[16] In these cases,

the mere fact that the nonprofit sponsor has received some federal housing subsidies has been deemed insufficient to demonstrate that the organization was engaged in purely charitable activities. In North Carolina, GS 105-278.6(2) makes clear that exemption is afforded to property of a nonprofit organization that provides housing for families with low or moderate incomes.

Faith-based organizations may seek exemptions provided for in GS 105-278.3. However, the North Carolina Supreme Court recently struck down a state law that provided a tax exemption for religious or Masonic organizations operating homes for senior citizens while denying the benefit to secular institutions offering the same services.[17] The court found that the provision violated the in the affordable housing market. Typical resale formulas permit the owner of the home to capitalize on a percentage of the increase in the appraised property value over the course of ownership. This allows the owner a modest appreciation on the home investment, while restricting the owner's ability to capitalize on the market rate, thus keeping the property affordable.

Community Land Trusts are democratically operated organizations in which all participating residents are members. The organization is typically administered by an executive director chosen by an elected board of directors. Membership of this board usually varies. It should be balanced so as to reflect the interests of residents and of the community as a whole. Thus it can include members representing residents, external interests, or public interests at large. The board is usually a diverse collection of backgrounds and professions, reflecting the needs of the organization. Attorneys, bankers, and government officials often serve, bringing areas of expertise to the organization.

Community Land Trust organizations may provide additional services for CLT home owners, including

- Homeowner training and assistance
- Home repair loan funds
- Emergency assistance funding
- Home sale assistance (which reduces the real estate transaction costs associated with home sales)

CLT property may be acquired through direct purchase, individual or corporate gifts and transfers, or grants from governmental entities. These properties may be used for almost any community need, including housing, community centers, business incubators, and common space. CLT organizational costs are usually offset by the lease fees charged to program participants through the land lease arrangements.[b]

Community Land Trusts often benefit from association with local governments. Property conveyed by developers in accordance with a local government's inclusionary zoning requirements may be donated by the local government to a CLT organization. In addition to land contributions, local governments may assist CLTs with funding for site acquisition, infrastructure improvements, and homeowner assistance through the Community Development Block Grant program, HOME funding, and other programs aimed at benefiting low- to moderate-income individuals.[c]

---

a. These organizations must conform to rules established in I.R.C. 501(c)(3).

b. Residents owning homes are liable for property taxes on the homes they own. Property taxes on the land owned by the CLT may be reduced if the CLT and residents request and receive reduced property tax assessments based upon the decreased resale value associated with the provisions of the CLT resale agreement.

c. *See generally* policy link, Community Land Trusts, *at* http://www.policylink.org/Equitable Development/content/tools/39/8-all.asp (last visited Jan. 13, 2005); Tom Peterson, *Community Land Trusts: An Introduction*, Planners Web http://www.plannersweb.com/articles/petllv.html (last visited Feb. 28, 2005).

freedom of religion clauses of both the state and federal constitutions.

*Other Forms of Local Government Support for Nonprofit Organizations*

Local governments may support nonprofit efforts to provide affordable housing in a number of ways beyond the provision of direct funding and tax exemptions.[18] For example, a local unit might include nonprofit staff in its training programs or use its purchasing power to purchase goods or services on behalf of a nonprofit for use in programs that the local government has authority to fund. Further, a local government may make the expertise of its staff available to a nonprofit as a form of in-kind assistance that can save money for both the local government and the nonprofit. In each case, subject to requirements of public purpose and statutory authority, local governments may provide in-kind support of whatever nature they choose. Although the state constitution generally prohibits a local government from giving public money or property to a private person or entity, North Carolina court cases have recognized that a promise to use property for a public purpose is legally sufficient consideration to support its conveyance. This means that as long as the proposed use is one for which the local government has authority to spend money, the local government may provide in-kind support as an outright donation in lieu of or in addition to a cash appropriation.

## Faith-Based Organizations

Faith-based nonprofit organizations have been involved in providing housing opportunities for lower-income persons since the eighteenth century; and local government agencies have long funded religiously affiliated organizations such as Catholic Charities, Lutheran Social Services, the Salvation Army, and others. Recent laws and federal policies go beyond this, however, mandating government funding of programs sponsored by pervasively sectarian organizations such as congregations, whose primary purpose is to provide religious instruction and spiritual support to their members rather than social services to clients.[19] Such laws and policies (including HUD policies) make clear that

- faith-based organizations are eligible for federal funding on an equal basis with other organizations;
- faith-based organizations are no longer required to form a separate, secular organization to receive federal funds;
- faith-based organizations that receive public funding remain independent in matters relating to governance and expression of beliefs;
- direct federal funds may not be used to support inherently religious activities such as worship, religious instruction, or proselytization; and
- federal provisions apply to state or local funds in cases where a state or local government commingles its own funds with the federal funds covered by the regulations.

The Establishment Clause of the First Amendment to the United States Constitution ultimately controls the legality of contracts with faith-based organizations. It dictates that "Congress shall make no law respecting an establishment of religion." Although some have viewed the First Amendment as a wall of separation between the government and religion, the courts never have interpreted it so literally. Under the test articulated by the United States Supreme Court in *Lemon v Kurtzman*, a local government may contract with a faith-based institution if the contract

1. has a secular purpose,
2. has a primary effect of neither advancing nor inhibiting religion, and
3. does not create an excessive entanglement between the government and religion.[20]

Although the Supreme Court has modified the *Lemon* test over the years, it still appears to set the parameters for analyzing government contracts with religious institutions.

In considering the limitations on a local government's ability to contract with a faith-based organization, officials also must take the North Carolina Constitution into consideration. Article I, section 13, states that "all persons have a natural and inalienable right to worship Almighty God according to the dictates of their own consciences, and no human authority shall, in any case whatever, control

or interfere with the rights of conscience." Although the state and federal constitutional provisions are not identical, state courts have said that the two provisions secure similar rights. Thus cases involving the state constitution are usually analyzed using the federal tests. A challenge to a local government's contract with a religious organization may come under the federal or state constitution, or both.

Given the guidelines provided by HUD and other federal funding agencies, local governments that contract with faith-based organizations willing to accept government funds to provide services to the needy must ensure that the contract (1) has the effect of safeguarding the religious integrity and character of the faith-based organization and protecting the religious freedoms of program participants and (2) that it does not require excessive involvement of the government in the internal affairs of the faith-based organization.

Although the Supreme Court has allowed some accommodations to safeguard the religious integrity of faith-based service providers, it has also recognized that too much accommodation can become favoritism toward a religion and thus violate the Establishment Clause. Thus the Court signaled how it might resolve the question of whether religious organizations are entitled to mandatory exemptions from government regulations when it held, in *Employment Division v. Smith*,[21] that religious groups are subject to neutral laws of general application. The holding makes it unlikely that claims for mandatory exemptions from regulations will prevail. Moreover, in *Texas Monthly v. Bullock*,[22] the Court struck down a sales tax exemption for religious periodicals because the exemption benefited only religious groups. The Court made clear that even permissive accommodations designed to alleviate a government-created burden on religion cannot favor particular sects and cannot favor religious groups over nonreligious groups or result in a burden on nonbeneficiaries.

The use of public funds to promote religious doctrine violates the effects test of the Establishment Clause. Because the constitutionality of public funding to religious organizations is measured at least in part by how the recipient uses that funding, the government must monitor the activities supported by the funding. The two other competing constitutional concerns implicated by monitoring are (1) whether the monitoring amounts to excessive entanglement[23] and (2) whether the monitoring results in government-sponsored religious indoctrination. But while careful governmental regulation and oversight are necessary to avoid claims of the former, such regulation and oversight are likely to result in complaints of the latter, as governmental control and surveillance are hallmarks of excessive church-state entanglement.[24]

A recent case, *Freedom from Religion Foundation v. McCallum*,[25] illustrates this conflict. In *McCallum* a federal district court held unconstitutional the state of Wisconsin's funding of Faith Works of Milwaukee (Faith Works), a program providing residential substance abuse treatment and employment assistance to criminal offenders and welfare recipients. Faith Works did not discriminate against potential clients based on religion and did not require clients to convert to any particular religion. Faith Works did, however, include topics related to faith and spirituality in its twelve-step recovery program. After reviewing the applicable federal and state laws and the grant agreement (all of which included prohibitions against the use of funds to promote religion), as well as the oversight provisions (which permitted monthly visits by the state to organizations receiving funds), the court was not troubled by the prospect of excessive entanglement.[26] On the other hand, when addressing the issue of state-sponsored religious indoctrination, the court held that public funding of the program violated the Establishment Clause. The court was particularly troubled by the ineffectiveness of the government's monitoring of this pervasively sectarian organization.[27] The court noted that despite the restrictions in federal and state law and in the grant agreement, the grant agreement failed to include any consequences for noncompliance. It concluded the state had not put in place adequate safeguards "to insure that direct, public funds are restricted to secular purposes."[28] Indeed, once the court determined that Faith Works subjected participants to religious indoctrination, it easily went one step further to find that this indoctrination could be attributed to the government because the rules prohibiting the use of grant money for religious activities "exist[ed] only on paper." Notably, the court compared pervasively sectarian organizations, such as Faith Works, to nonprofits that are merely religiously affiliated, and suggested that because pervasively sectarian organizations are more likely to engage in religious worship, proselytization, and religious education as part of their social service programs, compliance with the constitutional prohibition against government-sponsored indoctrination will require more than merely stating that public funds should not be used to support religious activities.[29]

## Notes

Some parts of this chapter appear in Anita R. Brown-Graham and David Lawrence, "Community and Economic Development," *Municipal Governments.* Some parts of that chapter benefited from an earlier edition of the same publication authored by Kurt Jenne.

1. In making these determinations, the governing board must take into consideration the physical age and condition of the buildings, the degree of overcrowding, the percentage of land coverage, the light and air available to the inhabitants, the size and arrangement of rooms in these dwellings, the sanitary conditions, and the extent to which conditions exist in the dwellings that pose a threat to life or property by fire or other causes. N.C. GEN. STAT. 157-4 & 157-33 (hereinafter G.S.).

2. G.S. 157-33.

3. There shall be no requirement to appoint such a person if the authority has fewer than 300 public housing units and makes the resident advisory board aware of the opportunity for the appointment, but no one indicates an interest in serving. G.S. 157-5.

4. G.S. 157-8.

5. G.S. 157-36.

6. The public housing program has been controversial from its inception. For reviews of the program, see L. FREEDMAN, PUBLIC HOUSING: THE POLITICS OF POVERTY (1969); *see also* E. MEEHAN, PUBLIC HOUSING POLICY: CONVENTION VERSUS REALITY (1975).

7. A governing board may abolish a housing authority by resolution. The abolition may not be made effective less than ninety days after adoption of the resolution.

8. G.S. 157-4.1; G.S. 157-33. *See also* G.S. 153A-376(b) and G.S. 160A-476.

9. The legislature has made clear its intent to afford broad authority to public housing authorities, in particular to acquire and dispose of property. In G.S. 157-9, the General Assembly has provided that "no provision with respect to the acquisition, operation or disposition of property by other public bodies shall be applicable to an authority unless the legislature shall specifically so state."

10. G.S. 157-4.1; G.S. 157-33. *See also* G.S. 153A-376(b) and 160A-476.

11. G.S. 14-234 makes it unlawful for a public official to benefit from a contract with the unit he or she represents. *See generally* Frayda S. Bluestein and Anita R. Brown-Graham, *Local Government Contracts with Nonprofit Organizations,* POPULAR GOVERNMENT, Fall 2001, at 32.

12. These organizations are founded by, and grounded in, the communities they serve and are believed by some to be more likely than local governments alone to be successful in supporting community needs.

13. The provision of housing for low-income persons is not designated tax-exempt activity as are religious, scientific, literary, or educational activities, so nonprofit housing organizations must seek to qualify for tax-exempt status as "[c]orporations . . . organized and operated exclusively for . . . charitable . . . purposes" under I.R.C. 501(c)(3) (1994). While there is little case law directly deciding the question of whether a nonprofit housing corporation qualifies under the "charitable purpose" test, the U.S. Treasury Department regulations and revenue rulings issued by the Internal Revenue Service give some guidance. In an important ruling, the IRS concluded:

> [W]here an organization is formed for charitable purposes and accomplishes its charitable purposes through aprogram of providing housing for low- and, in certain circumstances moderate-income families, it is entitled to exemption . . . . The fact that an organization receives public funds under State or Federal programs for housing is not determinative; qualification is based on whether or not the organization is charitable within the meaning of section 501(c)(3). Rev. Rul. 70-585, 1970-2C.B; see also Rev. Proc. 96-32, 1996-1 C.B. 717 setting forth a safe harbor under which

organizations that provide low-income housing will be considered charitable under 501(c)(3).

14. *See, e.g.,* I.R.C. 42(h)(5) (at least 10 percent of tax credit allocations to each state must be set aside for low-income housing projects in which 501(c)(3) tax exempt nonprofit organizations, whose exempt purposes include "the fostering of low income housing," materially participate).

15. *See* G.S. 105-278.6(a)(8); *see also* S. Iowa Methodist Homes Inc. v. Bd. of Review, 173 N.W. 2d 526 (Iowa 1970); Banahan v. Presbyterian Hous. Corp., 553 S.W.2d at 48 (Ky. 1977); Pentecostal Church of God v. Hughlett, 601 S.W.2d 666 (Mo. 1987); *contra* Clark v. Marian Park, Inc., 80 Ill. App. 3d. 1010, 400 N.E.2d 661 (1980); Rio Vista Non-Profit Hous. Corp. v. County of Ramsey, 277 N.W.2d 187 (Minn. 1979); *contra* Note, *Real Estate Tax Exemption for Low-Income Housing Corporation: Rio Vista Non-Profit Housing Corp. v. County of Ramsey*, 64 MINN. L. REV. 1094, 1103–5 (1980) (criticizing the Minnesota Supreme Court's decision as ill-advised because of the potential for forcing municipalities to subsidize low-income housing by providing services without receiving property tax revenues).

16. Clark v. Marian Park, Inc., 80 Ill. App. 3d 1010, 400 N.E.2d 661 (1980); Mountain View Homes, Inc. v. State Tax Comm'n, 77 N.M. 649, 427 P.2d 13 (1967); Metro. Pittsburgh Nonprofit Hous. Corp. v. Bd. of Prop. Assessment, 28 Pa. Commw. 356, 368 A.2d 837 (1977), *aff'd*, 480 Pa. 622, 391 A.2d 1059 (1978).

17. *In re* Springmoor, Inc., 348 N.C. 1, 498 S.E. 177 (1998).

18. *See generally* Bluestein and Brown-Graham, *Local Government Contracts, supra* note 11.

19. Substantial arguments exist to suggest that some of these "Charitable Choice" provisions may be unconstitutional under current Supreme Court jurisprudence. *See, e.g.,* Alan Brownstein, *Constitutional Questions about Charitable Choice, in* WELFARE REFORM AND FAITH BASED ORGANIZATIONS 219 (Derek H. Davis and Barry Hankins eds., 1999). The Court's interpretation of the Establishment Clause, however, does not represent stable doctrine. While this article focuses on what the law is presently, it also relies heavily on more recent jurisprudence to analyze how the Court might interpret both the new mandates and any resulting accountability measures that local governments might impose.

20. *See* Lemon v. Kurtzman, 403 U.S. 602, 612–13 (1971). The *Lemon* test was modified for cases involving aid to religious schools in *Agostini v. Felton*, 521 U.S. 203, 232–33 (1997). Under the modified *Lemon–Agostini* test, a faith-based publicly funded program does not violate the Establishment Clause if

1. it has a secular purpose,
2. it does not result in governmental indoctrination,
3. it does not define its participants by reference to religion, and
4. it does not create excessive government entanglement with religion.

Under *Employment Division v. Smith*, 494 U.S. 872, 890 (1990), generally applicable government regulations, even those that arguably burden religious groups, are presumptively valid unless

1. the Free Exercise Clause is linked with another constitutional violation (a hybrid claim);
2. the regulation at issue requires some form of individualized determination;
3. the law at issue is not neutral; or
4. the regulations violate the Establishment Clause by excessively entangling church and state.

21. *Smith*, 494 U.S. at 890. It should be noted that *Smith* did not involve a religious institution seeking exemption from regulation. Rather, the case involved two Native Americans who were fired by a private drug rehabilitation organization after they used peyote at a Native American church ceremony. The state denied their unemployment compensation applications pursuant to a state law that disqualified employees discharged for work-related conduct. The court reasoned that if the state could criminalize conduct, it could also penalize the conduct in its unemployment scheme. The court recognized two exceptions to its holding, however. First, where violation of the Free Exercise claim is joined with a claim of the violation of another constitutional protection, that hybrid claim might be entitled to an exemption. Second, where the law at issue provides for a system of individualized determinations of the exemption, the government may not, without compelling reason, refuse to apply that system in cases involving religious expression.

22. 489 U.S. 1, 8 (1989).

23. The Court noted in *Agostini* that entanglement exists if "(i) the program would require 'pervasive monitoring by public authorities' to ensure [that the public funds were not being used] . . . to inculcate religion; (ii) the program would require 'administrative cooperation' between the [government and sectarian organizations]; and (iii) the program might increase the dangers of 'political divisiveness.'" *Agostini*, 521 U.S. at 233 (citing Aguilar v. Felton, 473 U.S. 402, 413–14 (1985)).

24. "Pervasively sectarian," a vaguely defined term of art, has its roots in the Supreme Court's recognition that government must not engage in detailed supervision of the inner workings of religious institutions, and the Court's distaste for the picture of state inspectors prowling the halls of parochial schools and auditing classroom instruction. Under the "effects" prong of the *Lemon* test, the Court has used one variant or another of the "pervasively sectarian" concept to explain why any but the most indirect forms of government aid to such institutions would necessarily have the effect of advancing religion. Bowen v. Kendrick, 487 U.S. 589, 631 (1988) (Blackmun, J., dissenting); *see Lemon*, 403 U.S. at 612–13; *Agostini*, 521 U.S. at 232–33.

25. 179 F. Supp. 2d 950 (W.D. Wis. 2002). *Bowen v. Kendrick* is the only recent case in which the United States Supreme Court has addressed the issue of direct public funding of a religious organization. 487 U.S. 589 (1988) (upholding federal grants for teenage sexuality counseling, including counseling offered by faith-based organizations). The *Bowen* Court held that the Adolescent Family Life Act (AFLA) could not be deemed unconstitutional on its face because

1. the statute was clearly motivated primarily, if not entirely, by a legitimate secular purpose—the elimination or reduction of social and economic problems caused by teenage sexuality, pregnancy, and parenthood;
2. religion is no more than incidentally advanced by Congress's requirement that grantees involve religious and other charitable organizations as part of a broad-based community support system, or by Congress's willingness to allow religious organizations that are not pervasively sectarian to compete for grants; and
3. the monitoring involved was not intensive and therefore did not result in excessive entanglement of the state with religion.

Although the case concerned the constitutionality of a statute rather than a specific contract, and the faith-based organizations involved were not pervasively sectarian, the Court's decision is nonetheless instructive on the need to balance the prohibitions against excessive entanglement and indoctrination. The specific monitoring mechanisms involved in *Bowen* included grantee disclosures on application forms as to the nature of the services that would be provided, government evaluation of the services, and required reports from grantees. In attempting to balance the competing interests, the Court acknowledged that grant monitoring might also require a review of the educational materials or a visit to the site, but it dismissed the idea that such inspections alone would intrude on religious practice. The *Bowen* Court summarily noted that because the government was not monitoring pervasively sectarian grantees, "intensive monitoring" was unnecessary.

The *Bowen* Court noted in dictum the "risk that government funding, even if it is designated for specific secular purposes, may nonetheless advance [a] pervasively sectarian institution's religious mission." *Id.* at 610. The Court further noted the dilemma of governments, that "the very supervision of the aid to assure that it does not further religion renders [an agreement] . . . invalid." *Id.* at 615. If the programs of these pervasively sectarian organizations require clients to obey religious teachings, attend religious services, or study a particular religious doctrine, local governments will have "to tread an extremely narrow line" between the entanglement and the effects tests in their monitoring activities. *Id.* at 616. To ensure that public funding is not used to advance religion, governments must engage in ongoing surveillance of the programs. That very surveillance, however, may well constitute excessive entanglement.

26. *McCallum*, 179 F. Supp. 2d at 967 (citing *Agostini*, 521 U.S. 203, 234).

27. The court in *McCallum* found that simply because a social service program had secular purposes did not mean that it was not permeated by religion. The court noted that the religious organization had "used the integration of religion into [its program] as a strong selling point for obtaining funding," and that it could not "now try to excise religion from its offerings, saying that it contracted with the state to provide . . . wholly secular services . . . without any reference to religion." *McCallum*, 179 F. Supp. 2d at 969–70.

28. *Id.* at 975.

29. Earlier Supreme Court cases have also focused on these distinctions. So, for example, Roman Catholic elementary and secondary schools were often classified as pervasively sectarian because they tended to be "located close to parish churches," to have school buildings filled with "identifying religious symbols" (crosses, crucifixes, religious paintings, religious statues), to make "instruction in faith and morals [a] part of the total educational process," to sponsor "religiously oriented extracurricular activities," to have faculties composed substantially of nuns or priests, and to be "dedicated . . . [to] provid[ing] an atmosphere in which religious instruction and religious vocations are natural and proper parts of life." *See Lemon*, 403 U.S. at 615–16. By contrast, religiously affiliated colleges have not been labeled pervasively sectarian unless they have tended to "impose[ ] religious restrictions on admissions, require[ ] attendance at religious activities, compel[ ] obedience to the doctrines and dogmas of the faith, require[ ] instruction in theology and doctrine, and . . . propagate [a] particular religion." *See* Tilton v. Richardson, 403 U.S. 672, 682 (1971).

# 5 Local Government Responses to Specific Housing Conditions and Needs

## Housing Characteristics in North Carolina

As compared with the rest of the nation, North Carolina added the fourth highest number of housing units (705,751) between 1990 and 2000, behind only Florida, Texas, and California.[1] The dramatic increase of roughly 25 percent from about 2.8 million units in 1990 to 3.5 million in 2000 means that one out of every four housing units in the state was built during the 1990s. Single-family, detached units still comprise a large majority of housing. In 1990 these units made up 65.2 percent of all units, and in 2000 that percentage held constant at 65 percent. Meanwhile, the percentage of units in two- to four-unit structures increased by 2.8 percent, and the percentage of units in structures with five or more units increased by 0.3 percent. Finally, there continues to be a significant increase in the percentage of mobile homes within the state. In 1980 mobile homes represented 10 percent of all housing units; in 1990 this had increased to 15 percent; and in 2000, mobile homes comprised 16.4 percent of all housing units in North Carolina. The increase of mobile homes between 1990 and 2000 represented 155,859 units, which was second in the nation only to Texas. (See Figure 5-1.)

Beyond the increased numbers of housing units in North Carolina lie significant affordable housing problems. Despite the state's overall economic growth of the past two decades, many North Carolinians are unable to secure decent, safe, affordable housing. As a result of the housing squeeze, families are being forced to commute long distances from home to work,[2] live in substandard or overcrowded housing, or pay burdensome percentages of their household income for the cost of housing. The extent of housing problems differs based on the race and income of households. (See Figure 5-2.)

This chapter seeks to chronicle the state's affordable housing needs through the use of various data sources, including the dicennial census, the American Housing Survey, and the North Carolina Housing Finance Agency (NCHFA). Information on the extent of local government activities that respond to the identified affordable housing needs is derived from a community development survey of 652 local governments in North Carolina. The results

of the survey, which was conducted by the School of Government in March 2004, illustrate local governments' efforts to end homelessness, manage public housing, provide rental and home ownership assistance, encourage the development of affordable housing, eliminate regulatory barriers to affordable housing, and demolish substandard housing. The data on housing problems and local responses are divided into four categories: affordability, physical adequacy, overcrowding, and accessibility.

## Affordability

Under the standard definition of affordability, a household paying more than 30 percent of its gross household income for housing costs is considered to be experiencing affordability problems. Households paying more than 50 percent of their incomes for housing are considered to be experiencing severe affordability problems. Local governments are aware that many North Carolina households are facing affordability problems. As a result, there are local affordable housing programs targeted to helping lower-income households absorb the ever-increasing costs of housing.

The affordable housing squeeze has led to a particularly significant increase in housing costs for many renters. Between 1990 and 2000, the median rent and utility costs for renter households not living in subsidized housing rose from $382 a month to $548 a month after adjusting for inflation, an increase of 8.9 percent. The rising housing costs have forced many renters to spend large percentages of their income on housing. Some 31.5 percent of renters—302,138 households—spent at least 30 percent of their income on rent and utilities in 2000. The trend has continued past 2000. According to the National Low Income Housing Coalition's 2003 *Out of Reach* report, a household would need to earn $11.61 per hour in order to afford a two-bedroom apartment at North Carolina's average fair market rent.[3] Under this standard, 41 percent of the state's renter households (over 393,000 households) were unable to afford a two-bedroom unit in 2003.

**Figure 5-1.** North Carolina housing stock by type

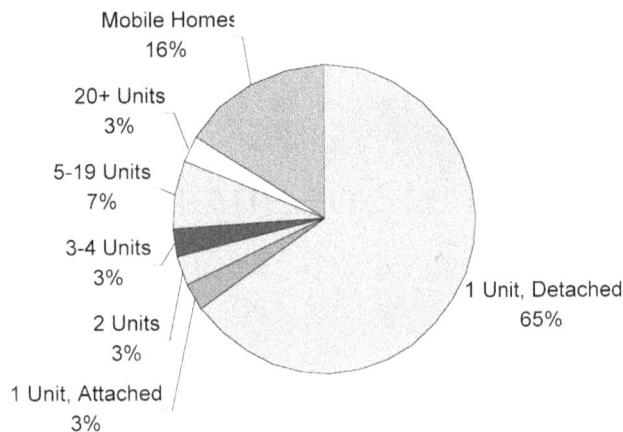

Source: North Carolina Housing Finance Agency, Housing Markets & Needs Analysis (2004)

**Figure 5-2.** Specific North Carolina households with housing problems

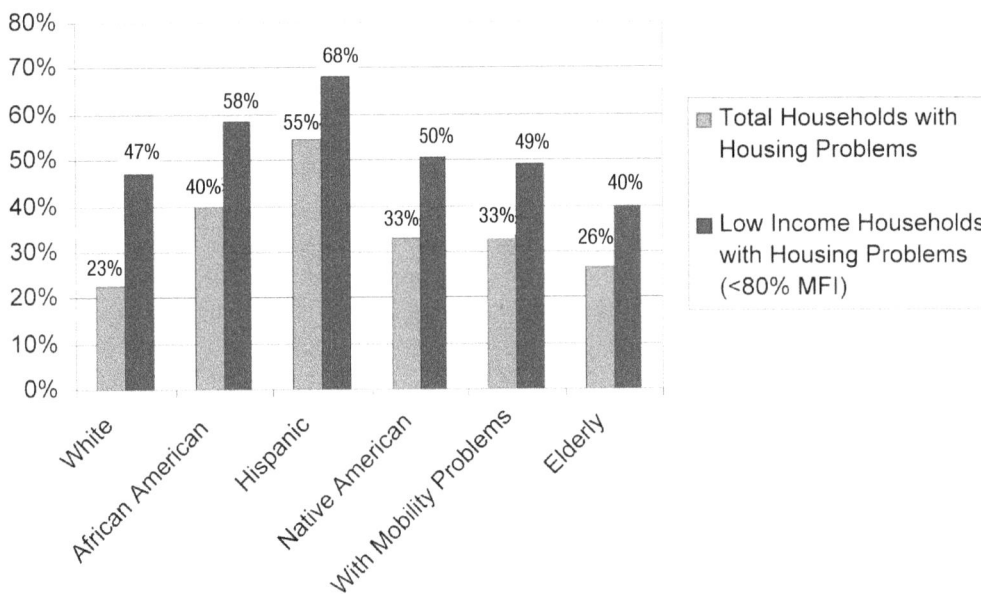

Source: North Carolina Housing Finance Agency, House Markets & Needs Analysis 2004

The state's rents are highest in its urban areas. In the Triangle metropolitan area (Chatham, Durham, Franklin, Johnston, Orange, and Wake counties), rents rose more than 95 percent between 1990 and 1998. By 2000 the region had the highest rents in the state. Indeed, the 2000 census shows that, despite relatively high incomes, 40 percent of Triangle metropolitan renters pay more than 30 percent of their income for rent. Of that number, almost one third pay more than 35 percent of their income for rent.[4]

The rental unaffordability statistics are starker when one considers the plight of renters with the lowest incomes—those defined by HUD to be very low income. According to the census, some 52.7 percent of these poorer-renter households in North Carolina, or 110,485 households, spent more than half of their income on housing in 2000.

Local governments have sought to provide affordable rental housing opportunities through both supply- and

**Figure 5-3.** With what frequency has your community engaged in affordable housing programs by income levels (percentage of area median income) in the last five years?

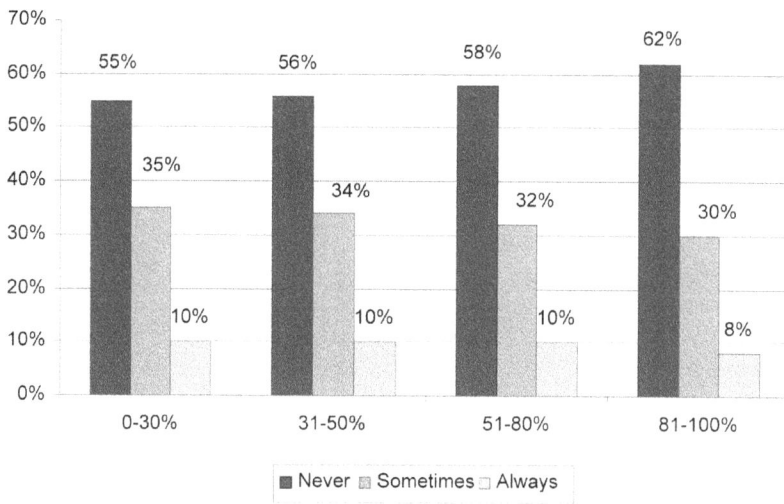

■ Never ▦ Sometimes □ Always

Source: School of Government, Community Development Survey (2004)

**Figure 5-4.** With what frequency has your community engaged in subsidy programs for low-income renters in the last five years?

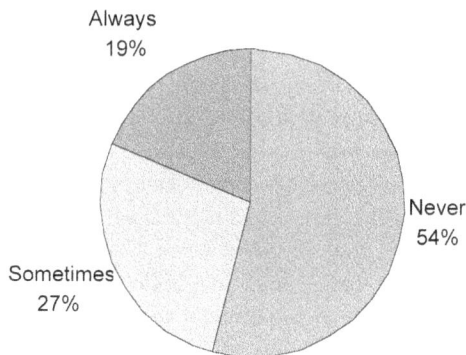

Source: School of Government, Community Development Survey (2004)

**Figure 5-5.** With what frequency has your community provided local government support for development of rental housing?

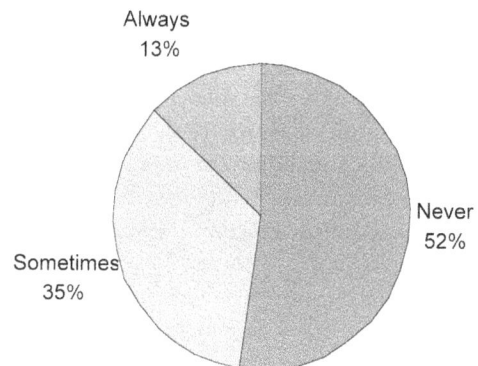

Source: School of Government, Community Development Survey (2004)

demand-side programs. (See Figure 5-3.) In addition to the direct ownership and operation of housing for low- and moderate-income persons, 46 percent of local governments also support programs that provide rent subsidies (which may be local or federal funds) to lower-income persons (see Figure 5-4), and 48 percent provide support for the development of rental housing for low- and moderate-income persons (See Figure 5-5).

Home ownership has long been a cherished part of the American dream. As one observer has noted, "It is important not only because of the potential for accumulation of wealth or 'equity' through monthly payments on a mortgage rather than monthly payments of rent, but also because of the deep psychological need for most Americans to 'own' their home as a sign of control over destinies."[5]

In North Carolina in 2000, 69.4 percent of all occupied units were owned by their residents. This is slightly more than the 1990 ownership rate of 68 percent, and it is greater than the national average of 52.3 percent. However, substantial differences exist in the home ownership rates of the state's various racial and ethnic groups. For example, in 2000 the home ownership rate for white households was the highest at 76 percent; the rate among African American households was 53 percent; and the rate for Hispanic households was 32 percent. Among all other races the home ownership rate was 58 percent in 2000. (See Figure 5-7.)

For many potential homeowners who can afford the monthly mortgage payment, the down payment and other financing requirements to secure a loan pose insurmountable barriers to home ownership. Some 41 percent of local governments provide assistance to low-income, usually first-time home buyers. (See Figure 5-6.) This assistance might include down payment assistance, loan products, or the subsidization of private market interest rates.

For other lower-income households that are able to own their homes, the cost of home ownership, including the cost of repairs, often exceeds the household's available resources. Local governments sometimes seek to preserve home ownership by providing assistance to low-income home owners to rehabilitate their substandard homes. (See Figure 5-8.)

## The Homeless

The most common definition of homelessness includes only those people who are literally homeless—that is, on the streets or in shelters—and persons who face imminent eviction (within a week) from a private dwelling or institution and who have no subsequent residence or resources to obtain housing.[6] Even with this narrow definition, the precise number of homeless persons is difficult to determine because the transience of this population likely results in undercounting.

There are two primary sources of data on the state's homeless population: a statewide point-in-time count and the performance reports of nonprofit organizations and units of local governments that receive Emergency Shelter Grant (ESG) Program funding from the N.C. Department of Health and Human Services. The first source of data is a snapshot count; the second source looks at the problem over the course of a year. On December 15, 2003, 9,687 homeless persons were counted in the point-in-time count. From July 1, 2002, to June 30, 2003, the 135 ESG-funded facilities for the homeless operated in communities in fifty-four of the state's counties and served over 45,666 persons. The ESG count is regarded as a more accurate estimate of who is homeless and how many people are homeless overall. (See Figure 5-11.)

The specific causes of homelessness are often disputed. Some argue that homelessness is not a housing problem, but rather it is a manifestation of mental incapacity, drug abuse, and other health-related causes. National studies indicate that about a third of persons who are homeless have a serious mental illness. Relatedly, national estimates indicate that nearly half of homeless persons have a substance use disorder. While these statistics call for a response to homelessness that includes both shelter and services, affordable housing advocates point out that some portion of the homeless population is homeless solely because of economic circumstances.

**Figure 5-6.** With what frequency has your community provided local government assistance to low-income homeowners (loans, subsidized interest rates, etc.)?

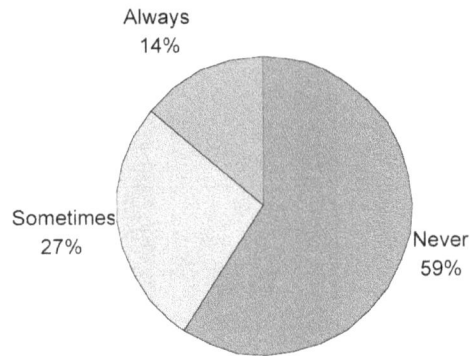

Always 14%

Sometimes 27%

Never 59%

Source: School of Government, Community Development Survey (2004)

The National Coalition for the Homeless, for example, has noted that "[t]he leading cause of contemporary homelessness is the lack of affordable housing. . . . Whenever there is a shortage, there is competition. When there is competition, someone loses. In this case, losing means being pushed out of one's home."[7] National data supports this perspective. Homeless people typically have had less income for longer periods of time than other poor people. They have less work experience and less education than do the poor who manage to avoid becoming homeless. Taken together with the diminished number of low-wage jobs for the unskilled, these factors create a destitute poor—those with incomes so meager that paying for food and other daily necessities leaves too little for shelter.

Club Nova Apartments, Carrboro, North Carolina, are efficiency apartments for individuals with mental illness.

**Figure 5-7.** North Carolina home ownership by race

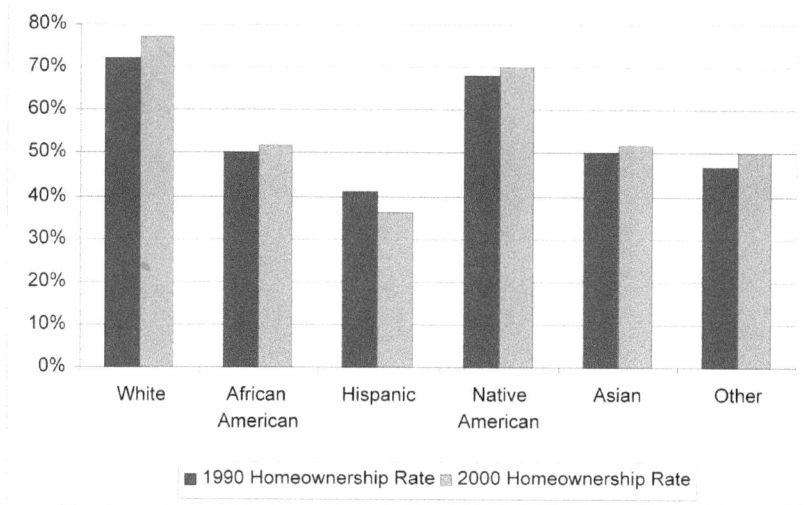

Source: North Carolina Housing Finance Agency, *Housing Markets & Needs Analysis* (2004)

**Figure 5-8.** With what frequency has your community provided local government assistance to low-income homeowners for rehabilitation?

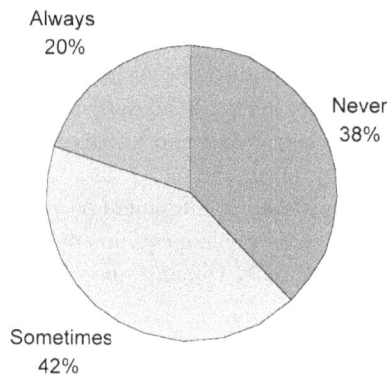

Source: School of Government, Community Development Survey (2004)

**Figure 5-9.** With what frequency has your community engaged in local government affordable housing programs for the homeless?

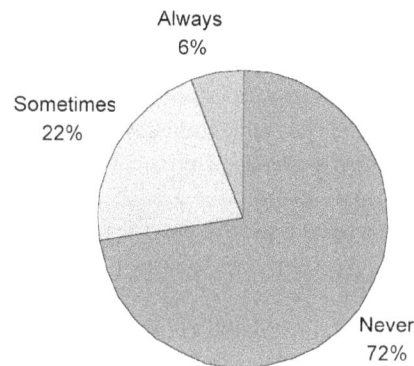

Source: School of Government, Community Development Survey (2004)

Less than 30 percent of local governments have responded to the plight of the homeless by operating housing shelters. (See Figure 5-9.) According to the NCHFA, the average daily occupancy in the state's 135 ESG-funded shelters in program year 2002–2003 ranged from 5 people in Cherokee and Hertford counties to 425 people in Wake and Mecklenburg counties.

## The Elderly

The United States, as a nation, is graying. North Carolina is no exception. This demographic shift is creating pressing challenges to providing safe, quality, affordable housing to the elderly.[8] According to HUD in 2000, 26.4 percent of all elderly households in the state had at least one housing problem. Fully 41 percent (53,000) of all elderly rental households had housing problems and 23 percent (128,400) of all elderly owner households had problems.

When looking at the particular housing problem of affordability, the census reflects that 12.6 percent of North Carolina's elderly live in poverty, and an even greater percent live in "shelter poverty," as the high cost of housing leaves little to pay for other essential needs. In addition, 25.7 percent of elderly households spent greater than 30 percent of their income on housing costs. Finally, since very little research has been done on the housing problems of elderly people, housing researchers speculate that they may well face housing problems beyond the traditional issues of unaffordability, inadequacy, inaccessibility, and homelessness.[9]

Historic Dallas Senior High School has been converted into a senior living facility in Dallas, North Carolina.

North Carolina Rural Communities Assistance Project, Inc.'s Safe Housing Initiative focuses on families living without indoor plumbing or who currently have inadequate water or wastewater facilities in Chatham and Randolph counties.

## Physical Inadequacy

The physical inadequacy of housing is difficult to analyze at the state level. Each of the primary sources of data is problematic. The census provides indicators only on the conditions of kitchen facilities and plumbing facilities, and the American Housing Survey does not make its data available at the state level. Thus, while local governments might be interested in other evidence of physical inadequacy beyond kitchens and plumbing, such as unsafe wiring or ventilation, that data is available at the state level only from estimates based on the American Housing Survey.

Focusing first on the more reliable census data, a unit is defined as having complete kitchen facilities when it has all of the following: (1) a sink with piped water; (2) a range, or cook top, and an oven; and (3) a refrigerator. A housing unit with complete plumbing facilities must have (1) hot and cold piped water; (2) a flush toilet; and (3) a bathtub or shower. In 1970, 20.2 percent of the total housing units in North Carolina were deemed to have inadequate kitchen and/or plumbing facilities. By 1980 that number had dropped dramatically to 7.9 percent. In 1990 the number again dropped (to 3.9 percent), but by 2000, the number had risen slightly to 4 percent. (See Figure 5-10.)

In 1980, 4.4 percent of all occupied housing units in North Carolina lacked complete kitchen facilities. By 1990, this figure had dropped to 1.2 percent. In 2000, the figure remained at 1.2 percent. The number of units without complete plumbing reflects a similar trend in the state. The percentage of all occupied units in the state that lacked complete plumbing dropped from 4.0 percent in 1980 to 1.3 percent in 1990 to 1.2 percent in 2000.

An analysis of the race and ethnicity of households lacking complete plumbing shows that in 2000, 1.3 percent of African American households and 1.2 percent of Hispanic households and 1.1 percent of Native American households lacked plumbing. At the same time, less than 0.7 percent of Asian households and 0.4 percent of white households lacked complete plumbing.

Estimates derived from the 2001 American Housing Survey[10] suggest that there are 2,221 housing units with no electrical wiring in North Carolina and 17,936 units with exposed wiring. Estimates from the survey also suggest that in 8,063 units there is no heating equipment of any type, in 118,475 units the primary heating equipment is a room heater without a flue, and in 91,160 units there is no room with air conditioning.

As indicated by the statistics on rehabilitation activity, the School of Government's survey suggests that local governments are actively engaged in efforts to improve the condition of housing units with problems. These efforts are not limited to units that are defined as physically inadequate by either the census or the American Housing Survey. Moreover, many local governments are demolishing units that pose health or safety risks to inhabitants and the community at large. (See Figure 5-12.)

## Overcrowding

An overcrowded unit is often defined as one that contains more than one person per room. According to a more technical HUD definition, the term *overcrowding* applies to a unit that has more than 1.01 persons per room.[11] By HUD's definition, in 1980, 4.5 percent of all occupied housing units in North Carolina were overcrowded. By 1990 this figure had dropped to 2.9 percent. But in 2000, 3.4 percent of households in the state were overcrowded. (See Figure

**Figure 5-10.** Percentage of North Carolina housing units deemed inadequate

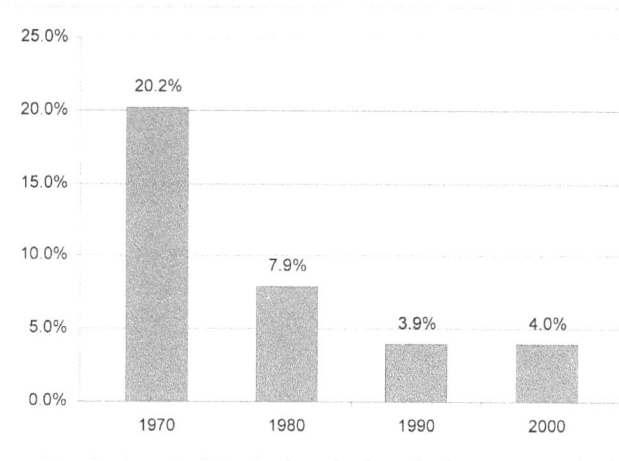

Source: North Carolina Housing Finance Agency

**Figure 5-11.** North Carolina's metropolitan counties have the highest average daily occupancy of ESG-funded shelters.

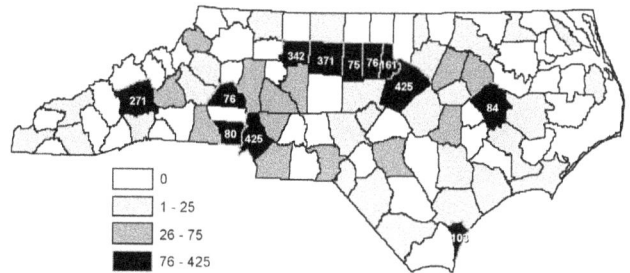

Source: North Carolina Housing Finance Agency

**Figure 5-12.** With what frequency has your community engaged in local government demolition programs?

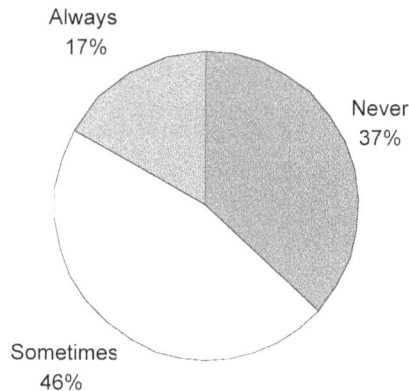

Source: School of Government, Community Development Survey (2004)

A handicapped accessible, affordable unit in Glenwood Place, Hickory, North Carolina.

5-13.) While overcrowding rates are dropping in some parts of the state, the rates are rising in many places—especially in urban areas. Orange County, for example, experienced a 398 percent increase in overcrowded units between 1990 and 2000.[12] In addition, while overcrowding is a more significant problem in rental housing, the NCHFA reports that even owner-occupied households are experiencing increased overcrowding in certain areas.

## Accessibility

As used in this chapter, accessibility refers to the "access" that individuals have to the full range of housing choices. The term covers individuals protected under the Fair Housing Act, as amended in 1988. (The Fair Housing Act and its amendments are discussed in detail in Chapter 2.) In essence, then, the term accessibility covers (1) efforts to make housing physically accessible to the disabled;

## A Case in Point: City of Greenville, North Carolina

### Programs to Address Housing Conditions and Needs

*Substandard Owner-Occupied Housing Rehabilitation Activity*

The city of Greenville, through qualified program rehabilitation contractors, provides housing rehabilitation assistance for repairs to owner-occupied homes. All rehabilitation activity takes place within a forty-five-block revitalization area, which includes the neighborhoods that comprise West Greenville. Homeowners with annual incomes below 80 percent of the median area income qualify for assistance.

*Acquisition of Substandard/Dilapidated Properties Activity*

Greenville has a minimum housing standards code, which it aggressively enforces. Through the code, the city acquires and demolishes substandard and dilapidated properties that present a risk of blight to the forty-five-block revitalization area. The city's acquisition activity focuses on vacant rental properties or vacant parcels. However, the city sometimes acquires blighted occupied rental units. Relocation assistance is provided to tenants that are displaced by such acquisitions. Acquired parcels of land are often combined for the construction of new, affordable housing units.

*Down Payment Assistance Activity*

The city places a high priority on activities that create home ownership opportunities within the forty-five-block revitalization area. Efforts to help low- and moderate-income tenants become home owners include down payment assistance funding.[a]

*Special Population Activities*

Greenville has engaged in an analysis of the impediments to fair housing. Through that analysis Greenville has identified a significant need for affordable housing programs targeted to those persons afflicted with AIDS and HIV, the homeless, the elderly, and the mentally ill and developmentally disabled. However, the city has no such programs for any group other than the homeless.

Since 2001, the city of Greenville has actively assisted with the creation and development of a continuum of care for Pitt County to address the issue of homelessness. The continuum includes the city of Greenville as lead entity; the towns of Farmville, Ayden, Bethel, Grifton, and Winterville; and Pitt County. The group received funding in 2003 after submitting its first application. City and county staff, as well as nonprofit and for-profit representatives, meet monthly to discuss the ever-growing homeless population in their communities. According to the city of Greenville's 2004 Annual Action Plan as provided to HUD, the group will continue to develop the continuum and prepare applications to secure funds for activities in Pitt County. Activities will include a needs assessment, procurement of a consultant to assist with the planning process, and continued internal development of a core committee and advisory committee. All actions by the continuum of care group will address obstacles to meet the underserved needs in the community, assist with the reduction of poverty, assist with the development of "institutional structures," and enhance coordination between public and private housing and social service providers. Other actions will include marketing the continuum among surrounding communities to promote regional participation.

*Housing Conditions and Needs*

The city of Greenville, North Carolina, is often referred to as the "hub" of Eastern North Carolina. From 1990 to 2000, the population of the city increased by 31 percent (from 52,789 to 60,476), making Greenville the thirteenth largest city in North Carolina. Greenville's dramatic growth over the past two decades marks the transformation of the city from a small, rural, farming community to the regional focal point of Eastern North Carolina.

Housing units in Greenville are relatively new. The 2000 U.S. Census reported that 1983 was the median year of construction for housing. The census also reported that the median size of all dwelling units was 4.5 rooms. With a mean dwelling size of 2.16 persons, overcrowding does not appear to be a significant problem in Greenville.

On the other hand, affordability and adequacy pose significant problems, particularly for renters. An analysis of the monthly cost of housing expenses related to owner-occupied units reflects that, in large part, home ownership is affordable. Seventy-nine percent of households spent less than 30 percent of their income for housing according to the 2000 census. In contrast, 52 percent of renters were paying in excess of 30 percent of their income for housing costs.

The rental squeeze in Greenville is directly related to the composition of the city's households. Of the 25,204 total households in Greenville, 12,003 were identified in the census as family households, while non-family households (unrelated people living together) represented 13,201 households. The high percentage of non-family households seeking housing makes Greenville fairly atypical of North Carolina communities. The demographic reflects the presence of East Carolina University (ECU), the third largest university in the state. The 2004 fall enrollment at the university was almost 22,000, and enrollment is expected to increase by 5,500 by the end of the decade. ECU provides housing in dormitories for only 24 percent of its current student population. The remaining students must seek housing within the city. Thus, the demand in Greenville for affordable rental units is high, and the housing market has responded to the demand. Because many property owners target students for rental properties, non-student residents of Greenville with low and very low incomes are often simply priced out of the market or forced to accept properties not desirable to the students.

In addition to its rental market trends, Greenville is also plagued with a home ownership rate for whites that is double (60 percent) that of its home ownership rate for African Americans (30 percent) and ten times the rate for Hispanics (6 percent). Moreover, suburbanization and poor maintenance practices by absentee landowners are causing significant deterioration in Greenville's older neighborhoods. The most significant rates of deterioration are found in the neighborhoods located to the west of the central business district in an area known as West Greenville. This area is comprised of fourteen different neighborhoods and has a combined population of 5,197. The median household income for the area is $17,716, with 42.8 percent of residents at or below the poverty level. Absentee landlords own over 70 percent of the homes. The other units are occupied by primarily low to very low-income home owners who often lack the financial resources to make needed repairs to their homes.

### Table 5-A. Households reporting housing problems in Greenville in the 2000 U.S. Census

| Household type reporting problems | Number of Households | Percentage |
|---|---|---|
| Elderly renters with incomes less than 80% of the area median income | 577 | (6.8%) |
| Elderly homeowners with incomes less than 80% of the area median income | 486 | (5.7%) |
| Owners other than elderly owners with incomes less than 80% of the area median income | 1,079 | (12.6%) |
| Renters other than elderly renters with incomes less than 80% of the area median income | 6,388 | (74.9%) |
| Total | 8,530 | |

### Table 5-B. Households reporting housing problems in Greenville in the 2000 U.S. Census by race

| Household type reporting problems | White | African American | Hispanic | Other |
|---|---|---|---|---|
| Elderly renters with incomes less than 80% of the area median income | 209 (36%) | 360 (62%) | 0 (0%) | 8 (2%) |
| Elderly owners with incomes less than 80% of the area median income | 366 (75%) | 120 (25%) | 0 (0%) | 0 (0%) |
| Owners other than elderly with incomes less than the area median income | 714 (66%) | 335 (31%) | 16 (1.5%) | 14 (1.5%) |
| Renters other than elderly with incomes less than 80% of the area median income | 3,843 (60%) | 2,257 (35%) | 105 (2%) | 183 (3%) |
| Total | 5,132 | 3,072 | 121 | 205 |

The city also notes particular housing problems for those with special needs, which the city describes as persons with AIDS or HIV, the homeless, the elderly, and the mentally ill and developmentally disabled.

---

a. This information is derived from the city of Greenville's Consolidated Plan and Annual Plan of Work. Both plans are required from jurisdictions receiving block grant funding from HUD. The Consolidated Plan consists of the jurisdiction's planning, application, and performance reporting. It includes an assessment of housing and community development needs and a long-term strategy for addressing those needs with the use of HUD and other sources of funding. The Annual Plan of Work includes a more detailed description of how the community intends to address the needs prioritized in the Consolidated Plan over the course of a particular fiscal year.

**Figure 5-13.** Average overcrowding of North Carolina occupied housing units

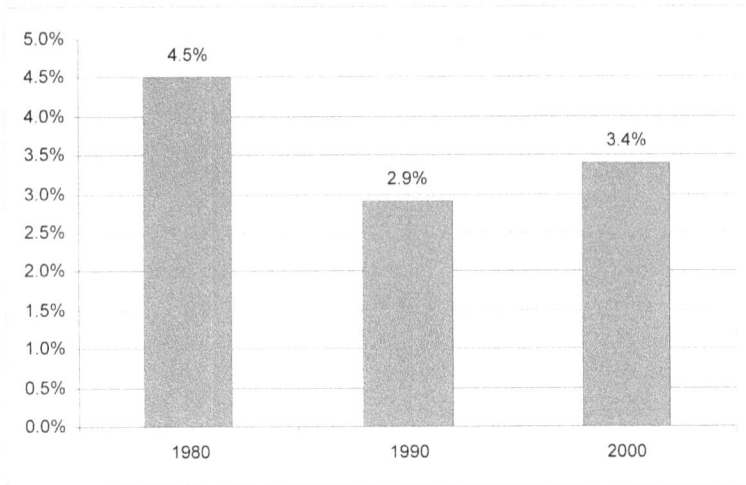

Source: School of Government, Community Development Survey (2004)

(2) activities to eradicate illegal discrimination in the housing markets based on race, religion, gender, familial status, and disability; and (3) efforts to affirmatively expand housing opportunities for groups that have traditionally been discriminated against.

The best statewide source of information on barriers to housing access is the North Carolina Human Relations Commission, which was created in 1963 to promote civil rights and equal opportunities for the residents of North Carolina. In addition to other functions, the NCHRC enforces the State Fair Housing Act by receiving and investigating housing discrimination complaints. The NCHRC received housing discrimination complaints from seventy-five counties between 2000 and 2004. The counties with the highest number of complaints were Wake, Guilford, and Pitt. The most common basis for fair housing complaints over the same period was race or color (40 percent). In order of frequency, race was followed by disability/handicap (26 percent ), familial status (14 percent), sex (11 percent), nation of origin (8 percent), and religion (1 percent).

The School of Government survey did not ask questions about efforts to provide housing for the disabled or other specific populations. The single "accessibility" question in this area asked whether local governments had engaged in studies of the impediments to fair housing or actions to affirmatively further fair housing opportunities in the past five years. The vast majority of local governments reported that they had not engaged in either studies of the impediments to fair housing or actions to affirmatively further fair housing opportunities.

## Notes

1. North Carolina Housing Finance Agency, Housing Market and Needs Analysis, Raleigh, N.C. September 2004.

2. In 1975 almost all of Raleigh's police officers lived in the city. By 2000, only 15 percent did. "Every day Raleigh cops put their lives on the line to protect neighborhoods they can never call home," observed a Raleigh columnist. Dennis Rogers, *City's Finest Have to Live Elsewhere*, NEWS AND OBSERVER, Sept. 23, 2000, at B1.

3. The Department of Housing and Urban Development (HUD) sets fair market rents for the state and its counties. These rents are approximations of the gross rent (rent for the unit plus utilities) of a less-than-average standard unit in the area. *See* www.huduser.org/datasets/fmr.html (last visited November 21, 2004).

4. TRIANGLE J COUNCIL OF GOV'TS, CENTER FOR AFFORDABLE LIVING, HOUSING OPPORTUNITY IN THE TRIANGLE: THE GROWING GAP BETWEEN HOUSEHOLD INCOMES AND HOUSING COSTS (2003).

5. Peter W. Salsich Jr., *Nonprofit Housing Organizations*, 4 NOTRE DAME J.L. ETHICS & PUB. POL'Y, 227 (1989).

6. Mckinney-Vento Homeless Assistance Act, 42 U.S.C.A. 11301 (1995).

7. NATIONAL COALITION FOR THE HOMELESS, HOMELESSNESS IN AMERICA: A SUMMARY, at 2–3 (1988).

8. Statistics regarding the elderly assume those individuals are sixty-five years and older.

9. *See* John I. Gilderbloom & R.L. Mullins Jr., *Elderly Housing Needs: An Examination of the American Housing Survey*, 40 INT. J. AGING & HUM. DEV. 57–72 (1995).

10. These estimates were calculated by the North Carolina Housing Finance Agency.

11. Severe overcrowding occurs when a unit has more than 1.51 persons per room.

12. U.S. Census, 2000.

# Appendix 1 | Glossary of Affordable Housing Terms

**Accessory Dwelling Units.** Complete and separate housing created in the surplus space of single-family homes. With its own kitchen and bath and almost always its own separate entrance, this housing is sometimes referred to as "mother-in-law" units or single-family conversions.

**Affordability.** Housing affordability is the relation of a consumer's housing costs to his or her available resources. Current federal standards suggest, as a rule of thumb, that a household should pay no more than 30 percent of its income for housing.

**Assisted Living.** A planned retirement housing option in the United States offering shelter, protective oversight, personalized assistance, and health care for physically or mentally vulnerable older people. Ideally, assisted living seeks to promote the maximum independence and personal autonomy of its residents in a homelike environment.

**Blight.** A condition of an area defined by a pattern of deterioration and decay of economic vitality. A determination of blight for federal funding purposes is based on state statutory definitions. Although *blight* and *slum* are often used interchangeably or together, *blight* is an economic term and *slum* a social one.

**Blockbusting.** Blockbusting is a now-illegal scare tactic used by real estate speculators to acquire property from owners in segregated neighborhoods and manipulate a decline in housing values. After one house is sold to a minority family, nonminority families in the neighborhood are contacted and pressured to sell their homes at below-market value to avoid living among minorities. After a number of such homes are acquired, real estate agents sell the homes at higher prices to minorities and keep the panic differential as profits. Blockbusting was made an illegal practice under Title VIII, section 804, of the federal Civil Rights Act of 1968.

**Board and Care Homes.** The forerunner of congregate housing and assisted living, board and care homes provide food, shelter, some protective oversight, and oftentimes personal care to residents.

**Building Codes.** State law that regulates the construction of new buildings. Building codes include regulations of materials and workmanship.

**Community Development Block Grant.** Since 1975, the federal government has supported most of local governments' community and economic development efforts, including affordable housing, through the Community Development Block Grant program (CDBG). HUD's Community Planning and Development Office administers and allocates these CDBG funds to states and units of general local government.

**Community Development Corporations.** A community development corporation (CDC) is a tax-exempt (501)(c)(3) nonprofit, community-based organization. Although they often address issues such as job training and development and commercial revitalization, CDCs are best known for creating affordable housing opportunities through the development of new housing and rehabilitation of substandard housing.

**Congregate-Housing Residences.** In this housing option, residents have their own apartments. However, they come together for meals and recreation, and they may receive limited services.

**Continuing-Care Retirement Communities.** These communities provide a continuum of care, including independent housing, congregate housing, assisted living, and nursing care.

**Demand-side Subsidies.** Demand-side subsidies go to consumers and reduce the costs of consumption. They can take the form of a direct cash payment by the government or involve preferential tax treatment that reduces the payments a household would otherwise have to make. The principal forms of demand-side subsidies for affordable housing are housing vouchers or housing certificates.

**Density Bonus.** Density bonuses are incentives given by local governments to developers to encourage the inclusion of affordable housing in otherwise market-rate developments. A density bonus enables a builder to develop a parcel of land more intensively than existing zoning rules would allow.

**Eviction.** The forced removal of people from their homes. Generally played out as a conflict between an individual tenant and landlord, eviction is usually the result of the tenant's failure to pay rent or some other material breach of the lease.

**Exclusionary Zoning.** An ordinance containing restrictive regulations of land use that has the effect of excluding low-income groups from a community by driving up the cost of housing.

**Fair Housing.** Laws that protect against discrimination in the housing market and often impose an affirmative obligation on those administering federal funds to act to eradicate policies and programs that are either intentionally discriminatory or that have a discriminatory effect.

**Fair Market Rent.** Published annually by HUD, this is the gross rent (shelter plus utilities) of privately owned, decent, safe, and sanitary housing of a modest nature with suitable amenities.

**Foreclosure.** The borrower who does not make a scheduled mortgage payment (or fulfill any covenant of the mortgage agreement) is technically in default. Default-foreclosure is a legal process that transfers ownership of the property from the borrower to the lender.

**Gentrification.** The process by which central urban neighborhoods that have undergone disinvestment and economic decline experience a reversal, reinvestment, and the in-migration of a relatively well-off, middle- and upper-middle-class population.

**Group Home.** A group home is one in which unrelated persons operate as a single housekeeping unit in a conventional residential structure.

**Home Equity.** The value of home ownership that is the net amount of money that home owners would receive if their house were sold at any given point in time.

**HOME Funds.** The Home Program (HOME) is a federal program designed to increase the supply of housing for low-income persons by providing funds to states and local governments to implement local housing strategies. HOME provides funds to states and local governments to implement local housing strategies, which may include tenant-based rental assistance, assistance to home buyers, property acquisition, new construction, rehabilitation, site improvements, demolition, relocation, and administrative costs. After certain mandated set-asides, the balance of HOME funds is allocated by formula with 60 percent going to cities, urban counties, and consortia (contiguous units of local government) and 40 percent to states to be reallocated to remaining jurisdictions.

**Homelessness.** Homelessness refers to people who lack regular access to conventional housing. This includes people sleeping on sidewalks, in parks, in public places, and in emergency shelters. It does not include people who may not have a home of their own but are temporarily living with family members or friends.

**Household.** This is a research term used to describe all persons who occupy the same housing unit. The Bureau of the Census divides households into two major categories: *family* and *nonfamily*. *Family households* include the person by whom the unit is rented or owned and at least one relative. *Nonfamily households* include no relatives.

**HUD.** The U.S. Department of Housing and Urban Development is a federal agency created in 1965, under President Lyndon B. Johnson. HUD is charged by law with providing local communities with assistance for housing and the development of urban areas. HUD articulates its mission as "to increase homeownership, support community development and increase access to affordable housing free from discrimination."

**Impact Fees.** Local governments sometimes levy cash assessments against developers to pay for the off-site infrastructure—including sewer, water supply, and storm drainage facilities; parks; and roads—necessitated by the development.

**Linkage.** This refers to the practice by local governments of making land use and zoning approval for nonresidential development contingent on the provision of affordable housing. For this practice to be legal, localities need to have studied and documented the link between the nonresidential development and affordable housing needs.

**Low-income Housing Tax Credits.** These tax credits are provided through the federal and state tax codes to investors in the construction of low-income rental housing.

**Manufactured Housing.** Housing that is produced in enclosed factories using assembly-line techniques and constructed in compliance with U.S. Housing and Urban Development (HUD) Construction and Safety Standards. The HUD code preempts state and local codes that usually govern building construction.

**Modular Homes.** Like manufactured housing, modular homes and other types of industrialized housing are factory-built, but rather than comply with the HUD codes, they must comply with state building codes.

**Mortgage Credit Certificate.** One particularly effective bond-driven housing program is the mortgage credit certificate (MCCs). MCCs are federal income tax credits issued through state housing agencies to eligible first-time home buyers. Authorized by the Tax Reform Act of 1984, MCCs have the effect of increasing home buyers' purchasing power by reducing their tax liability by a percentage of the mortgage interest.

**Public Housing Authorities.** (PHA) (sometimes referred to as local housing authorities) are created by local governments under state enabling legislation. PHAs' primary purpose is to provide low-rent housing to low-income households.

**Rent Control.** Price controls on rents may take different forms. The government might set the level of rents or seek to control increases in rent. With some limited exceptions, the policy of rent control of private markets is illegal in North Carolina.

**Residential Segregation.** Segregated housing exists wherever the residential distribution of one population group differs from that of another population group. The most prevalent form of segregation in the United States is segregation by race. Two of the most commonly used ways to measure segregation are the dissimilarity index, which measures the unevenness in the distribution of two groups among subareas, and the isolation index, which measures the exposure of whites to ethnic minorities.

**Single Room Occupancy Housing.** This is housing in which units consist of a single furnished room with no private kitchen.

**Supply-side Subsidies.** Supply-side subsidies are provided by the government to the suppliers of housing to reduce the costs of provision. These subsidies make it cheaper for builders and landlords to provide housing. Governments may provide direct subsidies through the explicit expenditure of funds or they may provide indirect subsidies through the use of tax benefits.

**Tax-exempt Mortgage Revenue Bonds.** State and local governments may use their borrowing capacity by selling mortgage revenue bonds to fund mortgage loans for households unable to afford conventional mortgage loans.

The government may either serve as the direct lender to these households or it may make funds available to conventional lenders on the agreement that the funds be used to make loans to qualified households.

**Tax Increment Financing.** Tax Increment Financing (TIF) raises development/redevelopment funds through the use of bonds later retired from the incremental tax revenue generated from the improved property. Across the country, TIF funds are sometimes used to fund affordable housing for lower-income households, particularly when the TIF district includes commercial areas that undergo revitalization, thereby increasing property values and the tax increment.

*Note:* For additional definitions of common affordable housing terms, see *The Encyclopedia of Housing*, Wilem van Vliet (ed.), Sage Publications, Inc., California, 1998.

# Appendix 2 | Federal Housing Legislation with Significant Effects on Local Government Housing Activity

**1933.** The National Industrial Recovery Act of 1933 (Public law 73-67) authorized federal funds to be used to finance low-rent housing and slum clearance.

**1937.** The United States Housing Act of 1937 (Public Law 75-412) established a permanent public housing program.

**1949.** The Housing Act of 1949 (Public Law 81-171) established the national housing policy of "a decent home and a suitable living environment for every American family."

**1954.** The Housing Act of 1954 (Public Law 83-560) extended the federal housing focus to include the prevention of slum and blight through rehabilitation and conservation. The law conditioned the receipt of federal funds on the enactment of a "workable program" in which localities adopted and enforced housing, zoning, building, and other codes.

**1955.** The Housing Amendment of 1955 (Public Law 84-345) established a new federal public facilities loan program.

**1956.** The Housing Act of 1956 (Public Law 84-1020) authorized relocation payments to persons and businesses displaced by urban renewal.

**1961.** The Housing Act of 1961 (Public Law 87-70) provided a below-market interest rate mortgage program for moderate-income families and made direct loan funding available to public agencies seeking to provide housing for the elderly.

**1964.** The Civil Rights Act of 1964 (Public Law 88-352) prohibited discrimination on the basis of race, color, religion, or national origin against persons eligible to participate in and receive the benefits of any program receiving federal financial assistance.

**1964.** The Housing Act of 1964 (Public Law 88-560) provided direct low-interest loans for eligible families to enable them to rehabilitate their residential and business structures.

**1965.** The Housing Act of 1965 (Public Law 89-4) established federal assistance, administered through local public housing authorities, to provide rehabilitation grants for home repairs and rehabilitation, demolition grants for unsound structures, and federally assisted code enforcement. This act also authorized the leasing of existing private housing by local housing authorities.

**1966.** The Demonstration Cities (later Model Cities) and Metropolitan Development Act of 1966 (Public Law 89-754) authorized federal grants and technical assistance to local communities to plan, develop, and carry out comprehensive city programs for rebuilding or restoring entire sections and neighborhoods characterized by slums and blighted areas. This act also authorized an FHA insurance program for rehabilitation of housing by nonprofit groups.

**1968.** The 1968 Housing and Urban Development Act (Public Law 90-448) authorized the Neighborhood Development Program under which urban renewal activities could be carried out in annual increments. It also authorized the federal government to guarantee loans for private developers of new communities and created the National Housing Partnerships to encourage greater use of private financial resources in affordable housing.

**1968.** The Fair Housing Act of 1968 (Public Law 90-284) established federal fair housing policy for the nation. The law made it illegal to discriminate in housing on the basis of race, color, religion, or national origin. In 1974 Congress amended the Fair Housing Act to prohibit gender discrimination.

**1970.** The Uniform Relocation Assistance and Real Property Acquisition Policy Act (Public Law 91-646) makes federal funds available to reimburse relocation cost incurred by persons displaced by federal housing and community development programs.

**1974.** The Housing and Community Development Act of 1974 (Public Law 93-383) consolidated five major categories of assistance programs into a new Community Development Block Grant program. States and local governments were authorized as the direct recipients of assistance. Eligible activities for use of CDBG funds included a broad range of physical improvement activities. The act also created a new federally assisted housing program—Section 8—which authorized federal housing assistance payment contracts to sponsors to develop, rehabilitate, or lease existing housing for lower-income families. Also, the act required a local Housing Assistance Plan as a condition of CDBG assistance.

**1977.** The Housing and Community Development Act of 1977 (Public Law 95-128) authorized federal urban development action grants to severely distressed cities and urban counties to help alleviate physical and economic deterioration through coordination with private investment and reinvestment opportunities.

**1977.** The Community Reinvestment Act of 1977 was enacted by Congress to encourage banks to lend equitably throughout their communities. CRA was a response to redlining—the practice of not lending in particular geographic areas. However, CRA does not dictate specific actions, activities, products, or services. Generally a bank negotiates with community groups to determine appropriate CRA activity.

**1978.** The Housing and Community Development Amendments of 1978 (Public Law 95-557) established a new "moderate rehabilitation" category under the Section 8 existing housing program; it also authorized a new system of operating subsidies for troubled multi-family projects and enacted a program to provide grants to neighborhood development organizations. It also established the livable cities program, which provided funding to enhance the artistic, cultural, and historic resources of neighborhoods.

**1980.** The Housing and Community Development Act of 1980 (Public Law 96-399) established national standards for condominium and cooperative conversions.

**1986.** The Law-Income Tax Credit Program of 1986 (Public Law 99-514) provided an incentive for the construction and rehabilitation of affordable housing by allowing owners of qualified rental properties to claim tax credits.

**1988.** The Fair Housing Amendments Act (Public Law 100-430) made it unlawful to discriminate in housing on the basis of disability or familial status. The act makes clear that discrimination against the disabled includes a refusal to make reasonable accomodations in rules, policies, practices or services when such accomodations are necessary to afford a disabled person an equal opportunity to use and enjoy the dwelling.

# Appendix 3 | A Sample of Funding Sources Available for Affordable Housing Programs

A detailed or comprehensive listing of funding sources for affordable housing activity is beyond the scope of this book. However, many funding programs are referenced in the book's chapters and this appendix aims to give more context to those programs and others that are closely related.

Each funding program's description has been derived from the description listed on the funding agency's Web site. However, because the regulations governing funding programs change constantly, readers are urged to visit the Web sites listed for the most current information on each program.

## Federal Funding Sources

The U.S. Department of Housing and Urban Development (HUD) administers a wide variety of programs including thirty-two housing programs and seven homeless assistance programs. HUD has field offices spread throughout the country, with at least one in every state. The HUD office for North Carolina is in Greensboro. The programs listed below are administered by HUD unless otherwise noted. (www.hud.gov.progdesc)

## Programs for Housing and Community Development Generally

*Community Development Block Grants/Small Cities Program*
The Community Development Block Grant (CDBG) program provides grants to cities and counties to develop viable urban communities by providing decent housing and a suitable living environment and by expanding economic opportunities. The program is also intended to help prevent community deterioration and to address serious threats to community health or welfare. At least 70 percent of a Community Development Block Grant must benefit low- and moderate-income persons.

Under the CDBG program, cities over 50,000 in population and urban counties are "entitled" to an annual grant. Communities under 50,000 are eligible to compete within their respective states for non-entitlement CDBG funds. States may elect to administer the "Small Cities" or non-entitlement portion of the CDBG funds. All states except Hawaii have chosen to do so. These states are responsible for designing and implementing their own programs and for administering their own funding competitions. In North Carolina the Small Cities Program is administered by the North Carolina Department of Commerce, Division of Community Assistance. The Small Cities program is discussed further in this appendix under the category State Sources of Funding.

In 2004 there were twenty-three entitlement cities in North Carolina and two entitlement counties. These entitlement communities develop their own programs and funding priorities. However, HUD requires them to give maximum feasible priority to activities which benefit low- and moderate-income persons. Entitlement communities may also carry out activities that aid in the prevention or elimination of slums or blight. Additionally, they may fund activities when they certify that the activities meet other community development needs having a particular urgency because existing conditions pose a serious and immediate threat to the health or welfare of the community where other financial resources are not available to meet such needs. CDBG funds may not be used for activities that do not meet these broad national objectives.

CDBG funds may be used for activities which include, but are not limited to

- relocation and demolition;
- rehabilitation of residential and nonresidential structures;
- construction of public facilities and improvements, such as water and sewer facilities, streets, neighborhood centers, and the conversion of school buildings for eligible purposes;
- public services, within certain limits;
- activities relating to energy conservation and renewable energy sources; and
- job creation/retention activities.

Generally, the following types of activities are ineligible:

- buildings for the general conduct of government;
- political activities;
- certain income payments; and
- construction of new housing by units of general local government.

### Indian Community Development Block Grant Program

Indian tribes and Alaska Natives may use this program to improve the housing stock, provide community facilities, make infrastructure improvements, and expand job opportunities by supporting the economic development of their communities. Eligible activities include housing rehabilitation programs, acquisition of land for housing, direct assistance to facilitate home ownership among low- and moderate-income persons, construction of tribal and other facilities for single- or multi-use, streets and other public facilities, and economic development projects. Construction and improvement of government facilities, the purchase of equipment, general government expenses, operating and maintenance expenses, political activities, new housing construction (except through community-based development organizations), or income payments are ineligible activities.

Any Indian tribe, band, group, or nation (including Alaska Indians, Aleuts, and Eskimos) and any Alaska Native Village is eligible for assistance. Low- to moderate-income persons may receive assistance under this program.

### HOME Investment Partnerships Program

HOME is the largest federal block grant to state and local governments designed exclusively to create affordable housing for low-income households. Each year it allocates approximately $2 billion as formula grants among the states and hundreds of localities nationwide known as participating jurisdictions (PJs). HUD establishes HOME Investment Trust Funds for each grantee, providing a line of credit that the jurisdiction may draw upon as needed. The program's flexibility allows states and local governments to use HOME funds for grants, direct loans, loan guarantees or other forms of credit enhancement, or rental assistance or security deposits.

States are automatically eligible for HOME funds and receive either their formula allocation or $3 million, whichever is greater. North Carolina's HOME funds are administered by the North Carolina Housing Finance Agency. Some local jurisdictions are eligible for at least $500,000 under the formula ($335,000 in years when Congress appropriates less than $1.5 billion for HOME). Communities that do not qualify for an individual allocation under the formula can join with one or more neighboring localities in a legally binding consortium whose members' combined allocation would meet the threshold for direct funding.

Housing developed with HOME funds must serve low- and very-low-income families. At least 90 percent of HOME funds used for rental housing must be invested in affordable units that are occupied by families whose incomes are at or below 60 percent of area median income. The remaining 10 percent must be invested in units occupied by families at or below 80 percent of area median income. Home owners assisted with HOME funds must have incomes at or below 80 percent of the area median income and the residence must be valued at or below 95 percent of the median area purchase price.

Funds may also be used for site acquisition, site improvements, demolition, and relocation. The provision of transitional and/or permanent housing for the homeless is an eligible activity. Participating jurisdictions determine how their HOME funds will be spent through a consolidated planning process that requires public participation.

Some special conditions apply to the use of HOME funds. PJs must match every dollar of HOME funds used (except for administrative costs) with 25 cents from nonfederal sources, which may include donated materials or labor, the value of donated property, proceeds from bond financing, and other resources. The match requirement may be reduced if the PJ is distressed or has suffered a presidentially declared disaster. In addition, PJs must reserve at least 15 percent of their allocations to fund housing to be owned, developed, or sponsored by experienced, community-driven nonprofit groups designated as Community Housing Development Organizations (CHDOs). PJs must ensure that HOME-funded housing units remain affordable in the long term (twenty years for new construction of rental housing; five to fifteen years for construction of home ownership housing and housing rehabilitation, depending on the amount of HOME subsidy). PJs have two years to commit funds (including reserving funds for CHDOs) and five years to spend funds.

### Self-Help Homeownership Opportunity Program

The Self-Help Homeownership Opportunity Program (SHOP) provides funds for land acquisition and infrastructure improvements for sites on which self-help housing will be developed. Low-income home buyers contribute "sweat equity" toward the construction of their homes.

Funds are available to nonprofit national or regional organizations or consortia that have experience in providing self-help housing homeownership opportunities based upon submission and approval of an expression of interest.

Low-income families who are unable to afford to purchase dwellings, and who provide significant amounts of sweat equity or volunteer labor to the development of the dwellings, are the ultimate beneficiaries.

## Programs for Public, Indian, and Assisted Housing

### Public Housing

Public Housing Authorities established in accordance with state law are eligible for this program. Public housing occupants include mostly very-low-income tenants who pay no more than 30 percent of their adjusted income for rent. These persons may include families, singles, eligible immigrants, individuals who are sixty-two years old or older, persons with disabilities, or the remaining members of a tenant family. Other low-income individuals may be served under certain limited circumstances.

HUD makes annual contributions to PHAs for debt service payments for commitments approved on or prior to September 30, 1986. HUD provides direct funding of capital costs (grants) to PHAs for commitments approved after September 30, 1986.

Previously PHAs were eligible for additional capital grant funding for modernization. This program has been combined with HUD's public housing development for operating subsidies to help defray the difference between income from tenant charges and the costs of operation and management, including reserve funds.

Because public housing serves mostly very-low-income tenants, operating subsidies are essential if PHAs are to provide cost-effective, decent, safe, and affordable dwellings. HUD provides these operating subsidies to help PHAs meet operating and maintenance expenses. Annual subsidy requirements are calculated on the basis of the Performance Funding System Formula (PFS), which takes into account what it would cost a comparable, well-managed PHA to operate its units.

Under the Native American Housing Assistance and Self-Determination Act of 1996, Indian Housing Authorities are no longer eligible for funds for public housing.

### Public Housing Capital Fund Program

The Public Housing Capital Fund Program (CFP) makes funds available to public housing agencies for capital and management activities. Funds can also be used for modernization and development of public housing.

### Section 8 Housing Choice Vouchers

This program combines the Section 8 Rental Voucher Program (CFDA 14.855) and the Section 8 Certificate Program (CFDA 14.857). The housing choice voucher program is the federal government's major program for assisting very-low-income families, the elderly, and the disabled to afford decent, safe and sanitary housing in the private market. According to the legislation enacting the change, it was meant to "assist in making tenant-based rental assistance more successful at helping low-income families obtain affordable housing and [to] increase housing choice for low-income families." Since housing assistance is provided on behalf of the family or individual, participants are able to find their own housing.

Applicants are limited to public housing authorities (PHAs). The primary beneficiaries of the program are very-low-income families, those with incomes below 50 percent of area median income. Rental vouchers are assigned to specific families. The amount of federal subsidy is based on the family's income and a payment standard that reflects the average costs of standard rental units for a given market area. The amount of assistance a family receives generally equals the difference between the payment standard and 30 percent of the family's monthly income, with allowable adjustments. The tenant is responsible for any remaining amount that is due the landlord. A participating family is free to pay more than 30 percent of its adjusted income for rent as long as the unit meets HUD's Housing Quality Standards. A participating family can pay less than 30 percent of its adjusted income for rent if the family is able to rent a standard unit for less than the predetermined payment standard.

Eligibility for a housing voucher is determined by the PHA based on the total annual gross income and family size and is limited to U.S. citizens and specified categories of non-citizens who have eligible immigration status. In general, the family's income may not exceed 50 percent of the median income for the county or metropolitan area in which the family chooses to live. By law, a PHA must provide 75 percent of its voucher to applicants whose incomes do not exceed 30 percent of the area median income.

### Resident Opportunity and Supportive Services

The Resident Opportunity and Supportive Services (ROSS) program provides supportive services and resident empowerment activities to residents of public housing, and assists them in becoming economically self-sufficient. The primary focus of the program is on "welfare to work" and on independent living for the elderly and persons with disabilities. Grant funds may be used for economic development and supportive services activities, organizational development, mediation, and the employment of service coordinators/case managers.

Public and Indian housing agencies and tribally designated housing entities, resident management corporations, resident councils or resident organizations, including nonprofit entities supported by residents, may administer ROSS programs. Residents of conventional public housing are eligible to receive benefits from the ROSS program.

### Family Self-Sufficiency

Administered by public housing agencies (PHAs), the Family Self-Sufficiency (FSS) program encourages communities to develop local strategies to help assisted families obtain employment that will lead to economic independence and self-sufficiency. Families who receive assistance under the Section 8 voucher program are eligible to participate in the FSS program.

Under the FSS program, the PHA establishes an interest-bearing escrow account for each participating family. As the family's earned income increases, the PHA credits additional funds to the escrow account. If the family successfully completes the five-year FSS contract, the family receives the money in the account. The PHA may also make a portion of the account available during the contract to enable the family to complete an interim goal such as education. Even after successful completion of a contract, the family may still be eligible for housing assistance if needed.

*Indian Housing Block Grants*
The Indian Housing Block Grant program (IHBG) was created by the Native American Housing Assistance and Self-Determination Act of 1996 (NAHASDA), which separated housing for Native Americans from other public housing. Under NAHASDA, most HUD funds for native American housing are provided to tribes or tribally designated housing entities (TDHEs). Recipients may use the funds in a variety of ways, including for development of new units, assistance to residents of existing units, provision of services, management, crime prevention and safety, and more. A Native American tribe or TDHE is eligible for housing block grant funds when it submits a housing plan that complies with NAHASDA requirements. Funds are to aid families with incomes below 80 percent of area median. Ten percent of each grant can be used to serve families between 80 and 100 percent of area median income. Families who exceed 100 percent of the median income can apply for funding if approved by HUD's headquarters office.

*Loan Guarantees for Indian Housing (Section 184)*
The Section 184 program provides home-ownership opportunities to Native Americans, tribes, tribally designated housing entities, and housing authorities on Native American land. It guarantees mortgage loans made by private financial institutions for the acquisition or rehabilitation of existing homes or construction of new homes. The home owner is the ultimate beneficiary of the program. The loan applicant must be a Native American, including Alaska Natives, or a Tribally Designated Housing Entity (TDHE), tribe, or housing authority (IHA) that meets certain requirements.

*Title VI Federal Guarantees for Financing Tribal Housing Activities*
In 1992, Congress established the section 184 Indian Housing Loan Guarantee Program. By issuing guaranteed/insured loans, this program assists Native American tribes and TDHEs in obtaining private financing for affordable housing activities under the Indian Housing Block Grant

program. The borrower must be a federally recognized Native American tribe or TDHE that is an approved recipient for Indian Housing Block Grant funds. Borrowers may be required to pledge security in addition to IHBG funds.

*Demolition and Revitalization of Severely Distressed Public Housing (HOPE VI)*
The HOPE VI Program was developed as a result of recommendations by the National Commission on Severely Distressed Public Housing, which was charged with proposing a national action plan to eradicate severely distressed public housing. The commission recommended revitalization in three general areas: physical improvements, management improvements, and social and community services to address resident needs.

HOPE VI provides grants that enable PHAs to amend the living environment for public housing residents of severely distressed public housing projects. There are two types of HOPE VI grants: revitalization and demolition.

HOPE revitalization grants fund

- Capital costs of major rehabilitation, new construction, and other physical improvements
- Demolition of severely distressed public housing
- Acquisition of sites for off-site construction
- Community and supportive service programs for residents, including those relocated as a result of revitalization efforts

HOPE VI demolition grants fund the demolition of severely distressed public housing, relocation, and supportive services for relocated residents. PHAs operating public housing units are eligible. Indian Housing Authorities and PHAs that administer only the Section 8 program are not eligible to apply.

## Programs for Weatherization

*Weatherization Assistance for Low-Income Persons (administered by the Department of Energy, www.energy.gov)*
The objective of this program is to provide adequate insulation in order to conserve energy for homes in which low-income people live, particularly the elderly and persons with disabilities. Such insulation may include caulking windows, installing storm windows, and replacing furnaces or boilers.

States, the District of Columbia, and, in certain instances, Indian tribal organizations are eligible. If a state does not apply, local governments, community action agencies, and/or other nonprofit agencies within that state become eligible to apply. In most areas, community action agencies or other community-based organizations administer the program.

*Low-Income Home Energy Assistance (administered by Health and Human Services, www.hhs.gov )*

The Low-Income Home Energy Assistance Program (LIHEAP) makes grants available to states and other jurisdictions to assist eligible households to meet the costs of home energy. Supplemental Leveraging Incentive Funds may be awarded to reward states and other jurisdictions that provide additional benefits, and services to LIHEAP-eligible households beyond what can be provided with federal funds.

States, the District of Columbia, federal and state-recognized tribal governments that request direct funding, and specified territories are eligible applicants. In North Carolina, this program is administered by the Department of Health and Human Services. Ultimate beneficiaries are households with incomes less than 150 percent of the poverty level or 60 percent of state median income.

## Programs for Housing Target Populations

*Rural Housing Programs (administered by the U.S. Department of Agriculture, www.rurdev.usda.gov/rhs/)*

With the exception of its farm labor housing program (Sections 514/516), which is also available in urban areas, Rural Housing Services from the U.S. Department of Agriculture makes housing loans and grants only in rural areas. For all housing programs, RHS defines rural as (1) open country that is not part of or associated with an urban area or (2) any town, village, city, or place, including the immediately adjacent densely settled area, that

- has a population not in excess of 2,500 and is not part of or associated with an urban area;
- has a population under 10,000 and is rural in character;
- has a population under 20,000, is outside a Metropolitan Statistical Area (MSA), and has a serious lack of mortgage credit for low-income families, as agreed to by the secretaries of Agriculture and Housing and Urban Development (Rural Development district or local offices provide a listing of eligible areas with populations under 20,000); or
- was determined to be rural prior to October 1, 1990, and whose population after the 1990 decennial Census did not exceed 25,000 (this provision may be changed, either to update it when data from the 2000 Census becomes available or, as proposed in Congress in 2000, to maintain eligibility based on the 1980 Census through 2010).

Specifically accepted as rural are Pajero, California; Guadalupe, Arizona; Plainsview, Texas; and Altus, Oklahoma.

Rural Housing programs include the following for single family housing:

- Rural Housing Guaranteed Loan
- Rural Housing Direct Loan

- Housing Repair and Rehabilitation Loan
- Housing Repair and Rehabilitation Grant
- Self-Help Technical Assistance Grant
- Mutual Self-Help Loans
- Rural Housing Site Loans
- Individual Water and Waste Grants
- Housing Application Packaging Grants
- Homes for Sale

and for multi-family housing:

- Farm Labor Housing Loans and Grants
- Rural Rental Housing
- Housing Preservation Grant
- Guaranteed Rental Housing
- Rental Assistance Program

Two programs are specifically designed to assist rural households to recover from the effects of a natural disaster:

- Direct Housing Natural Disaster Loans and Grants (Section 504 Disaster Loans and Grants)
- Direct Housing Natural Disaster (Section 502 Disaster Loans).

There is also a Rural Capacity Development Initiative (RCDI), created in 2000, and intended to develop the capacity and ability of nonprofit community-based housing and community development organizations and low-income rural communities to improve housing, community facilities, and community and economic development projects in rural areas. Through RCDI, RHS provides grants to intermediaries to provide technical assistance to qualified organizations.

*Persons with AIDS*

The Housing Opportunities for Persons with AIDS (HOPWA) program provides states and localities with the resources and incentives to devise long-term comprehensive strategies for meeting the housing needs of persons with AIDS or related diseases and their families. Program activities include counseling, information, and referral services to assist eligible individuals to locate, acquire, finance, and maintain housing; developing housing assistance resources; acquiring and rehabilitating buildings; constructing single room occupancy dwellings and community residences; providing rental assistance or short-term financial assistance or supportive services; and covering operating costs, technical assistance, and administrative expenses.

Entitlement grants are awarded to states and cities with the largest number of AIDS cases. Other states, local governments, and nonprofit organizations are eligible to compete for funding. In North Carolina the HOPWA program is administered by the North Carolina Department of Health and Human Services.

The program's beneficiaries are low-income persons with AIDS or related diseases, including HIV infection, and their families. However, all persons with AIDS, regardless of income, may receive housing information. Persons living near community residences may also receive educational information.

### Supportive Housing for Persons with Disabilities (Section 811)

The Section 811 program provides grant funds to finance the construction or rehabilitation of supportive housing for people with disabilities, including the purchase of buildings without rehabilitation or with moderate rehabilitation for use as group homes. Private nonprofit corporations with Section 501(c)(3) tax-exempt status are eligible for Section 811 grants. This program is for very-low-income, physically disabled, developmentally disabled, or chronically mentally ill persons, eighteen years of age or older.

### Housing for the Elderly (Section 202)

The Section 202 program provides capital grants to private nonprofit sponsors and consumer cooperatives for the construction or substantial rehabilitation of residential projects and related facilities for elderly persons, which may include the cost of real property acquisition, site improvement, conversion, demolition, relocation, and other expenses of supportive housing for elderly persons.

Private nonprofit corporations and consumer cooperatives may participate in this program. Public bodies and their instrumentalities are not eligible Section 202 applicants. Beneficiaries of housing developed under this program must be elderly (sixty-two years old or older) and have very low incomes.

## Homeless Programs

### Emergency Food and Shelter National Board (www.fema.gov) (administered by the Federal Emergency Management Agency)

This program supplements and expands ongoing efforts that provide shelter, food, and supportive services for needy families and individuals. The program provides assistance for

- food and feeding-related expenses such as transport of food, food preparation, and serving equipment;
- mass shelter, other shelter such as hotels and motels, and rent and/or mortgage assistance for one month only per individual/family per year; and
- utility assistance and limited repairs to feeding and sheltering facilities.

Local boards are formed and approved by a national board. Local boards then distribute formula-allocated program funds to Local Recipient Organizations (LROs) or sponsor organizations—private nonprofit organizations or public organizations. Emphasis is placed on domestic violence centers, Native American organizations, and organizations providing food or shelter to AIDS patients, persons with disabilities, the elderly, teenage runaways, and many other groups with emergency needs.

### Emergency Shelter Grants (administered by HUD)

This program is designed to help improve the quality of existing emergency shelters for homeless people, to make additional shelters available, to meet the costs of operating shelters and of providing essential social services to homeless individuals, and to help prevent homelessness. Eligible activities include renovation, major rehabilitation or conversion of buildings for use as emergency shelters, provision of essential services to homeless people, shelter operating costs such as maintenance, insurance, utilities, rent and furnishings, and homeless prevention efforts.

Grants are provided to states, metro cities, urban counties, and territories. Local governments receiving formula allocations may distribute all or part of their grants to nonprofit recipients to be used for ESG activities. Only local governments and nonprofit organizations may apply for ESG funds directly from states. The territories receive their allocations based on their population. The Cranston-Gonzalez National Affordable Housing Act established a separate set-aside of 1 percent of the total ESG appropriation for tribes and Alaska Native Villages. ESG funds are used to serve homeless families and individuals and low-income persons at immediate risk of losing their housing due to eviction, foreclosure, or utility shutoffs.

### Projects for Assistance in Transition from Homelessness (administered by Health and Human Services)

The Projects for Assistance in Transition from Homelessness (PATH) program provides financial assistance to states to support services for individuals who are suffering from serious mental illness, or serious mental illness and substance abuse, and who are homeless or at imminent risk of becoming homeless. Programs and activities include (1) outreach services; (2) screening and diagnostic treatment services; (3) habilitation and rehabilitation services; (4) community mental health services; (5) alcohol or drug treatment services; (6) staff training; (7) case management services; (8) supportive and supervisory services in residential settings; (9) referrals for primary health services, job training, educational services, and relevant housing services; and (10) a prescribed set of housing services.

States, the District of Columbia, Guam, American Samoa, the Commonwealths of Puerto Rico and the Northern Mariana Islands, and the U.S. Virgin Islands are eligible to receive funds. Eligible beneficiaries are individuals who have a serious mental illness, or serious mental illness and substance abuse, and who are homeless or at imminent risk of becoming homeless.

### Section 8 Moderate Rehabilitation Single-Room Occupancy Component

The Section 8 Moderate Rehabilitation Single-Room Occupancy Program provides rental assistance to homeless individuals. Under the program, HUD enters into annual contributions contracts with public housing agencies in connection with the moderate rehabilitation of residential properties that, when rehabilitation is completed, will contain single room occupancy (SRO) dwelling units. SRO housing is defined as residential property that includes multiple dwelling units designed for occupancy by individuals. Each unit need not, but may, contain food preparation or sanitary facilities or both. Efficiency apartments are eligible, but one-bedroom units are not. Public housing authorities or private nonprofit organizations are eligible applicants. Nonprofits are, however, required to subcontract with local or state housing authorities, which administer SRO housing assistance payments.

*Shelter Plus Care*

This program provides rental assistance, in connection with supportive services funded from other sources, to homeless people with disabilities and their families. The program has four components: Tenant-based Rental Assistance (TRA), Sponsor-based Rental Assistance (SRA), Project-based Rental Assistance (PRA), and Single Room Occupancy (SRO) Dwellings. States, local governments, tribes, and public housing agencies are eligible. Nonprofits are eligible PRA and SRO subrecipients. The SRO program requires a public housing authority as co-applicant. Eligible participants are homeless individuals with disabilities and their families, except in single room occupancy dwellings, which are only for homeless persons with disabilities.

*Supportive Housing Program*

The Supportive Housing Program (SHP) is designed to promote the development of housing and supportive services for assisting homeless persons to transition from homelessness and to live as independently as possible. Funds may be used to provide

- transitional housing designed to enable homeless persons and families to move to permanent housing within a twenty-four-month period, which may include up to six months of follow-up services;
- permanent housing provided in conjunction with appropriate supportive services designed to maximize the ability of persons with disabilities to live as independently as possible within permanent housing;
- supportive housing that is, or is part of, a particularly innovative project for, or alternative methods of, meeting the immediate and long-term needs of homeless individuals and families;
- supportive services for homeless individuals not provided in conjunction with supportive housing; and
- safe havens for homeless individuals with serious mental illness currently residing on the streets who may not yet be ready for supportive services.

Eligible activities are acquisition of structures for supportive housing and/or services, rehabilitation of structures, new construction (under limited circumstances), leasing of structures, supportive housing operating costs for a new or expanded project, supportive services costs, and administrative costs up to 5 percent of the SHP grant.

States, local governments, other governmental entities, Indian tribes, private nonprofits, and community mental health associations that are public nonprofits are eligible to compete for grant funds through HUD's Continuum of Care process.

## Programs for Veterans

*Veterans Homeless Providers Grant and per Diem Program (Department for Veteran Affairs)*

This program serves to assist public and nonprofit private organizations in creating new programs and service centers to furnish supportive services and housing for homeless veterans through grants. Grants can be used to acquire, renovate, or alter facilities and to provide per diem payments, or similar assistance in place of per diem payments, to eligible entities with established programs. Grants can also be used to purchase vans for outreach and transportation.

Eligible applicants include public and nonprofit private entities with the capacity to administer a grant. Programs eligible for funding must have been established after November 10, 1992. Eligible beneficiaries include veterans who served in the active military naval or air service, and who were discharged or released under conditions other than dishonorable.

## Programs Involving Mortgages

The Federal Housing Administration (FHA), a part of HUD, was created to encourage lenders to make loans by insuring the borrower's payment to the lender if the borrower defaults on the loan. FHA insures mortgages on single family and multi-family homes (including manufactured homes) and hospitals. It is the largest insurer of mortgages in the world, insuring nearly 33 million properties since its inception in 1934.

*Mortgage Insurance—Homes (Section 203(b))*

Section 203(b) is the best-known FHA mortgage program. Through this program, the FHA insures mortgages made by qualified lenders to people purchasing or refinancing a home. The program helps low- and moderate-income families to become home owners by lowering some of the costs of their mortgage loans. Additionally, the program encourages lenders to make loans to otherwise creditworthy borrowers and projects that might not be able to meet conventional underwriting requirements, by protecting the lender against loan default on mortgages.

FHA-approved lending institutions, such as banks, mortgage companies, and savings and loan associations, can make insured Section 203(b) loans. Eligible borrowers include anyone who buys a home costing less than the Section 203(b) limits and intends to occupy it as their principal residence. The home buyer applies to the mortgage lender, not directly to HUD.

*Manufactured Home Loan Insurance—Financing Purchase of Manufactured Homes as Principal Residences of Borrowers (Title I) (CFDA 14.110)*
This program, popularly known as the Title I manufactured housing program, insures lenders against loss on loans to purchase manufactured homes that are to be principal residences for the borrowers. The maximum loan limit is $48,600. The borrower must give assurance that the site complies with local zoning and land development requirements. This program has no income limits; all persons are eligible to apply.

*Mortgage Insurance—Manufactured Home Parks (CFDA 14.127)*
This program provides insurance on mortgages to finance the construction or rehabilitation of manufactured home parks of five or more spaces. The maximum mortgage limit is $9,000 per space, except in high-cost areas where the limit may be increased by up to 140 percent on a case-by-case basis. Eligible applicants are investors, builders, developers, and others who meet HUD requirements.

*Mortgage Insurance—Combination and Manufactured Home Lot Loans (CFDA 14.162)*
Insured loans under this program may be used to purchase manufactured homes and lots for buyers intending to use them as their principal place of residence. This program has no income limits; all persons are eligible to apply.

## Programs Involving Historic Preservation
*National Parks Service—Historic Preservation Fund Grants-in-Aid (administered by the Department of the Interior)*
The Historic Preservation Fund program is administered by the National Parks Service, an agency within the Department of the Interior. It provides funds matching grants-in-aid for identification, evaluation, and protection of historic properties. Funds to states may be used to expand the National Register of Historic Places and for historic preservation activities. Funds to Indian Tribes and Alaskan Native Corporations may be used to preserve their culture.

States, territories, and federally recognized Indian Tribes, Alaska Native corporations, and Native Hawaiian organizations are eligible. They may subcontract to public and private organizations, individuals, and, in some instances, owners of historic properties.

*Federal Historic Preservation Tax Credits*
The 20 percent Rehabilitation Tax Credit is jointly administered by the U.S. National Park Service and the Internal Revenue Service. Although tax credits for historic preservation are available from the federal government in both 10 percent and 20 percent programs, only the 20 percent program permits commercial residential (rental) use of rehabilitated properties. In order to qualify for the 20 percent preservation tax credit, a property must conform to the tax requirements of the Internal Revenue Code.[1]

- The structure must either be listed individually on the *National Register of Historic Places* or be located in a registered historic district and certified by the National Park Service as contributing to the historic significance of that district.
- The structure being renovated must be a building—not a bridge, ship, railroad, car, or dam.
- The building may not be used exclusively as an owner's private residence.
- The building must be depreciable, in that it must be used for a commercial purpose. It may be used for offices, industrial or agricultural enterprises, or for rental housing.[2]
- The total rehabilitation expenditures for the rehabilitation project must exceed the greater of $5,000 or the adjusted basis of the building and its structural components.[3]
- The rehabilitation project must be completed within a twenty-four-month period, as selected by the taxpayer.
- The building must be returned to use following the qualifying rehabilitation project.

Properties rehabilitated using the 20 percent federal historic preservation tax credit must be retained for five years by the owner claiming the credit. Should an owner dispose of a property within a year of the property's placement into service, the owner must repay 100 percent of the credit. Following the first year, the amount of the tax credit due for repayment is prorated by 20 percent each year.

Developments involving the production of large numbers of affordable housing units using historic preservation tax credits commonly use limited partnerships as a vehicle for syndication of credits.[4] In this arrangement, the limited partnership will combine resources to finance the project, assuming 99 percent ownership of the project (the general partner running the project and managing the partnership typically retains 1 percent ownership). A credit syndicator will typically assess the value of the project and sell the credits based upon their future value to the investor, that is, based upon how much the investor is willing to pay for the future value of the credit.

Properties used by governmental bodies, nonprofit organizations, or other tax-exempt entities are not eligible for the rehabilitation tax credit if the tax-exempt entity enters into a disqualified lease for more than 35 percent of the property. Such leases exist under any of the following conditions:

- Part or all of the property is financed by the tax-exempt entity (either directly or indirectly) by an obligation in which the interest is tax-exempt.
- The tax-exempt entity (or a related entity) is granted a fixed or determinable price for purchase or an option to buy under the provisions of the lease.
- The lease term is in excess of twenty years.
- The lease occurs after a sale or lease of the property and the lessee used the property before the sale or lease.

## Housing Counseling Programs

*Housing Counseling Assistance Program*

The Housing Counseling Assistance Program is not a housing development program but provides grant funds to HUD-approved housing counseling agencies to counsel home owners, home buyers, prospective renters, and tenants under HUD and other programs and in conventionally financed homes. Counseling is to assure successful home ownership or tenancy and prevent delinquencies, defaults, foreclosures, and other losses.

Agencies applying for a HUD housing counseling grant must first become HUD-approved counseling agencies. An applicant agency must be a national, regional, or multi-state intermediary or a state housing finance agency.

## State Sources of Funding

### Historic Preservation Tax Incentives

The state of North Carolina in 1998 created a historic preservation tax credit of 20 percent for income-producing structures to augment the federal tax credit program. The requirements of the North Carolina tax credit program mirror those of the federal program, using the standards established by the U.S. secretary of the interior as guidelines for rehabilitation projects. These tax credits are administered by the North Carolina State Historic Preservation Office.

Historic preservation tax incentive programs encourage the rehabilitation and restoration of historic properties for both commercial and residential uses. Both the federal and North Carolina tax incentive programs recognize rental housing as a commercial use of historic properties, qualifying housing developers of designated historic structures for reductions in federal and state tax liability. These credits do not require that rental housing rehabilitated using the tax credit programs be occupied by individuals of specified income levels, though many projects which do contain restrictions on tenant income

are developed in conjunction with the federal and North Carolina low-income housing credit programs.

Historic preservation projects in both the federal and North Carolina tax credit programs may be subject to a lengthy certification process. Plans for rehabilitation of historic properties must conform to the standards established by the U.S. secretary of the interior. Technical assistance in applying for tax credit projects is provided by both the National Park Service and the North Carolina State Historic Preservation Office.

### Small Cities Community Development Block Grant Program

The state of North Carolina administers Community Development Block Grants (CDBG) to communities in the state that do not receive CDBG funding directly from the U.S. Department of Housing and Urban Development (HUD) as part of the CDBG entitlement program. In 2004 the grant programs and their purposes were as follows.

**Community Revitalization (Concentrated Needs and Revitalization Strategies).** To strengthen neighborhoods and rehabilitate homes of low- to moderate-income citizens

**Scattered Site Housing.** To address the most critical housing needs of families

**Infrastructure.** To provide public water or sewer to correct severe health or environmental problems

**Economic Development.** To provide grants or loans to local governments for creating and retaining jobs

**Housing Development.** To support development of single family and rental housing

**Urgent Needs.** To help communities recover from disasters that threaten public health and safety where insufficient or no local or other funds are available

**Capacity Building.** To help nonprofits design and carry out CDBG activities in partnership with units of local government

All Small City CDBG funding from the state must be granted to and administered by a local government entity. Community-based nonprofit groups may receive assistance through the program, but these organizations may not receive funding directly from the state.

In order for a project to qualify for CDBG funding, it must meet one of the following broad criteria established by HUD (as of January, 2003):

1. Fifty-one percent of the funding must benefit low- to moderate-income households, calculated as a percentage of the Area Median Income (AMI)
2. Help to prevent or eliminate slums or blight
3. Address a community's urgent needs

In addition, CDBG recipient projects must meet all federal and state administrative requirements. These requirements include disclosure of conflicts of interest, certification of compliance with equal opportunity and nondiscrimination laws in program design, certification of compliance with citizen participation requirements, certification of compliance with fair housing and nondiscrimination regulations, description of local economic benefits derived from CDBG program funding, completion of the Environmental Review Record (ERR), completion of residential anti-displacement and relocation assistance plans, compliance with Section 504 of the Rehabilitation Act of 1973, compliance with Title I of the Americans with Disabilities Act, compliance with labor standards under the Davis-Bacon Act and related acts, and compliance with elimination standards for lead-based paint hazards.

### The North Carolina Low Income Housing Tax Credit

The North Carolina Low Income Housing Credit program is structured to allow differing levels of subsidy depending upon the geographic area in which the affordable housing development occurs. The program allows a tax credit equal to 10, 20, or 30 percent of the development's eligible basis, depending upon the location of the housing project. The levels of tax credit correspond to the project's location in high-, moderate-, or low-income areas.

North Carolina tax credit benefits do not flow from the LLC to its members or partners. These credits are either claimed directly by the pass-through entity or are transferred to the North Carolina Housing Finance Agency. Qualifying recipients receive tax credit allocations over a five-year period. These credits cannot be used to offset more than 50 percent of an investor's tax liability in a single year. Should a taxpayer have excess credits after the five-year period, the credits may be carried forward

for a maximum of five years. North Carolina low-income housing credits may not be carried back to offset tax liability in years prior to the original investment in the eligible development.

### The North Carolina Housing Trust Fund

The General Assembly created a fund separate and distinct from the General Fund to be used to increase the supply of decent, affordable, and energy-efficient housing for low-, very-low-, and moderate-income residents of the state. The fund is available for loans, grants, interest-reduction payments or other comparable forms of assistance. In recent years, the fund has received a $3 million annual appropriation.

*Note:* For more information on federal funding sources, see http://www.huduser.org/whatsnew/ProgramsHUD05.pdf, www.hud.gov/offices/hsg/mfh/prodesc, and http://www.assetbuilding.org/AssetBuilding/index.cfm?pg=docs&SecID=2&TopID=3.

### Notes

1. *See* I.R.C.§ 47.

2. Credits cannot be claimed against the cost of acquisition, new additions, site work, or personal property.

3. The adjusted basis is generally the purchase price, minus the cost of the land, plus improvements already made, minus depreciation already taken.

4. Such arrangements are usually structured in such a manner as to allow a loss for each year of the project, generating positive tax impact and little or no additional tax liability associated with cash distributions.

# Appendix 4 | Statutes

## Minimum Housing Statutes

G.S. Chapter 160A.
Cities and Towns.
Article 19.
Planning and Regulation of Development.
Part 6. Minimum Housing Standards.

### § 160A-441. Exercise of police power authorized.

It is hereby found and declared that the existence and occupation of dwellings in this State that are unfit for human habitation are inimical to the welfare and dangerous and injurious to the health, safety and morals of the people of this State, and that a public necessity exists for the repair, closing or demolition of such dwellings. Whenever any city or county of this State finds that there exists in the city or county dwellings that are unfit for human habitation due to dilapidation, defects increasing the hazards of fire, accidents or other calamities, lack of ventilation, light or sanitary facilities, or due to other conditions rendering the dwellings unsafe or unsanitary, or dangerous or detrimental to the health, safety, morals, or otherwise inimical to the welfare of the residents of the city or county, power is hereby conferred upon the city or county to exercise its police powers to repair, close or demolish the dwellings in the manner herein provided. No ordinance enacted by the governing body of a county pursuant to this Part shall be applicable within the corporate limits of any city unless the city council of the city has by resolution expressly given its approval thereto.

In addition to the exercise of police power authorized herein, any city may by ordinance provide for the repair, closing or demolition of any abandoned structure which the city council finds to be a health or safety hazard as a result of the attraction of insects or rodents, conditions creating a fire hazard, dangerous conditions constituting a threat to children or frequent use by vagrants as living quarters in the absence of sanitary facilities. Such ordinance, if adopted, may provide for the repair, closing or demolition of such structure pursuant to the same provisions and procedures as are prescribed herein for the repair, closing or demolition of dwellings found to be unfit for human habitation. (1939, c. 287, s. 1; 1969, c. 913, s. 1; 1971, c. 698, s. 1; 1973, c. 426, s. 60; 1975, c. 664, s. 15.)

### § 160A-442. Definitions.

The following terms shall have the meanings whenever used or referred to as indicated when used in this Part unless a different meaning clearly appears from the context:

(1) "City" means any incorporated city or any county.

(2) "Dwelling" means any building, structure, manufactured home or mobile home, or part thereof, used and occupied for human habitation or intended to be so used, and includes any outhouses and appurtenances belonging thereto or usually enjoyed therewith, except that it does not include any manufactured home or mobile home, which is used solely for a seasonal vacation purpose.

(3) "Governing body" means the council, board of commissioners, or other legislative body, charged with governing a city or county.

(3a) "Manufactured home" or "mobile home" means a structure as defined in G.S. 143-145(7).

(4) "Owner" means the holder of the title in fee simple and every mortgagee of record.

(5) "Parties in interest" means all individuals, associations and corporations who have interests of record in a dwelling and any who are in possession thereof.

(6) "Public authority" means any housing authority or any officer who is in charge of any department or branch of the government of the city, county, or State relating to health, fire, building regulations, or other activities concerning dwellings in the city.

(7) "Public officer" means the officer or officers who are authorized by ordinances adopted hereunder to exercise the powers prescribed by the ordinances and by this Part. (1939, c. 287, s. 2; 1941, c.140; 1953, c. 675, s. 29; 1961, c. 398, s. 1;

1969, c. 913, s. 2; 1971, c. 698, s. 1; 1973, c. 426, s. 60; 1983, c. 401, ss. 1, 2.)

## § 160A-443. Ordinance authorized as to repair, closing, and demolition; order of public officer.

Upon the adoption of an ordinance finding that dwelling conditions of the character described in G.S. 160A-441 exist within a city, the governing body of the city is hereby authorized to adopt and enforce ordinances relating to dwellings within the city's territorial jurisdiction that are unfit for human habitation. These ordinances shall include the following provisions:

(1) That a public officer be designated or appointed to exercise the powers prescribed by the ordinance.

(2) That whenever a petition is filed with the public officer by a public authority or by at least five residents of the city charging that any dwelling is unfit for human habitation or whenever it appears to the public officer (on his own motion) that any dwelling is unfit for human habitation, the public officer shall, if his preliminary investigation discloses a basis for such charges, issue and cause to be served upon the owner of and parties in interest in such dwellings a complaint stating the charges in that respect and containing a notice that a hearing will be held before the public officer (or his designated agent) at a place within the county in which the property is located fixed not less than 10 days nor more than 30 days after the serving of the complaint; that the owner and parties in interest shall be given the right to file an answer to the complaint and to appear in person, or otherwise, and give testimony at the place and time fixed in the complaint; and that the rules of evidence prevailing in courts of law or equity shall not be controlling in hearings before the public officer.

(3) That if, after notice and hearing, the public officer determines that the dwelling under consideration is unfit for human habitation, he shall state in writing his findings of fact in support of that determination and shall issue and cause to be served upon the owner thereof an order,

  a. If the repair, alteration or improvement of the dwelling can be made at a reasonable cost in relation to the value of the dwelling (the ordinance of the city may fix a certain percentage of this value as being reasonable), requiring the owner, within the time specified, to repair, alter or improve the dwelling in order to render it fit for human habitation or to vacate and close the dwelling as a human habitation; or

  b. If the repair, alteration or improvement of the dwelling cannot be made at a reasonable cost in relation to the value of the dwelling (the ordinance of the city may fix a certain percentage of this value as being reasonable), requiring the owner, within the time specified in the order, to remove or demolish such dwelling. However, notwithstanding any other provision of law, if the dwelling is located in a historic district of the city and the Historic District Commission determines, after a public hearing as provided by ordinance, that the dwelling is of particular significance or value toward maintaining the character of the district, and the dwelling has not been condemned as unsafe, the order may require that the dwelling be vacated and closed consistent with G.S. 160A-400.14(a).

(4) That, if the owner fails to comply with an order to repair, alter or improve or to vacate and close the dwelling, the public officer may cause the dwelling to be repaired, altered or improved or to be vacated and closed; that the public officer may cause to be posted on the main entrance of any dwelling so closed, a placard with the following words: "This building is unfit for human habitation; the use or occupation of this building for human habitation is prohibited and unlawful." Occupation of a building so posted shall constitute a Class 1 misdemeanor.

(5) That, if the owner fails to comply with an order to remove or demolish the dwelling, the public officer may cause such dwelling to be removed or demolished. The duties of the public officer set forth in subdivisions (4) and (5) shall not be exercised until the governing body shall have by ordinance ordered the public officer to proceed to effectuate the purpose of this Article with respect to the particular property or properties which the public officer shall have found to be unfit for human habitation and which property or properties shall be described in the ordinance. No such ordinance shall be adopted to require demolition of a dwelling until the owner has first been given a reasonable opportunity to bring it into conformity with the housing code. This ordinance shall be recorded in the office of the register of deeds in the county wherein the property or properties are located and shall be indexed in the name of the property owner in the grantor index.

(5a) If the governing body shall have adopted an ordinance, or the public officer shall have:

  a. In a municipality located in counties which have a population in excess of 71,000 by the last federal census (including the entirety of any municipality located in more than one county at least one county of which has a population in excess of 71,000), other than municipalities with a population in excess of 190,000 by the last federal census, issued an order, ordering a dwelling to be repaired or vacated and closed, as provided in subdivision (3)a, and if the owner has vacated and closed such dwelling and kept such dwelling vacated and closed for a period of one year pursuant to the ordinance or order;

b. In a municipality with a population in excess of 190,000 by the last federal census, commenced proceedings under the substandard housing regulations regarding a dwelling to be repaired or vacated and closed, as provided in subdivision (3)a., and if the owner has vacated and closed such dwelling and kept such dwelling vacated and closed for a period of one year pursuant to the ordinance or after such proceedings have commenced,

then if the governing body shall find that the owner has abandoned the intent and purpose to repair, alter or improve the dwelling in order to render it fit for human habitation and that the continuation of the dwelling in its vacated and closed status would be inimical to the health, safety, morals and welfare of the municipality in that the dwelling would continue to deteriorate, would create a fire and safety hazard, would be a threat to children and vagrants, would attract persons intent on criminal activities, would cause or contribute to blight and the deterioration of property values in the area, and would render unavailable property and a dwelling which might otherwise have been made available to ease the persistent shortage of decent and affordable housing in this State, then in such circumstances, the governing body may, after the expiration of such one year period, enact an ordinance and serve such ordinance on the owner, setting forth the following:

a. If it is determined that the repair of the dwelling to render it fit for human habitation can be made at a cost not exceeding fifty percent (50%) of the then current value of the dwelling, the ordinance shall require that the owner either repair or demolish and remove the dwelling within 90 days; or

b. If it is determined that the repair of the dwelling to render it fit for human habitation cannot be made at a cost not exceeding fifty percent (50%) of the then current value of

the dwelling, the ordinance shall require the owner to demolish and remove the dwelling within 90 days.

This ordinance shall be recorded in the Office of the Register of Deeds in the county wherein the property or properties are located and shall be indexed in the name of the property owner in the grantor index. If the owner fails to comply with this ordinance, the public officer shall effectuate the purpose of the ordinance.

This subdivision only applies to municipalities located in counties which have a population in excess of 71,000 by the last federal census (including the entirety of any municipality located in more than one county at least one county of which has a population in excess of 71,000).

[This subdivision does not apply to the local government units listed in subdivision (5b) of this section.]

(5b) If the governing body shall have adopted an ordinance, or the public officer shall have:

a. In a municipality other than municipalities with a population in excess of 190,000 by the last federal census, issued an order, ordering a dwelling to be repaired or vacated and closed, as provided in subdivision (3)a, and if the owner has vacated and closed such dwelling and kept such dwelling vacated and closed for a period of one year pursuant to the ordinance or order;

b. In a municipality with a population in excess of 190,000 by the last federal census, commenced proceedings under the substandard housing regulations regarding a dwelling to be repaired or vacated and closed, as provided in subdivision (3)a., and if the owner has vacated and closed such dwelling and kept such dwelling vacated and closed for a period of one year pursuant to the ordinance or after such proceedings have commenced,

then if the governing body shall find that the owner has abandoned the intent and purpose to repair, alter or improve the dwelling in order to render it fit for human habitation and that the continuation of the dwelling in its vacated and closed status would be inimical to the health, safety, morals and welfare of the municipality in that the dwelling would continue to deteriorate, would create a fire and safety hazard, would be a threat to children and vagrants, would attract persons intent on criminal activities, would cause or contribute to blight and the deterioration of property values in the area, and would render unavailable property and a dwelling which might otherwise have been made available to ease the persistent shortage of decent and affordable housing in this State, then in such circumstances, the governing body may, after the expiration of such one year period, enact an ordinance and serve such ordinance on the owner, setting forth the following:

    a. If it is determined that the repair of the dwelling to render it fit for human habitation can be made at a cost not exceeding fifty percent (50%) of the then current value of the dwelling, the ordinance shall require that the owner either repair or demolish and remove the dwelling within 90 days; or

    b. If it is determined that the repair of the dwelling to render it fit for human habitation cannot be made at a cost not exceeding fifty percent (50%) of the then current value of the dwelling, the ordinance shall require the owner to demolish and remove the dwelling within 90 days.

This ordinance shall be recorded in the Office of the Register of Deeds in the county wherein the property or properties are located and shall be indexed in the name of the property owner in the grantor index. If the owner fails to comply with this ordinance, the public officer shall effectuate the purpose of the ordinance. This subdivision applies to the Cities of Eden, Greenville, Lumberton, Roanoke Rapids, and Whiteville, to the municipalities in Lee County, and the Towns of Bethel, Farmville, Newport, and Waynesville only.

(6) Liens.

    a. That the amount of the cost of repairs, alterations or improvements, or vacating and closing, or removal or demolition by the public officer shall be a lien against the real property upon which the cost was incurred, which lien shall be filed, have the same priority, and be collected as the lien for special assessment provided in Article 10 of this Chapter.

    b. If the real property upon which the cost was incurred is located in an incorporated city, then the amount of the cost is also a lien on any other real property of the owner located within the city limits or within one mile thereof except for the owner's primary residence. The additional lien provided in this sub-subdivision is inferior to all prior liens and shall be collected as a money judgment.

    c. If the dwelling is removed or demolished by the public officer, he shall sell the materials of the dwelling, and any personal property, fixtures or appurtenances found in or attached to the dwelling, and shall credit the proceeds of the sale against the cost of the removal or demolition and any balance remaining shall be deposited in the superior court by the public officer, shall be secured in a manner directed by the court, and shall be disbursed by the court to the persons found to be entitled thereto by final order or decree of the court. Nothing in this section shall be construed to impair or limit in any way the power of the city to define and declare nuisances and to cause their removal or abatement by summary proceedings, or otherwise.

(7) If any occupant fails to comply with an order to vacate a dwelling, the public officer may file a civil action in the name of the city to remove such occupant. The action to vacate the dwelling shall be in the nature of summary ejectment and shall be commenced by filing a complaint naming as parties-defendant any person occupying such dwelling. The clerk of superior court shall issue a summons requiring the defendant to appear before a magistrate at a certain time, date and place not to exceed 10 days from the issuance of the summons to answer the complaint. The summons and complaint shall be served as provided in G.S. 42-29. The summons shall be returned according to its tenor, and if on its return it appears to have been duly served, and if at the hearing the public officer produces a certified copy of an ordinance adopted by the governing body pursuant to subdivision (5) authorizing the officer to proceed to vacate the occupied dwelling, the magistrate shall enter judgment ordering that the premises be vacated and that all persons be removed. The judgment ordering that the dwelling be vacated shall be enforced in the same manner as the judgment for summary ejectment entered under G.S. 42-30. An appeal from any judgment entered hereunder by the magistrate may be taken as provided in G.S. 7A-228, and the execution of such judgment may be stayed as provided in G.S. 7A-227. An action to remove an occupant of a dwelling who is a tenant of the owner may not be in the nature of a summary ejectment proceeding pursuant to this paragraph unless such occupant was served with notice at least 30 days before the filing of the summary ejectment proceeding that the governing body has ordered the public officer to proceed to exercise his duties under subdivisions (4) and (5) of this section to vacate and close or remove and demolish the dwelling.

(8) That whenever a determination is made pursuant to subdivision (3) of this section that a dwelling must be vacated and closed, or removed or demolished, under the provisions of this section, notice of the order shall be given by first-class mail to any organization involved in providing or restoring dwellings for affordable housing that has filed a written request for such notices. A minimum period of 45 days from the mailing of such notice shall be given before removal or demolition by action of the public officer, to allow the opportunity for any organization to negotiate with the owner to make repairs, lease, or purchase the property for the purpose of providing affordable housing. The public officer or clerk shall certify the mailing of the notices, and the certification shall be conclusive in the absence of fraud. Only an organization that has filed a written request for such notices may raise the issue of failure to mail such notices, and the sole remedy shall be an order requiring the public officer to wait 45 days before causing removal or demolition. (1939, c. 287, s. 3; 1969, c. 868, ss. 1, 2; c. 1065, s. 2; 1971, c. 698, s. 1; 1973, c. 426, s. 70; 1983, c. 698; 1987, c. 542; 1989, c. 562; 1991, c. 208, s. 1; c. 315, s. 1; c. 581, s. 1; 1993, c. 539, s. 1095; c. 553, ss. 58, 59; 1994, Ex. Sess., c. 24, s. 14(c); 1995, c. 347, s. 1; c. 509, s. 112; c. 733, ss. 1, 2; 1997-101, ss. 1, 2; 1997-414, s. 1; 1997-449, s. 1; 1998-26, s. 1; 1998-87, s. 1; 2000-186, s. 1; 2001-283, s. 1; 2001-448, s. 3; 2002-118, s. 3.)

## § 160A-443.1. Heat source required.

(a) A city shall, by ordinance, require that by January 1, 2000, every dwelling unit leased as rental property within the city shall have, at a minimum, a central or electric heating system or sufficient chimneys, flues, or gas vents, with heating appliances connected, so as to heat at least one habitable room, excluding the kitchen, to a minimum temperature of 68 degrees Fahrenheit measured three feet above the floor with an outside temperature of 20 degrees Fahrenheit.

(b) If a dwelling unit contains a heating system or heating appliances that meet the requirements of subsection (a) of this section, the owner of the dwelling unit shall not be required to install a new heating system or heating appliances, but the owner shall be required to maintain the existing heating system or heating appliances in a good and safe working condition. Otherwise, the owner of the dwelling unit shall install a heating system or heating appliances that meet the requirements of subsection (a) of this section and shall maintain the heating system or heating appliances in a good and safe working condition.

(c) Portable kerosene heaters are not acceptable as a permanent source of heat as required by subsection (a) of this section but may be used as a supplementary source in single family dwellings and duplex units. An owner who has complied with subsection (a) shall not be held in violation of this section where an occupant of a dwelling unit uses a kerosene heater as a primary source of heat.

(d) This section applies only to cities with a population of 200,000 or over, according to the most recent decennial federal census.

(e) Nothing in this section shall be construed as:
(1) Diminishing the rights of or remedies available to any tenant under a lease agreement, statute, or at common law; or
(2) Prohibiting a city from adopting an ordinance with more stringent heating requirements than provided for by this section. (1999-14, s. 1.)

## § 160A-444. Standards.

An ordinance adopted by a city under this Part shall provide that the public officer may determine that a dwelling is unfit for human habitation if he finds that conditions exist in the dwelling that render it dangerous or injurious to the health, safety or morals of the occupants of the dwelling, the occupants of neighboring dwellings, or other residents of the city. Defective conditions may include the following (without limiting the generality of the foregoing): defects therein increasing the hazards of fire, accident, or other calamities; lack of adequate ventilation, light, or sanitary facilities; dilapidation; disrepair; structural defects; uncleanliness. The ordinances may provide additional standards to guide the public officers, or his agents, in determining the fitness of a dwelling for human habitation. (1939, c. 287, s. 4; 1971, c. 698, s. 1; 1973, c. 426, s. 60.)

## § 160A-445. Service of complaints and orders.

(a) Complaints or orders issued by a public officer pursuant to an ordinance adopted under this Part shall be served upon persons either personally or by registered or certified mail. When service is made by registered or certified mail, a copy of the complaint or order may also be sent by regular mail. Service shall be deemed sufficient if the registered or certified mail is unclaimed or refused, but the regular mail is not returned by the post office within 10 days after the mailing. If regular mail is used, a notice of the pending proceedings shall be posted in a conspicuous place on the premises affected.

(a1) If the identities of any owners or the whereabouts of persons are unknown and cannot be ascertained by the public officer in the exercise of reasonable diligence, or, if the owners are known but have refused to accept service by registered or certified mail, and the public officer makes an affidavit to that effect, then the serving of the complaint or order upon the owners or other persons may be made by publication in a newspaper having general circulation in the city at least once no later than the time at which personal service would be required under the provisions of this Part. When service is made by publication, a notice of the pending proceedings shall be posted in a conspicuous place on the premises thereby affected.

(b) Repealed by Session Laws 1997, c. 201, s. 1. (1939, c. 287, s. 5; 1965, c. 1055; 1969, c. 868, ss. 3, 4; 1971, c. 698, s. 1; 1973, c. 426, s. 60; 1977, c. 912, s. 14; 1979, 2nd Sess., c. 1247, s. 38; 1991, c. 526, s. 1; 1997-201, s. 1.)

## § 160A-446. Remedies.

(a) The governing body may provide for the creation and organization of a housing appeals board to which appeals may be taken from any decision or order of the public officer, or may provide for such appeals to be heard and determined by its zoning board of adjustment.

(b) The housing appeals board, if created, shall consist of five members to serve for three-year staggered terms. It shall have the power to elect its own officers, to fix the times and places for its meetings, to adopt necessary rules of procedure, and to adopt other rules and regulations for the proper discharge of its duties. It shall keep an accurate record of all its proceedings.

(c) An appeal from any decision or order of the public officer may be taken by any person aggrieved thereby or by any officer, board or commission of the city. Any appeal from the public officer shall be taken within 10 days from the rendering of the decision or service of the order by filing with the public officer and with the board a notice of appeal which shall specify the grounds upon which the appeal is based. Upon the filing of any notice of appeal, the public officer shall forthwith transmit to the board all the papers constituting the record upon which the decision appealed from was made. When an appeal is from a decision of the public officer refusing to allow the person aggrieved thereby to do any act, his decision shall remain in force until modified or reversed. When any appeal is from a decision of the public officer requiring the person aggrieved to do any act, the appeal shall have the effect of suspending the requirement until the hearing by the board, unless the public officer certifies to the board, after the notice of appeal is filed with him, that because of facts stated in the certificate (a copy of which shall be furnished the appellant), a suspension of his requirement would cause imminent peril to life or property. In that case the requirement shall not be suspended except by a restraining order, which may be granted for due cause shown upon not less than one day's written notice to the public officer, by the board, or by a court of record upon petition made pursuant to subsection (f) of this section.

(d) The appeals board shall fix a reasonable time for hearing appeals, shall give due notice to the parties, and shall render its decision within a reasonable time. Any party may appear in person or by agent or attorney. The board may reverse or affirm, wholly or partly, or may modify the decision or order appealed from, and may make any decision and order that in its opinion ought to be made in the matter, and to that end it shall have all the powers of the public officer, but the concurring vote of four members of the board shall be necessary to reverse or modify any decision or order of the public officer. The board shall have power also in passing upon appeals, when practical difficulties or unnecessary hardships would result from carrying out the strict letter of the ordinance, to adapt the application of the ordinance to the necessities of the case to the end that the spirit of the ordinance shall be observed, public safety and welfare secured, and substantial justice done.

(e) Every decision of the board shall be subject to review by proceedings in the nature of certiorari instituted within 15 days of the decision of the board, but not otherwise.

(f) Any person aggrieved by an order issued by the public officer or a decision rendered by the board may petition the superior court for an injunction restraining the public officer from carrying out the order or decision and the court may, upon such petition, issue a temporary injunction restraining the public officer pending a final disposition of the cause. The petition shall be filed within 30 days after issuance of the order or rendering of the decision. Hearings shall be had by the court on a petition within 20 days, and shall be given preference over other matters on the court's calendar. The court shall hear and determine the issues raised and shall enter such final order or decree as law and justice may require. It shall not be necessary to file bond in any amount before obtaining a temporary injunction under this subsection.

(g) If any dwelling is erected, constructed, altered, repaired, converted, maintained, or used in violation of this Part or of any ordinance or code adopted under authority of this Part or any valid order or decision of the public officer or board made pursuant to any ordinance or code adopted under authority of this Part, the public officer or board may institute any appropriate action or proceedings to prevent the unlawful erection, construction, reconstruction, alteration or use, to restrain, correct or abate the violation, to prevent the occupancy of the dwelling, or to prevent any illegal act, conduct or use in or about the premises of the dwelling. (1939, c. 287, s. 6; c. 386; 1969, c. 868, s. 5; 1971, c. 698, s. 1.)

## § 160A-447. Compensation to owners of condemned property.

Nothing in this Part shall be construed as preventing the owner or owners of any property from receiving just compensation for the taking of property by the power of eminent domain under the laws of this State, nor as permitting any property to be condemned or destroyed except in accordance with the police power of the State. (1939, c. 386; 1943, c. 196; 1971, c. 698, s. 1.)

## § 160A-448. Additional powers of public officer.

An ordinance adopted by the governing body of the city may authorize the public officer to exercise any powers necessary or convenient to carry out and effectuate the purpose and provisions of this Part, including the following powers in addition to others herein granted:

(1) To investigate the dwelling conditions in the city in order to determine which dwellings therein are unfit for human habitations;

(2) To administer oaths, affirmations, examine witnesses and receive evidence;

(3) To enter upon premises for the purpose of making examinations in a manner that will do the least possible inconvenience to the persons in possession;

(4) To appoint and fix the duties of officers, agents and employees necessary to carry out the purposes of the ordinances; and

(5) To delegate any of his functions and powers under the ordinance to other officers and other agents. (1939, c. 287, s. 7; 1971, c. 698, s. 1; 1973, c. 426, s. 60.)

## § 160A-449. Administration of ordinance.

The governing body of any city adopting an ordinance under this Part shall, as soon as possible thereafter, prepare an estimate of the annual expenses or costs to provide the equipment, personnel and supplies necessary for periodic examinations and investigations of the dwellings in the city for the purpose of determining the fitness of dwellings for human habitation, and for the enforcement and administration of its ordinances adopted under this Part. The city is authorized to make appropriations from its revenues necessary for this purpose and may accept and apply grants or donations to assist it in carrying out the provisions of the ordinances. (1939, c. 287, s. 8; 1971, c. 698, s. 1.)

## § 160A-450. Supplemental nature of Part.

Nothing in this Part shall be construed to abrogate or impair the powers of the courts or of any department of any city to enforce any provisions of its charter or its ordinances or regulations, nor to prevent or punish violations thereof; and the powers conferred by this Part shall be in addition and supplemental to the powers conferred by any other law. (1939, c. 287, s. 9; 1971, c. 698, s. 1.)

# Community Development Statutes: G.S. 160A

G.S. Chapter 160A.
Article 19.
Part 8. Miscellaneous Powers.

## § 160A-456. Community development programs and activities.

(a) Any city is authorized to engage in, to accept federal and State grants and loans for, and to appropriate and expend funds for community development programs and activities. In undertaking community development programs and activities, in addition to other authority granted by law, a city may engage in the following activities:

(1) Programs of assistance and financing of rehabilitation of private buildings principally for the benefit of low and moderate income persons, or for the restoration or preservation of older neighborhoods or properties, including direct repair, the making of grants or loans, the subsidization of interest payments on loans, and the guaranty of loans;

(2) Programs concerned with employment, economic development, crime prevention, child care, health, drug abuse, education, and welfare needs of persons of low and moderate income.

(b) Any city council may exercise directly those powers granted by law to municipal redevelopment commissions and those powers granted by law to municipal housing authorities, and may do so whether or not a redevelopment commission or housing authority is in existence in such city. Any city council desiring to do so may delegate to any redevelopment commission or to any housing authority the responsibility of undertaking or carrying out any specified community development activities. Any city council and any board of county commissioners may by agreement undertake or carry out for each other any specified community development activities. Any city council may contract with any person, association, or corporation in undertaking any specified community development activities. Any county or city board of health, county board of social services, or county or city board of education, may by agreement undertake or carry out for any city council any specified community development activities.

(c) Any city council undertaking community development programs or activities may create one or more advisory committees to advise it and to make recommendations concerning such programs or activities.

(d) Any city council proposing to undertake any loan guaranty or similar program for rehabilitation of private buildings is authorized to submit to its voters the question whether such program shall be undertaken, such referendum to be conducted pursuant to the general and local laws applicable to special elections in such city.

(d1) Any city may receive and dispense funds from the Community Development Block Grant Section 108 Loan Guarantee program, Subpart M, 24 CFR 570.700 et seq., either through application to the North Carolina Department of Commerce or directly from the federal government, in accordance with State and federal laws governing these funds. Any city that receives these funds directly from the federal government may pledge current and future CDBG funds for use as loan guarantees in accordance with State and federal laws governing these funds. A city may implement the receipt, dispensing, and pledging of CDBG funds under this subsection by borrowing CDBG funds and lending all or a portion of those funds to a third party in accordance with applicable laws governing the CDBG program.

Any city that has pledged current or future CDBG funds for use as loan guarantees prior to the enactment of this subsection is authorized to have taken such action. A pledge of future CDBG funds under this subsection is not a debt or liability of the State or any political subdivision of the State or a pledge of the faith and credit of the State or any political subdivision of the State. The pledging of future CDBG funds under this subsection does not directly, indirectly, or contingently obligate the State or any political subdivision of the State to levy or to pledge any taxes.

(e) Repealed by Session Laws 1985, c. 665, s. 5.

(e1) All program income from Economic Development Grants from the Small Cities Community Development Block Grant Program may be retained by recipient cities in "economically distressed counties," as defined in G.S. 143B-437A, for the purposes of creating local economic development revolving loan funds. Such program income derived through the use by cities of Small Cities Community Development Block Grant money includes but is not limited to: (i) payment of principal and interest on loans made by the county using Community Development Block Grant Funds; (ii) proceeds from the lease or disposition of real property acquired with Community Development Block Grant Funds; and (iii) any late fees associated with loan or lease payments in (i) and (ii) above. The local economic development revolving loan fund set up by the city shall fund only those activities eligible under Title I of the federal Housing and Community Development Act of 1974, as amended (P.L. 93-383), and shall meet at least one of the three national objectives of the Housing and Community Development Act. Any expiration of G.S. 143B-437A or G.S. 105-129.3 shall not affect this subsection as to designations of economically distressed counties made prior to its expiration. (1975, c. 435, s. 1; c. 689, s. 1; c. 879, s. 46; 1983, c. 908, s. 4; 1985, c. 665, s. 5; 1987, c. 464, s. 10; 1987 (Reg. Sess., 1988), c. 992, s. 2; 1995, c. 310, s. 3; 1995 (Reg. Sess., 1996), c. 13, s. 3.9; c. 575, s. 3.)

## § 160A-457. Acquisition and disposition of property for redevelopment.

In addition to the powers granted by G.S. 160A-456, any city is authorized, either as a part of a community development program or independently thereof, and without the necessity of compliance with the Urban Redevelopment Law, to exercise the following powers:

(1) To acquire, by voluntary purchase from the owner or owners, real property which is either:

a. Blighted, deteriorated, deteriorating, undeveloped, or inappropriately developed from the standpoint of sound community development and growth;

b. Appropriate for rehabilitation or conservation activities;

c. Appropriate for housing construction or the economic development of the community; or

d. Appropriate for the preservation or restoration of historic sites, the beautification of urban land, the conservation of open space, natural resources, and scenic areas, the provision of recreational opportunities, or the guidance of urban development;

(2) To clear, demolish, remove, or rehabilitate buildings and improvements on land so acquired; and

(3) To retain property so acquired for public purposes, or to dispose, through sale, lease, or otherwise, of any property so acquired to any person, firm, corporation, or governmental unit; provided, the disposition of such property shall be undertaken in accordance with the procedures of Article 12 of this Chapter, or the procedures of G.S. 160A-514, or any applicable local act or charter provision modifying such procedures; or subsection (4) of this section.

(4) To sell, exchange, or otherwise transfer real property or any interest therein in a community development project area to any redeveloper at private sale for residential, recreational, commercial, industrial or other uses or for public use in accordance with the community development plan, subject to such covenants, conditions and restrictions as may be deemed to be in the public interest or to carry out the purposes of this Article; provided that such sale, exchange or other transfer, and any agreement relating thereto, may be made only after approval of the municipal governing body and after a public hearing; a notice of the public hearing shall be given once a week for two successive weeks in a newspaper having general circulation in the municipality, and the notice shall be published the first time not less than 10 days nor

more than 25 days preceding the public hearing; and the notice shall disclose the terms of the sale, exchange or transfer. At the public hearing the appraised value of the property to be sold, exchanged or transferred shall be disclosed; and the consideration for the conveyance shall not be less than the appraised value. (1977, c. 660, s. 1; 1983, c. 797, ss. 1, 2.)

### § 160A-457.1. Urban Development Action Grants.

In addition to the powers granted by G.S. 160A-456 and G.S. 160A-457, any city is authorized, either as a part of a community development program or independently thereof, to enter into contracts or agreements with any person, association, or corporation to undertake and carry out specified activities in furtherance of the purposes of Urban Development Action Grants authorized by the Housing and Community Development Act of 1977 (P.L. 95-128) or any amendment thereto which is a continuation of such grant programs by whatever designation, including the authority to enter into and carry out contracts or agreements to extend loans, loan subsidies, or grants to persons, associations, or corporations and to dispose of real or personal property by private sale in furtherance of such contracts or agreements.

Any enabling legislation contained in local acts which refers to "Urban Development Action Grants" or the Housing and Community Development Act of 1977 (P.L. 95-128) shall be construed also to refer to any continuation of such grant programs by whatever designation. (1981, c. 865, ss. 1, 2.)

### § 160A-457.2. Urban homesteading programs.

A city may establish a program of urban homesteading, in which residential property of little or no value is conveyed to persons who agree to rehabilitate the property and use it, for a minimum number of years, as their principal place of residence. Residential property is considered of little or no value if the cost of bringing the property into compliance with the city's housing code exceeds sixty percent (60%) of the property's appraised value on the county tax records. In undertaking such a program a city may:

(1) Acquire by purchase, gift or otherwise, but not eminent domain, residential property specifically for the purpose of reconveyance in the urban homesteading program or may transfer to the program residential property acquired for other purposes, including property purchased at a tax foreclosure sale.

(2) Under procedures and standards established by the city, convey residential property by private sale under G.S. 160A-267 and for nominal monetary consideration to persons who qualify as grantees.

(3) Convey property subject to conditions that:

   a. Require the grantee to use the property as his or her principal place of residence for a minimum number of years,

   b. Require the grantee to rehabilitate the property so that it meets or exceeds minimum code standards,

   c. Require the grantee to maintain insurance on the property,

   d. Set out any other specific conditions (including, but not limited to, design standards) or actions that the city may require, and

   e. Provide for the termination of the grantee's interest in the property and its reversion to the city upon the grantee's failure to meet any condition so established.

(4) Subordinate the city's interest in the property to any security interest granted by the grantee to a lender of funds to purchase or rehabilitate the property. (1987, c. 464, s. 8; 1997-456, s. 27.)

## Community Development Statutes: G.S. 153A

G.S. Chapter 153A.
Counties.
Article 18.
Planning and Regulation of Development
Part 5. Community Development

### § 153A-376. Community development programs and activities.

(a) Any county is authorized to engage in, to accept federal and State grants and loans for, and to appropriate and expend funds for community development programs and activities. In undertaking community development programs and activities, in addition to other authority granted by law, a county may engage in the following activities:

(1) Programs of assistance and financing of rehabilitation of private buildings principally for the benefit of low and moderate income persons, or for the restoration or preservation of older neighborhoods or properties, including direct repair, the making of grants or loans, the subsidization of interest payments on loans, and the guaranty of loans;

(2) Programs concerned with employment, economic development, crime prevention, child care, health, drug abuse, education, and welfare needs of persons of low and moderate income.

(b) Any board of county commissioners may exercise directly those powers granted by law to county redevelopment commissions and those powers granted by law to county housing authorities. Any board of county commissioners desiring to do so may delegate to redevelopment commission or to any housing authority the responsibility of undertaking or carrying out any specified community development activities. Any board of county commissioners and any municipal governing body may by agreement undertake or carry out for each other any specified community development activities. Any board of county commissioners may contract with any person, association, or corporation in undertaking any specified community development activities. Any county or city board of health, county board of social services, or county or city board of education, may by agreement undertake or carry out for any board of county commissioners any specified community development activities.

(c) Any board of county commissioners undertaking community development programs or activities may create one or more advisory committees to advise it and to make recommendations concerning such programs or activities.

(d) Any board of county commissioners proposing to undertake any loan guaranty or similar program for rehabilitation of private buildings is authorized to submit to its voters the question whether such program shall be undertaken, such referendum to be conducted pursuant to the general and local laws applicable to special elections in such county.

(e) No state or local taxes shall be appropriated or expended by a county pursuant to this section for any purpose not expressly authorized by G.S. 153A-149, unless the same is first submitted to a vote of the people as therein provided.

(f) All program income from Economic Development Grants from the Small Cities Community Development Block Grant Program may be retained by recipient "economically distressed counties", as defined in G.S. 143B-437A for the purposes of creating local economic development revolving loan funds. Such program income derived through the use by counties of Small Cities Community Development Block Grant money includes but is not limited to: (i) payment of principal and interest on loans made by the county using Community Development Block Grant Funds; (ii) proceeds from the lease or disposition of real property acquired with Community Development Block Grant Funds; and (iii) any late fees associated with loan or lease payments in (i) and (ii) above. The local economic development revolving loan fund set up by the county shall fund only those activities eligible under Title I of the federal Housing and Community Development Act of 1974, as amended (P.L. 93-383), and shall meet at least one of the three national objectives of the Housing and Community Development Act. Any expiration of G.S. 143B-437A or G.S. 105-129.3 shall not affect this subsection as to designations of economically distressed counties made prior to its expiration.

(g) Any county may receive and dispense funds from the Community Development Block Grant Section 108 Loan Guarantee program, Subpart M, 24 CFR 570.700 et seq., either through application to the North Carolina Department of Commerce or directly from the federal government, in accordance with State and federal laws governing these funds. Any county that receives these funds directly from the federal government may pledge current and future CDBG funds for use as loan guarantees in accordance with State and federal laws governing these funds. A county may implement the receipt, dispensing, and pledging of CDBG funds under this subsection by borrowing CDBG funds and lending all or a portion of those funds to a third party in accordance with applicable laws governing the CDBG program.

Any county that has pledged current or future CDBG funds for use as loan guarantees prior to the enactment of this subsection is authorized to have taken such action. A pledge of future CDBG funds under this subsection is not a debt or liability of the State or any political subdivision of the State or a pledge of the faith and credit of the State or any political subdivision of the State. The pledging of future CDBG funds under this subsection does not directly, indirectly, or contingently obligate the State or any political subdivision of the State to levy or to pledge any taxes. (1975, c. 435, s. 2; c. 689, s. 2; 1987 (Reg. Sess., 1988), c. 992, s. 1; 1995, c. 310, s. 2; 1995 (Reg. Sess., 1996), c. 575, s. 2; 1996, 2nd Ex. Sess., c. 13, s. 3.8.)

## § 153A-377. Acquisition and disposition of property for redevelopment.

In addition to the powers granted by G.S. 153A-376, any county is authorized, either as a part of a community development program or independently thereof, and without the necessity of compliance with the Urban Redevelopment Law, to exercise the following powers:

(1) To acquire, by voluntary purchase from the owner or owners, real property which is either:
   a. Blighted, deteriorated, deteriorating, undeveloped, or inappropriately developed from the standpoint of sound community development and growth;
   b. Appropriate for rehabilitation or conservation activities;
   c. Appropriate for housing construction of the economic development of the community; or
   d. Appropriate for the preservation or restoration of historic sites, the beautification of urban land, the conservation of open space, natural resources, and scenic areas, the provision of recreational opportunities, or the guidance of urban development;

(2) To clear, demolish, remove, or rehabilitate buildings and improvements on land so acquired; and

(3) To retain property so acquired for public purposes, or to dispose, through sale, lease, or otherwise, of any property so acquired to any person, firm, corporation, or governmental unit; provided, the disposition of such property shall be undertaken in accordance with the procedures of G.S. 153A-176, or the procedures of G.S. 160A-514, or any applicable local act modifying such procedures. (1977, c. 660, s. 2.)

## § 153A-378. Low- and moderate-income housing programs.

In addition to the powers granted by G.S. 153A-376 an G.S. 153A-377, any county is authorized to exercise the following powers:

(1) To engage in and to appropriate and expend funds for residential housing construction, new or rehabilitated, for sale or rental to persons and families of low and moderate income. Any board of commissioners may contract with any person, association, or corporation to implement the provisions of this subdivision.

(2) To acquire real property by voluntary purchase from the owners to be developed by the county or to be used by the county to provide affordable housing to persons of low and moderate income.

(3) Under procedures and standards established by the county, to convey property by private sale to any public or private entity that provides affordable housing to persons of low or moderate income. The county shall include as part of any such conveyance covenants or conditions that assure the property will be developed by the entity for sale or lease to persons of low or moderate income.

(4) Under procedures and standards established by the county, to convey residential property by private sale to persons of low or moderate income in accordance with G.S. 160A-267 and any terms and conditions that the board of commissioners may determine. (1999-366, s. 2.)

# Urban Redevelopment Statutes

G.S. Chapter 160A.
Cities and Towns.
Article 22.
Urban Redevelopment Law.

## § 160A-500. Short title.

This Article shall be known and may be cited as the "Urban Redevelopment Law." (1951, c. 1095, s. 1; 1973, c. 426, s. 75.)

## § 160A-501. Findings and declaration of policy.

It is hereby determined and declared as a matter of legislative finding:

(1) That there exist in urban communities in this State blighted areas as defined herein.

(2) That such areas are economic or social liabilities, inimical and injurious to the public health, safety, morals and welfare of the residents of the State, harmful to the social and economic well-being of the entire communities in which they exist, depreciating values therein, reducing tax revenues, and thereby depreciating further the general community-wide values.

(3) That the existence of such areas contributes substantially and increasingly to the spread of disease and crime, necessitating excessive and disproportionate expenditures of public funds for the preservation of the public health and safety, for crime prevention, correction, prosecution, punishment and the treatment of juvenile delinquency and for the maintenance of adequate police, fire and accident protection and other public services and facilities, constitutes an economic and social liability, substantially impairs or arrests the sound growth of communities.

(4) That the foregoing conditions are beyond remedy or control entirely by regulatory processes in the exercise of the police power and cannot be effectively dealt with by private enterprise under existing law without the additional aids herein granted.

(5) That the acquisition, preparation, sale, sound replanning, and redevelopment of such areas in accordance with sound and approved plans for their redevelopment will promote the public health, safety, convenience and welfare.

Therefore, it is hereby declared to be the policy of the State of North Carolina to promote the health, safety, and welfare of the inhabitants thereof by the creation of bodies corporate and politic to be known as redevelopment commissions, which shall exist and operate for the public purposes of acquiring and replanning such areas and of holding or disposing of them in such manner that they shall become available for economically and socially sound redevelopment. Such purposes are hereby declared to be public uses for which public money may be spent, and private property may be acquired by the exercise of the power of eminent domain. (1951, c. 1095, s. 2; 1973, c. 426, s. 75.)

### § 160A-502. Additional findings and declaration of policy.

It is further determined and declared as a matter of legislative finding:

(1) That the cities of North Carolina constitute important assets for the State and its citizens; that the preservation of the cities and of urban life against physical, social, and other hazards is vital to the safety, health, and welfare of the citizens of the State, and sound urban development in the future is essential to the continued economic development of North Carolina, and that the creation, existence, and growth of substandard areas present substantial hazards to the cities of the State, to urban life, and to sound future urban development.

(2) That blight exists in commercial and industrial areas as well as in residential areas, in the form of dilapidated, deteriorated, poorly ventilated, obsolete, overcrowded, unsanitary, or unsafe buildings, inadequate and unsafe streets, inadequate lots, and other conditions detrimental to the sound growth of the community; that the presence of such conditions tends to depress the value of neighboring properties, to impair the tax base of the community, and to inhibit private efforts to rehabilitate or improve other structures in the area; and that the acquisition, preparation, sale, sound replanning and redevelopment of such areas in accordance with sound and approved plans will promote the public health, safety, convenience and welfare.

(3) That not only is it in the interest of the public health, safety, convenience and welfare to eliminate existing substandard areas of all types, but it is also in the public interest and less costly to the community to prevent the creation of new blighted areas or the expansion of existing blighted areas; that vigorous enforcement of municipal and State building standards, sound planning of new community facilities, public acquisition of dilapidated, obsolescent buildings, and other municipal action can aid in preventing the creation of new blighted areas or the expansion of existing blighted areas; and that rehabilitation, conservation, and reconditioning of areas in accordance with sound and approved plans, where, in the absence of such action, there

is a clear and present danger that the area will become blighted, will protect and promote the public health, safety, convenience and welfare.

Therefore it is hereby declared to be the policy of the State of North Carolina to protect and promote the health, safety, and welfare of the inhabitants of its urban areas by authorizing redevelopment commissions to undertake nonresidential redevelopment in accord with sound and approved plans and to undertake the rehabilitation, conservation, and reconditioning of areas where, in the absence of such action, there is a clear and present danger that the area will become blighted. (1961, c. 837, s. 1; 1973, c. 426, s. 75.)

### § 160A-503. Definitions.

The following terms where used in this Article, shall have the following meanings, except where the context clearly indicates a different meaning:

(1) "Area of operation" — The area within the territorial boundaries of the city or county for which a particular commission is created.

(2) "Blighted area" shall mean an area in which there is a predominance of buildings or improvements (or which is predominantly residential in character), and which, by reason of dilapidation, deterioration, age or obsolescence, inadequate provision for ventilation, light, air, sanitation, or open spaces, high density of population and overcrowding, unsanitary or unsafe conditions, or the existence of conditions which endanger life or property by fire and other causes, or any combination of such factors, substantially impairs the sound growth of the community, is conducive to ill health, transmission of disease, infant mortality, juvenile delinquency and crime, and is detrimental to the public health, safety, morals or welfare; provided, no area shall be considered a blighted area nor subject to the power of eminent domain, within the meaning of this Article, unless it is determined by the planning commission that at least two-thirds of the number of buildings within the area are of the character described in this subdivision and substantially contribute to the conditions making such area a blighted area; provided that if the power of eminent domain shall be exercised under the provisions of this Article, the property owner or owners or persons having an interest in property shall be entitled to be represented by counsel of their own selection and their reasonable counsel fees fixed by the court, taxed as a part of the costs and paid by the petitioners.

(3) "Bonds" — Any bonds, interim certificates, notes, debentures or other obligations of a commission issued pursuant to this Article.

(4) "City" — Any city or town. "The city" shall mean the particular city for which a particular commission is created.

(5) "Commission" or "redevelopment commission" — A public body and a body corporate and politic created and organized in accordance with the provisions of this Article.

(6) "Field of operation" — The area within the territorial boundaries of the city for which a particular commission is created.

(7) "Governing body" — In the case of a city or town, the city council or other legislative body. The board of county commissioners.

(8) "Government" — Includes the State and federal governments or any subdivision, agency or instrumentality corporate or otherwise of either of them.

(9) "Municipality" — Any incorporated city or town, or any county.

(10) "Nonresidential redevelopment area" shall mean an area in which there is a predominance of buildings or improvements, whose use is predominantly nonresidential, and which, by reason of:

  a. Dilapidation, deterioration, age or obsolescence of buildings and other structures,

  b. Inadequate provisions for ventilation, light, air, sanitation or open spaces,

  c. Defective or inadequate street layout,

  d. Faulty lot layout in relation to size, adequacy, accessibility, or usefulness,

  e. Tax or special assessment delinquency exceeding the fair value of the property,

  f. Unsanitary or unsafe conditions,

  g. The existence of conditions which endanger life or property by fire and other causes, or

  h. Any combination of such factors

    1. Substantially impairs the sound growth of the community,

    2. Has seriously adverse effects on surrounding development, and

    3. Is detrimental to the public health, safety, morals or welfare;

provided, no such area shall be considered a nonresidential redevelopment area nor subject to the power of eminent domain, within the meaning of this Article, unless it is determined by the planning commission that at least one-half of the number of buildings within the area are of the character described in this subdivision and substantially contribute to the conditions making such area a nonresidential redevelopment area; provided that if the power of eminent domain shall be exercised under the provisions of this

Article, the property owner or owners or persons having an interest in property shall be entitled to be represented by counsel of their own selection and their reasonable counsel fees fixed by the court, taxed as a part of the costs and paid by the petitioners.

(11) "Obligee of the commission" or "obligee" — Any bondholder, trustee or trustees for any bondholders, any lessor demising property to a commission used in connection with a redevelopment project, or any assignees of such lessor's interest, or any part thereof, and the federal government, when it is a party to any contract with a commission.

(12) "Planning commission" — Any planning commission established by ordinance for a municipality of this State. "The planning commission" shall mean the particular planning commission of the city or town in which a particular commission operates.

(13) "Real property" — Lands, lands under water, structures and any and all easements, franchises and incorporeal hereditaments and every estate and right therein, legal and equitable, including terms for years and liens by way of judgment, mortgage or otherwise.

(14) "Redeveloper" — Any individual, partnership or public or private corporation that shall enter or propose to enter into a contract with a commission for the redevelopment of an area under the provisions of this Article.

(15) "Redevelopment" — The acquisition, replanning, clearance, rehabilitation or rebuilding of an area for residential, recreational, commercial, industrial or other purposes, including the provision of streets, utilities, parks, recreational areas and other open spaces; provided, without limiting the generality thereof, the term "redevelopment" may include a program of repair and rehabilitation of buildings and other improvements, and may include the exercise of any powers under this Article with respect to the area for which such program is undertaken.

(16) "Redevelopment area" — Any area which a planning commission may find to be

  a. A blighted area because of the conditions enumerated in subdivision (2) of this section;

  b. A nonresidential redevelopment area because of conditions enumerated in subdivision (10) of this section;

  c. A rehabilitation, conservation, and reconditioning area within the meaning of subdivision (21) of this section;

d. Any combination thereof, so as to require redevelopment under the provisions of this Article.

(17) "Redevelopment contract" — A contract between a commission and a redeveloper for the redevelopment of an area under the provisions of this Article.

(18) "Redevelopment plan" — A plan for the redevelopment of a redevelopment area made by a "commission" in accordance with the provisions of this Article.

(19) "Redevelopment project" shall mean any work or undertaking:

a. To acquire blighted or nonresidential redevelopment areas or portions thereof, or individual tracts in rehabilitation, conservation, and reconditioning areas, including lands, structures, or improvements, the acquisition of which is necessary or incidental to the proper clearance, development, or redevelopment of such areas or to the prevention of the spread or recurrence of conditions of blight;

b. To clear any such areas by demolition or removal of existing buildings, structures, streets, utilities or other improvements thereon and to install, construct, or reconstruct streets, utilities, and site improvements essential to the preparation of sites for uses in accordance with the redevelopment plan;

c. To sell land in such areas for residential, recreational, commercial, industrial or other use or for the public use to the highest bidder as herein set out or to retain such land for public use, in accordance with the redevelopment plan;

d. To carry out plans for a program of voluntary or compulsory repair, rehabilitation, or reconditioning of buildings or other improvements in such areas; including the making of loans therefor; and

e. To engage in programs of assistance and financing, including the making of loans, for rehabilitation, repair, construction, acquisition, or reconditioning of residential units and commercial and industrial facilities in a redevelopment area.

The term "redevelopment project" may also include the preparation of a redevelopment plan, the planning, survey and other work incident to a redevelopment project, and the preparation of all plans and arrangements for carrying out a redevelopment project.

(20) "Redevelopment proposal" — A proposal, including supporting data and the form of a redevelopment contract for the redevelopment of all or any part of a redevelopment area.

(21) "Rehabilitation, conservation, and reconditioning area" shall mean any area which the planning commission shall find, by reason of factors listed in subdivision (2) or subdivision (10), to be subject to a clear and present danger that, in the absence of municipal action to rehabilitate, conserve, and recondition the area, it will become in the reasonably foreseeable future a blighted area or a nonresidential redevelopment area as defined herein. In such an area, no individual tract, building, or improvement shall be subject to the power of eminent domain, within the meaning of this Article, unless it is of the character described in subdivision (2) or subdivision (10) and substantially contributes to the conditions endangering the area; provided that if the power of eminent domain shall be exercised under the provisions of this Article, the respondent or respondents shall be entitled to be represented by counsel of their own selection and their reasonable counsel fees fixed by the court, taxed as part of the costs and paid by the petitioners. (1951, c. 1095, s. 3; 1957, c. 502, ss. 1-3; 1961, c. 837, ss. 2, 3, 4, 6; 1967, c. 1249; 1969, c. 1208, s. 1; 1973, c. 426, s. 75; 1981, c. 907, ss. 1, 2; 1985, c. 665, s. 6.)

## § 160A-504. Formation of commissions.

(a) Each municipality, as defined herein, is hereby authorized to create separate and distinct bodies corporate and politic to be known as the redevelopment commission of the municipality by the passage by the governing body of such municipality of an ordinance or resolution creating a commission to function within the territorial limits of said municipality. Notice of the intent to consider the passage of such a resolution or ordinance shall be published at least 10 days prior to the meeting.

(b) The governing body of a municipality shall not adopt a resolution pursuant to subsection (a) above unless it finds:

(1) That blighted areas (as herein defined) exist in such municipality, and

(2) That the redevelopment of such areas is necessary in the interest of the public health, safety, morals or welfare of the residents of such municipality.

(c) The governing body shall cause a certified copy of such ordinance or resolution to be filed in the office of the Secretary of State; upon receipt of the said certificate the Secretary of State shall issue a certificate of incorporation.

(d) In any suit, action or proceeding involving or relating to the validity or enforcement of any contract or act of a commission, a copy of the certificate of incorporation duly certified by the Secretary of State shall be admissible in evidence and shall be conclusive proof of the legal establishment of the commission. (1951, c. 1095, s. 4; 1973, c. 426, s. 75.)

### § 160A-505. Alternative organization.

(a) In lieu of creating a redevelopment commission as authorized herein, the governing body of any municipality may, if it deems wise, either designate a housing authority created under the provisions of Chapter 157 of the General Statutes to exercise the powers, duties, and responsibilities of a redevelopment commission as prescribed herein, or undertake to exercise such powers, duties, and responsibilities itself. Any such designation shall be by passage of a resolution adopted in accordance with the procedure and pursuant to the findings specified in G.S. 160A-504(a) and (b). In the event a governing body designates itself to perform the powers, duties, and responsibilities of a redevelopment commission under this subsection, or exercises those powers, duties, and responsibilities pursuant to G.S. 153A-376 or G.S. 160A-456, then where any act or proceeding is required to be done, recommended, or approved both by a redevelopment commission and by the municipal governing body, then the performance, recommendation, or approval thereof once by the municipal governing body shall be sufficient to make such performance, recommendation, or approval valid and legal. In the event a municipal governing body designates itself to exercise the powers, duties, and responsibilities of a redevelopment commission, it may assign the administration of redevelopment policies, programs and plans to any existing or new department of the municipality.

(b) The governing body of any municipality which has prior to July 1, 1969, created, or which may hereafter create, a redevelopment commission may, in its discretion, by resolution abolish such redevelopment commission, such abolition to be effective on a day set in such resolution not less than 90 days after its adoption. Upon the adoption of such a resolution, the redevelopment commission of the municipality is hereby authorized and directed to take such actions and to execute such documents as will carry into effect the provisions and the intent of the resolution, and as will effectively transfer its authority, responsibilities, obligations, personnel, and property, both real and personal, to the municipality. Any municipality which abolishes a redevelopment commission pursuant to this subsection may, at any time subsequent to such abolition or concurrently therewith, exercise the authority granted by subsection (a) of this section.

On the day set in the resolution of the governing body:

(1) The redevelopment commission shall cease to exist as a body politic and corporate and as a public body;

(2) All property, real and personal and mixed, belonging to the redevelopment commission shall vest in, belong to, and be the property of the municipality;

(3) All judgments, liens, rights of liens, and causes of action of any nature in favor of the redevelopment commission shall remain, vest in, and inure to the benefit of the municipality;

(4) All rentals, taxes, assessments, and any other funds, charges or fees, owing to the redevelopment commission shall be owed to and collected by the municipality;

(5) Any actions, suits, and proceedings pending against, or having been instituted by the redevelopment commission shall not be abated by such abolition, but all such actions, suits, and proceedings shall be continued and completed in the same manner as if abolition had not occurred, and the municipality shall be a party to all such actions, suits, and proceedings in the place and stead of the redevelopment commission and shall pay or cause to be paid any judgment rendered against the redevelopment commission in any such actions, suits, or proceedings, and no new process need be served in any such action, suit, or proceeding;

(6) All obligations of the redevelopment commission, including outstanding indebtedness, shall be assumed by the municipality, and all such obligations and outstanding indebtedness shall be constituted obligations and indebtedness of the municipality;

(7) All ordinances, rules, regulations and policies of the redevelopment commission shall continue in full force and effect until repealed or amended by the governing body of the municipality.

(c) Where the governing body of any municipality has in its discretion, by resolution, abolished a redevelopment commission pursuant to subsection (b) above, the governing body of such municipality may, at any time subsequent to the passage of a resolution abolishing a redevelopment commission, or concurrently therewith, by the passage of a resolution adopted in accordance with the procedures and pursuant to the findings specified in G.S. 160A-504(a) and (b), designate an existing housing authority created pursuant to Chapter 157 of the General Statutes to exercise the powers, duties, and responsibilities of a redevelopment commission. Where the governing body of any municipality designates, pursuant to this subsection, an existing housing authority created pursuant to Chapter 157 of the General Statutes to exercise the powers, duties, and responsibilities of a redevelopment commission, on the day set in the resolution of the governing body passed pursuant to subsection (b) of this section, or pursuant to subsection (c) of this section:

(1) The redevelopment commission shall cease to exist as a body politic and corporate and as a public body;

(2) All property, real and personal and mixed, belonging to the redevelopment commission or to the municipality as hereinabove provided in subsections (a) or (b), shall vest in, belong to, and be the property of the existing housing authority of the municipality;

(3) All judgments, liens, rights of liens, and causes of action of any nature in favor of the redevelopment commission or in favor of the municipality as hereinabove provided in subsections (a) or (b), shall remain, vest in, and inure to the benefit of the existing housing authority of the municipality;

(4) All rentals, taxes, assessments, and any other funds, charges or fees owing to the redevelopment commission, or owing to the municipality as hereinabove provided in subsections (a) or (b), shall be owed to and collected by the existing housing authority of the municipality;

(5) Any actions, suits, and proceedings pending against or having been instituted by the redevelopment commission, or the municipality, or to which the municipality has become a party, as hereinabove provided in subsections (a) or (b), shall not be abated by such abolition but all such actions, suits, and proceedings shall be continued and completed in the same manner as if abolition had not occurred, and the existing housing authority of the municipality shall be a party to all such actions, suits, and proceedings in the place and stead of the redevelopment commission, or the municipality, and shall pay or cause to be paid any judgments rendered in such actions, suits, or proceedings, and no new processes need be served in such action, suit, or proceeding;

(6) All obligations of the redevelopment commission, or the municipality as hereinabove provided in subsections (a) or (b), including outstanding indebtedness, shall be assumed by the existing housing authority of the municipality; and all such obligations and outstanding indebtedness shall be constituted obligations and indebtedness of the existing housing authority of the municipality.

(7) All ordinances, rules, regulations, and policies of the redevelopment commission, or of the municipality as hereinabove provided in subsections (a) or (b), shall continue in full force and effect until repealed and amended by the existing housing authority of the municipality.

(d) A housing authority designated by the governing body of any municipality to exercise the powers, duties and responsibilities of a redevelopment commission shall, when exercising the same, do so in accordance with Article 22 of Chapter 160A of the General Statutes. Otherwise the housing authority shall continue to exercise the powers, duties and responsibilities of a housing authority in accordance with Chapter 157 of the General Statutes. (1969, c. 1217, s. 1; 1971, c. 116, ss. 1, 2; 1973, c. 426, s. 75; 1981 (Reg. Sess., 1982), c. 1276, s. 13; 2003-403, s. 16.)

### § 160A-505.1. Commission budgeting and accounting systems as a part of municipality budgeting and accounting systems.

The governing body of a municipality may by resolution provide that the budgeting and accounting systems of the municipality's redevelopment commission or, if the municipality's housing authority is exercising the powers, duties, and responsibilities of a redevelopment commission, the budgeting and accounting systems of the housing authority, shall be an integral part of the budgeting and accounting systems of the municipality. If such a resolution is adopted:

(1) For purposes of the Local Government Budget and Fiscal Control Act, the commission or authority shall not be considered a "public authority," as that phrase is defined in G.S. 159-7(b), but rather shall be considered a department or agency of the municipality. The operations of the commission or authority shall be budgeted and accounted for as if the operations were those of a public enterprise of the municipality.

(2) The budget of the commission or authority shall be prepared and submitted in the same manner and according to the same procedures as are the budgets of other departments and agencies of the municipality; and the budget ordinance of the municipality shall provide for the operations of the commission or authority.

(3) The budget officer and finance officer of the municipality shall administer and control that portion of the municipality's budget ordinance relating to the operations of the commission or authority. (1971, c. 780, s. 37.2; 1973, c. 474, s. 30.)

### § 160A-506. Creation of a county redevelopment commission.

If the board of county commissioners of a county by resolution declares that blighted areas do exist in said county, and the redevelopment of such areas is necessary in the interest of public health, safety, morals, or welfare of the residents of such county, the county commissioners of said county are hereby authorized to create a separate and distinct body corporate and politic to be known as the redevelopment commission of said county by passing a resolution to create such a commission to function in the territorial limits of said county. Provided, however, that notice of the intent to consider passage of such a resolution or ordinance shall be published at least 10 days prior to the meeting of the board of county commissioners for such purposes, and further provided that the redevelopment commission shall not function in an area where such a commission exists or in the corporate limits of a municipality without resolution of agreement by said municipality.

All of the provisions of Article 22, Chapter 160A of the General Statutes, shall be applicable to county redevelopment commissions, including the formation, appointment, tenure, compensation, organization, interest and powers as specified therein. (1969, c. 1208, s. 2; 1973, c. 426, s. 75.)

## § 160A-507. Creation of a regional redevelopment commission.

If the board of county commissioners of two or more contiguous counties by resolution declare that blighted areas do exist in said counties and the redevelopment of such areas is necessary in the interest of public health, morals, or welfare of the residents of such counties, the county commissioners of said counties are hereby authorized to create a separate and distinct body corporate and politic to be known as the regional redevelopment commission by the passage of a resolution by each county to create such a commission to function in the territorial limits of the counties; provided, however, that notice of the intent to consider passage of such a resolution or ordinance shall be published at least 10 days prior to the meeting of the board of county commissioners for such purposes, and further provided that the redevelopment commission shall not function in an area where such a commission exists or in the corporate limits of a municipality without resolution of agreement by the municipality.

The board of county commissioners of each county included in the regional redevelopment commission shall appoint one person as a commissioner and such a person may be appointed at or after the time of the adoption of the resolution creating the redevelopment commission. The board of county commissioners shall have the authority to appoint successors or to remove persons for misconduct who are appointed by them. Each commissioner to the redevelopment commission shall serve for a five-year term except that initial appointments may be for less time in order to establish a fair donation system of appointments. In the event that a regional redevelopment commission shall have an even number of counties, the Governor of North Carolina shall appoint a member to the commission from the area to be served. The appointed members as commissioners shall constitute the regional redevelopment commission and certification of appointment shall be filed with the Secretary of State as part of the application for charter.

All provisions of the "Urban Redevelopment Law" as defined in Article 22 of Chapter 160A of the General Statutes, shall apply to the creation and operation of a regional redevelopment commission, and where reference is made to municipality, it shall be interpreted to apply to the area served by the regional redevelopment commission. (1969, c. 1208, s. 3; 1973, c. 426, s. 75.)

## § 160A-507.1. Creation of a joint county-city redevelopment commission.

A county and one or more cities within the county are hereby authorized to create a separate and distinct body corporate and politic to be known as the joint redevelopment commission by the passage of a resolution by the board of county commissioners and the governing body of one or more cities within the county creating such a commission to function within the territorial limits of such participating units of government; provided, however, that notice of the intent to consider passage of such a resolution or ordinance shall be published at least 10 days prior to the meeting of the affected governing boards for such purposes, and further provided that a joint redevelopment commission created hereunder shall have authority to operate in an area where there presently exists a redevelopment commission upon the approval of the municipality or county concerned. The governing body of each participating local government shall appoint one or more commissioners as such governing bodies shall determine; such persons may be appointed at or after the time of adoption of the resolution creating the joint redevelopment commission. The appointing authority shall have the authority to appoint successors or to remove persons for misfeasance, malfeasance or nonfeasance who are appointed by them. Each commissioner shall serve for a term designated by the governing bodies of not less than one nor more than five years. The appointed members as commissioners shall constitute the joint redevelopment commission and certification of appointment shall be filed with the Secretary of State as part of the application for charter.

All provisions of the "Urban Redevelopment Law" as defined in Article 22 of Chapter 160A of the General Statutes shall apply to the creation and operation of a joint redevelopment commission and where reference is made to municipality, it shall be interpreted to apply to the units of government creating a joint redevelopment commission. (1975, c. 407.)

## § 160A-508. Appointment and qualifications of members of commission.

Upon certification of a resolution declaring the need for a commission to operate in a city or town, the mayor and governing board thereof, respectively, shall appoint, as members of the commission, not less than five nor more than nine citizens who shall be residents of the city or town in which the commission is to operate. The governing body may at any time by resolution or ordinance increase or decrease the membership of a commission, within the limitations herein prescribed. (1951, c. 1095, s. 5; 1971, c. 362, ss. 6, 7; 1973, c. 426, s. 75.)

## § 160A-509. Tenure and compensation of members of commission.

The mayor and governing body shall designate overlapping terms of not less than one nor more than five years for the members who are first appointed. Thereafter, the term of office shall be five years. A member shall hold office until his successor has been appointed and qualified. Vacancies for the unexpired terms shall be promptly filled by the mayor and governing body. A member shall receive such compensation, if any, as the municipal governing board may provide for this service, and shall be entitled within the budget appropriation to the necessary expenses, including traveling expenses, incurred in the discharge of his duties. (1951, c. 1095, s. 6; 1967, c. 932, s. 4; 1971, c. 362, s. 8; 1973, c. 426, s. 75.)

## § 160A-510. Organization of commission.

The members of a commission shall select from among themselves a chairman, a vice-chairman, and such other officers as the commission may determine. A commission may employ a secretary, its own counsel, and such technical experts, and such other agents and employees, permanent or temporary, as it may require, and may determine the qualifications and fix the compensation of such persons. A majority of the members shall constitute a quorum for its meeting. Members shall not be liable personally on the bonds or other obligations of the commission, and the rights of creditors shall be solely against such commission. A commission may delegate to one or more of its members, agents or employees such of its powers as it shall deem necessary to carry out the purposes of this Article, subject always to the supervision and control of the commission. For inefficiency or neglect of duty or misconduct in office, a commissioner of a commission may be removed by the governing body, but a commissioner shall be removed only after a hearing and after he shall have been given a copy of the charges at least 10 days prior to such hearing and have had an opportunity to be heard in person or by counsel. (1951, c. 1095, s. 7; 1971, c. 362, s. 9; 1973, c. 426, s. 75.)

## § 160A-511. Interest of members or employees.

No member or employee of a commission shall acquire any interest, direct or indirect, in any redevelopment project or in any property included or planned to be included in any redevelopment area, or in any area which he may have reason to believe may be certified to be a redevelopment area, nor shall he have any interest, direct or indirect, in any contract or proposed contract for materials or services to be furnished or used by a commission, or in any contract with a redeveloper or prospective redeveloper relating, directly or indirectly, to any redevelopment project, except that a member or employee of a commission may acquire property in a residential redevelopment area from a person or entity other than the commission after the residential redevelopment plan for that area is adopted if:

(1) The primary purpose of acquisition is to occupy the property as his principal residence;

(2) The redevelopment plan does not provide for acquisition of such property by the commission; and

(3) Prior to acquiring title to the property, the member or employee shall have disclosed in writing to the commission and to the local governing body his intent to acquire the property and to occupy the property as his principal residence.

Except as authorized herein, the acquisition of any such interest in a redevelopment project or in any such property or contract shall constitute misconduct in office. If any member or employee of a commission shall have already owned or controlled within the preceding two years any interest, direct or indirect, in any property later included or planned to be included in any redevelopment project, under the jurisdiction of the commission, or has any such interest in any contract for material or services to be furnished or used in connection with any redevelopment project, he shall disclose the same in writing to the commission and to the local governing body. Any disclosure required herein shall be entered in writing upon the minute books of the commission. Failure to make disclosure shall constitute misconduct in office. (1951, c. 1095, s. 8; 1973, c. 426, s. 75; 1977, 2nd Sess., c. 1139.)

## § 160A-512. Powers of commission.

A commission shall constitute a public body, corporate and politic, exercising public and essential governmental powers, which powers shall include all powers necessary or appropriate to carry out and effectuate the purposes and provisions of this Article, including the following powers in addition to those herein otherwise granted:

(1) To procure from the planning commission the designation of areas in need of redevelopment and its recommendation for such redevelopment;

(2) To cooperate with any government or municipality as herein defined;

(3) To act as agent of the State or federal government or any of its instrumentalities or agencies for the public purposes set out in this Article;

(4) To prepare or cause to be prepared and recommend redevelopment plans to the governing body of the operation;

(5) Subject to the provisions of G.S. 160A-514(b) to arrange or contract for the furnishing or repair, by any person or agency, public or private, of services, privileges, works, streets, roads, public

utilities or other facilities for or in connection with a redevelopment project; and (notwithstanding anything to the contrary contained in this Article or any other provision of law), to agree to any conditions that it may deem reasonable and appropriate attached to federal financial assistance and imposed pursuant to federal law relating to the determination of prevailing salaries or wages or compliance with labor standards, in the undertaking or carrying out of a redevelopment project, and to include in any contract let in connection with such a project, provisions to fulfill such of said conditions as it may deem reasonable and appropriate;

(6) Within its area of operation, to purchase, obtain options upon, acquire by gift, grant, bequest, devise, eminent domain or otherwise, any real or personal property or any interest therein, together with any improvements thereon, necessary or incidental to a redevelopment project; to hold, improve, clear or prepare for redevelopment any such property, and subject to the provisions of G.S. 160A-514, and with the approval of the local governing body sell, exchange, transfer, assign, subdivide, retain for its own use, mortgage, pledge, hypothecate or otherwise encumber or dispose of any real or personal property or any interest therein, either as an entirety to a single "redeveloper" or in parts to several redevelopers; provided that the commission finds that the sale or other transfer of any such part will not be prejudicial to the sale of other parts of the redevelopment area, nor in any other way prejudicial to the realization of the redevelopment plan approved by the governing body; to enter into contracts, either before or after the real property that is the subject of the contract is acquired by the Commission (although disposition of the property is still subject to G.S. 160A-514), with "redevelopers" of property containing covenants, restrictions, and conditions regarding the use of such property for residential, commercial, industrial, recreational purposes or for public purposes in accordance with the redevelopment plan and such other covenants, restrictions and conditions as the commission may deem necessary to prevent a recurrence of blighted areas or to effectuate the purposes of this Article; to make any of the covenants, restrictions or conditions of the foregoing contracts covenants running with the land, and to provide appropriate remedies for any breach of any such covenants or conditions, including the right to terminate such contracts and any interest in the property created pursuant thereto; to borrow money and issue bonds therefor

and provide security for bonds; to insure or provide for the insurance of any real or personal property or operations of the commission against any risks or hazards, including the power to pay premiums on any such insurance; and to enter into any contracts necessary to effectuate the purposes of this Article;

(7) To invest any funds held in reserves or sinking funds or any funds not required for immediate disbursements, in such investments as may be lawful for guardians, executors, administrators or other fiduciaries under the laws of this State; to redeem its bonds at the redemption price established therein or to purchase its bonds at less than redemption price, all bonds so redeemed or purchased to be cancelled;

(8) To borrow money and to apply for and accept advances, loans evidenced by bonds, grants, contributions and any other form of financial assistance from the federal government, the State, county, municipality or other public body or from any sources, public or private for the purposes of this Article, to give such security as may be required and to enter into and carry out contracts in connection therewith; and, notwithstanding the provisions of any other law, may include in any contract for financial assistance with the federal government for a redevelopment project such conditions imposed pursuant to federal law as the commission may deem reasonable and appropriate and which are not inconsistent with the purposes of this Article;

(9) Acting through one or more commissioners or other persons designated by the commission, to conduct examinations and investigations and to hear testimony and take proof under oath at public or private hearings on any matter material for its information; to administer oaths, issue subpoenas requiring the attendance of witnesses or the production of books and papers;

(10) Within its area of operation, to make or have made all surveys, studies and plans (but not including the preparation of a general plan for the community) necessary to the carrying out of the purposes of this Article and in connection therewith to enter into or upon any land, building, or improvement thereon for such purposes and to make soundings, test borings, surveys, appraisals and other preliminary studies and investigations necessary to carry out its powers but such entry shall constitute no cause of action for trespass in favor of the owner of such land, building, or improvement except for injuries resulting from negligence, wantonness or malice; and to contract or cooperate with any and all persons or agencies

public or private, in the making and carrying out of such surveys, appraisals, studies and plans.

A redevelopment commission is hereby specifically authorized to make (i) plans for carrying out a program of voluntary repair and rehabilitation of buildings and improvements and (ii) plans for the enforcement of laws, codes, and regulations relating to the use of land and the use and occupancy of buildings and improvements, and to the compulsory repair, rehabilitation, demolition, or removal of buildings and improvements. The redevelopment commission is further authorized to develop, test and report methods and techniques, and carry out demonstrations and other activities, for the prevention and elimination of slums and urban blight.

(11) To make such expenditures as may be necessary to carry out the purposes of this Article; and to make expenditures from funds obtained from the federal government;

(12) To sue and be sued;

(13) To adopt a seal;

(14) To have perpetual succession;

(15) To make and execute contracts and other instruments necessary or convenient to the exercise of the powers of the commission; and any contract or instrument when signed by the chairman or vice-chairman and secretary or assistant secretary, or, treasurer or assistant treasurer of the commission shall be held to have been properly executed for and on its behalf;

(16) To make and from time to time amend and repeal bylaws, rules, regulations and resolutions;

(17) To make available to the government or municipality or any appropriate agency, board or commission, the recommendations of the commission affecting any area in its field of operation or property therein, which it may deem likely to promote the public health, morals, safety or welfare;

(18) To perform redevelopment project undertakings and activities in one or more contiguous or noncontiguous redevelopment areas which are planned and carried out on the basis of annual increments. (1951, c. 1095, s. 9; 1961, c. 837, ss. 5, 7; 1969, c. 254, s. 1; 1973, c. 426, s. 75; 1981 (Reg. Sess., 1982), c. 1276, s. 14; 2003-403, s. 17.)

## § 160A-513. Preparation and adoption of redevelopment plans.

(a) A commission shall prepare a redevelopment plan for any area certified by the planning commission to be a redevelopment area. A redevelopment plan shall be sufficiently complete to indicate its relationship to definite local objectives as to appropriate land uses, improved traffic, public transportation, public utilities, recreational and community facilities and other public improvements and the proposed land uses and building requirements in the redevelopment project area.

(b) The planning commission's certification of a redevelopment area shall be made in conformance with its comprehensive general plan, if any (which may include, inter alia, a plan of major traffic arteries and terminals and a land use plan and projected population densities) for the area.

(c) A commission shall not acquire real property for a development project unless the governing body of the community in which the redevelopment project area is located has approved the redevelopment plan, as hereinafter prescribed; provided, however, that the commission may acquire, through negotiation, specific pieces of property in the redevelopment area prior to the approval of such plan when the governing body finds that advance acquisition of such properties is in the public interest and specifically approves such action.

(d) The redevelopment commission's redevelopment plan shall include, without being limited to, the following:

(1) The boundaries of the area, with a map showing the existing uses of the real property therein;

(2) A land use plan of the area showing proposed uses following redevelopment;

(3) Standards of population densities, land coverage and building intensities in the proposed redevelopment;

(4) A preliminary site plan of the area;

(5) A statement of the proposed changes, if any, in zoning ordinances or maps;

(6) A statement of any proposed changes in street layouts or street levels;

(7) A statement of the estimated cost and method of financing redevelopment under the plan; provided, that where redevelopment activities are performed on the basis of annual increments, such statement to be sufficient shall set forth a schedule of the activities proposed to be undertaken during the incremental period, together with a statement of the estimated cost and method of financing such scheduled activities only;

(8) A statement of such continuing controls as may be deemed necessary to effectuate the purposes of this Article;

(9) A statement of a feasible method proposed for the relocation of the families displaced.

(e) The commission shall hold a public hearing prior to its final determination of the redevelopment plan. Notice of such hearing shall be given once a week for two successive calendar weeks in a newspaper published in the municipality, or if there be no newspaper published in the municipality, by posting such notice at four public places in the municipality, said notice to be published the first time or posted not less than 15 days prior to the date fixed for said hearing.

(f) The commission shall submit the redevelopment plan to the planning commission for review. The planning commission, shall, within 45 days, certify to the redevelopment commission its recommendation on the redevelopment plan, either of approval, rejection or modification, and in the latter event, specify the changes recommended.

(g) Upon receipt of the planning commission's recommendation, or at the expiration of 45 days, if no recommendation is made by the planning commission, the commission shall submit to the governing body the redevelopment plan with the recommendation, if any, of the planning commission thereon. Prior to recommending a redevelopment plan to the governing body for approval, the commission shall consider whether the proposed land uses and building requirements in the redevelopment project area are designed with the general purpose of accomplishing, in conformance with the general plan, a coordinated, adjusted and harmonious development of the community and its environs, which will in accordance with present and future needs promote health, safety, morals, order, convenience, prosperity and the general welfare, as well as efficiency and economy in the process of development, including, among other things, adequate provision for traffic, vehicular parking, the promotion of safety from fire, panic and other dangers, adequate provision for light and air, the promotion of the healthful and convenient distribution of population, the provision of adequate transportation, water, sewerage and other public utilities, schools, parks, recreational and community facilities and other public requirements, the promotion of sound design and arrangements, the wise and efficient expenditure of public funds, the prevention of the recurrence of insanitary or unsafe dwelling accommodations, slums, or conditions of blight.

(h) The governing body, upon receipt of the redevelopment plan and the recommendation (if any) of the planning commission, shall hold a public hearing upon said plan. Notice of such hearing shall be given once a week for two successive weeks in a newspaper published in the municipality, or, if there be no newspaper published in the municipality, by posting such notice at four public places in the municipality, said notice to be published the first time or posted not less than 15 days prior to the date fixed for said hearing. The notice shall describe the redevelopment area by boundaries, in a manner designed to be understandable by the general public. The redevelopment plan, including such maps, plans, contracts, or other documents as form a part of it, together with the recommendation (if any) of the planning commission and supporting data, shall be available for public inspection at a location specified in the notice for at least 10 days prior to the hearing.

At the hearing the governing body shall afford an opportunity to all persons or agencies interested to be heard and shall receive, make known, and consider recommendations in writing with reference to the redevelopment plan.

(i) The governing body shall approve, amend, or reject the redevelopment plan as submitted.

(j) Subject to the proviso in subsection (c) of this section, upon approval by the governing body of the redevelopment plan, the commission is authorized to acquire property, to execute contracts for clearance and preparation of the land for resale, and to take other actions necessary to carry out the plan, in accordance with the provisions of this Article.

(k) A redevelopment plan may be modified at any time by the commission; provided that, if modified after the sale of real property in the redevelopment project area, the modification must be consented to by the redeveloper of such real property or his successor, or their successors in interest affected by the proposed modification. Where the proposed modification will substantially change the redevelopment plan as previously approved by the governing body the modification must similarly be approved by the governing body as provided above. (1951, c. 1095, s. 10; 1961, c. 837, s. 8; 1965, c. 808; 1969, c. 254, s. 2; 1973, c. 426, s. 75.)

## § 160A-514. Required procedures for contracts, purchases and sales; powers of commission in carrying out redevelopment project.

(a) A commission may privately contract for engineering, legal, surveying, professional or other similar services without advertisement or bid.

(b) In entering and carrying out any contract for construction, demolition, moving of structures, or repair work or the purchase of apparatus, supplies, materials, or equipment, a commission shall comply with the provisions of Article 8 of Chapter 143 of the General Statutes. In construing such provisions, the commission shall be considered to be the governing board of a "subdivision of the State," and a contract for demolition or moving of structures, shall be treated in the same manner as a contract for construction or repair. Compliance with such provisions shall not be required, however, where the commission enters into contracts with the municipality which created it for the municipality to furnish any such services, work, apparatus, supplies, materials, or equipment; the making of these contracts without advertisement or bids is hereby specifically authorized. Advertisement or bids shall not be required for any contract for construction, demolition, moving of structures, or repair work, or for the purchase of apparatus, supplies, materials, or equipment, where such contract involves the expenditure of public money in an amount less than five hundred dollars ($500.00).

(c) A commission may sell, exchange, or otherwise transfer the fee or any lesser interest in real property in a redevelopment project area to any redeveloper for any public or private use that accords with the redevelopment plan, subject to such covenants, conditions and restrictions as the commission may deem to be in the public interest and in furtherance of the purposes of this Article. In the sale, exchange, or transfer of property, the commission shall exercise the authority and procedure set out in G.S. 160A-268, 160A-269, 160A-270, 160A-271, or 160A-279 for the disposition of property by a city council. Provided, however, that all sales, exchanges, or other transfers of real property from July 9, 1985, to December 31, 1987, in accordance with the provisions of this section prior to its revision on July 9, 1985, shall be and are valid in all respects.

(d) A commission may sell personal property having a value of less than five hundred dollars ($500.00) at private sale without advertisement and bids.

(e) In carrying out a redevelopment project, the commission may:

(1) With or without consideration and at private sale convey to the municipality in which the project is located such real property as, in accordance with the redevelopment plan, is to be laid out into streets, alleys, and public ways.

(2) With or without consideration, convey at private sale, grant, or dedicate easements and rights-of-way for public utilities, sewers, streets and other similar facilities, in accordance with the redevelopment plan.

(3) With or without consideration and at private sale convey to the municipality, county or other appropriate public body such real property as, in accordance with the redevelopment plan, is to be used for parks, schools, public buildings, facilities or other public purposes.

(4) In addition to other authority contained in this section, after a public hearing advertised in accordance with the provisions of G.S. 160A-513(e), and subject to the approval of the governing body of the municipality, convey to a nonprofit association or corporation organized and operated exclusively for educational, scientific, literary, cultural, charitable or religious purposes, no part of the net earnings of which inure to the benefit of any private shareholder or individual, such real property as, in accordance with the redevelopment plan, is to be used for the purposes of such associations or corporations. Such conveyance shall be for such consideration as may be agreed upon by the commission and the association or corporation, which shall not be less than the fair value of the property agreed upon by a committee of three professional real estate appraisers currently practicing in the State, which committee shall be appointed by the commission. All conveyances made under the authority of

this subsection shall contain restrictive covenants limiting the use of property so conveyed to the purposes for which the conveyance is made.

(f) After receiving the required approval of a sale from the governing body of the municipality, the commission may execute any required contracts, deeds, and other instruments and take all steps necessary to effectuate any such contract or sale. Any contract of sale between a commission and a redeveloper may contain, without being limited to, any or all of the following provisions:

(1) Plans prepared by the redeveloper or otherwise and such other documents as may be required to show the type, material, structure and general character of the proposed redevelopment;

(2) A statement of the use intended for each part of the proposed redevelopment;

(3) A guaranty of completion of the proposed redevelopment within specified time limits;

(4) The amount, if known, of the consideration to be paid;

(5) Adequate safeguards for proper maintenance of all parts of the proposed redevelopment;

(6) Such other continuing controls as may be deemed necessary to effectuate the purposes of this Article.

Any deed to a redeveloper in furtherance of a redevelopment contract shall be executed in the name of the commission, by its proper officers, and shall contain in addition to all other provisions, such conditions, restrictions and provisions as the commission may deem desirable to run with the land in order to effectuate the purposes of this Article.

(g) The commission may temporarily rent or lease, operate and maintain real property in a redevelopment project area, pending the disposition of the property for redevelopment, for such uses and purposes as may be deemed desirable even though not in conformity with the redevelopment plan. (1951, c. 1095, s. 11; 1961, c. 837, s. 9; 1963, c. 1212, ss. 1, 2; 1965, c. 679, s. 2; 1967, c. 24, s. 18; c. 932, s. 1; 1973, c. 426, s. 75; 1985, c. 665, ss. 1, 2; 1987, c. 364; 1989, c. 413; 2003-66, ss. 1, 2.)

## § 160A-515. Eminent domain.

The commission may exercise the right of eminent domain in accordance with the provisions of Chapter 40A. (1951, c. 1095, s. 12; 1965, c. 679, s. 3; c. 1132; 1967, c. 932, ss. 2, 3; 1973, c. 426, s. 75; 1981, c. 919, s. 30.)

## § 160A-515.1. Project development financing.

(a) Authorization. — A city may finance a redevelopment project and any related public improvements with the proceeds of project development financing debt instruments, issued pursuant to Article 6 of Chapter 159 of the General Statutes, together with any other revenues that are available to the city. Before it receives the approval of the Local Government Commission for issuance of project development financing debt instruments, the city's governing body must define a development financing district and adopt a development financing plan for the district. The city may act jointly with a county to finance a project, define a development financing district, and adopt a development financing plan for the district.

(b) Development Financing District.— A development financing district shall comprise all or portions of one or more redevelopment areas defined pursuant to this Article. The total land area within development financing districts in a city, including development financing districts created pursuant to G.S. 158-7.3, may not exceed five percent (5%) of the total land area of the city.

(c) Development Financing Plan. — The development financing plan must be compatible with the redevelopment plan or plans for the redevelopment area or areas included within the district. The development financing plan must include all of the following:

(1) A description of the boundaries of the development financing district.

(2) A description of the proposed development of the district, both public and private.

(3) The costs of the proposed public activities.

(4) The sources and amounts of funds to pay for the proposed public activities.

(5) The base valuation of the development financing district.

(6) The projected incremental valuation of the development financing district.

(7) The estimated duration of the development financing district.

(8) A description of how the proposed development of the district, both public and private, will benefit the residents and business owners of the district in terms of jobs, affordable housing, or services.

(9) A description of the appropriate ameliorative activities which will be undertaken if the proposed projects have a negative impact on residents or business owners of the district in terms of jobs, affordable housing, services, or displacement.

(10) A requirement that the initial users of any new manufacturing facilities that will be located in the district and that are included in the plan will comply with the wage requirements in subsection (d) of this section.

(d) Wage Requirements. — A development financing plan shall include a requirement that the initial users of a new manufacturing facility to be located in the district and included in the plan must pay its employees an average weekly manufacturing wage that is either above the average manufacturing wage paid in the county in which the district will be located or not less than ten percent (10%) above the average weekly manufacturing wage paid in the State. The plan may include information on the wages to be paid by the initial users of a new manufacturing facility to

its employees and any provisions necessary to implement the wage requirement. The issuing unit's governing body shall not adopt a plan until the Secretary of Commerce certifies that the Secretary has reviewed the average weekly manufacturing wage required by the plan to be paid to the employees of a new manufacturing facility and has found either (i) that the wages proposed by the initial users of a new manufacturing facility are in compliance with the amount required by this subsection or (ii) that the plan is exempt from the requirement of this subsection. The Secretary of Commerce may exempt a plan from the requirement of this subsection if the Secretary receives a resolution from the issuing unit's governing body requesting an exemption from the wage requirement and a letter from an appropriate State official, selected by the Secretary, finding that unemployment in the county in which the proposed district is to be located is especially severe. Upon the creation of the district, the unit of local government proposing the creation of the district shall take any lawful actions necessary to require compliance with the applicable wage requirement by the initial users of any new manufacturing facility included in the plan; however, failure to take such actions or obtain such compliance shall not affect the validity of any proceedings for the creation of the district, the existence of the district, or the validity of any debt instruments issued under Article 6 of Chapter 159 of the General Statutes. All findings and determinations made by the Secretary of Commerce under this subsection shall be binding and conclusive. For purposes of this section, the term "manufacturing facility" means any facility that is used in the manufacturing or production of tangible personal property, including the processing resulting in a change in the condition of the property.

(e) County Review. — Before adopting a plan for a development financing district, the city council shall send notice of the plan, by first-class mail, to the board of county commissioners of the county or counties in which the development financing district is located. The person mailing the notice shall certify that fact, and the date thereof, to the city council, and the certificate is conclusive in the absence of fraud. Unless the board of county commissioners (or either board, if the district is in two counties) by resolution disapproves the proposed plan within 28 days after the date the notice is mailed, the city council may proceed to adopt the plan.

(f) Environmental Review. — Before adopting a plan for development financing districts, the city council shall submit the plan to the Secretary of Environment and Natural Resources to review to determine if the construction and operation of any new manufacturing facility in the district will have a materially adverse effect on the environment and whether the company that will operate the facility has operated in substantial compliance with federal and State laws, regulations, and rules for the protection of the environment. If the Secretary finds that the new manufacturing facility will not have a materially adverse effect on the environment and that the company that will operate the facility has operated other facilities in compliance with environmental requirements, the Secretary shall approve the plan. In making the determination on environmental impact, the Secretary shall use the same criteria that apply to the determination under G.S. 159C-7 of whether an industrial project will have a materially adverse effect on the environment. The findings of the Secretary are conclusive and binding.

(g) Plan Adoption. — Before adopting a plan for a development financing district, the city council shall hold a public hearing on the plan. The council shall, no less than 30 days before the day of hearing, cause notice of the hearing to be mailed by first-class mail to all property owners and mailing addresses within the proposed development financing district. The council shall also, no more than 30 days and no less than 14 days before the day of the hearing, cause notice of the hearing to be published once in a newspaper of general circulation in the city. The notice shall state the time and place of the hearing, shall specify its purpose, and shall state that a copy of the proposed plan is available for public inspection in the office of the city clerk. At the public hearing, the council shall hear anyone who wishes to speak with respect to the proposed district and proposed plan. Unless a board of county commissioners or the Secretary of Environment and Natural Resources has disapproved the plan pursuant to subsection (e) or (f) of this section, the council may adopt the plan, with or without amendment, at any time after the public hearing. However, the plan and the district do not become effective until the city's application to issue project development financing debt instruments has been approved by the Local Government Commission, pursuant to Article 6 of Chapter 159 of the General Statutes.

(h) Plan Modification. — Subject to the limitations of this subsection, a city council may, after the effective date of the district, amend a development financing plan adopted for a development financing district. Before making any amendment, the city council shall follow the procedures and meet the requirements of subsections (d) through (g) of this section. The boundaries of the district may be enlarged only during the first five years after the effective date of the district and only if the area to be added has been or is about to be developed and the development is primarily attributable to development that has occurred within the district, as certified by the Local Government Commission. The boundaries of the district may be reduced at any time, but the city may agree with the holders of any project development financing debt instruments to restrict its power to reduce district boundaries.

(i) Plan Implementation. — In implementing a development financing plan, a city may act directly, through a redevelopment commission, through one or more contracts with private agencies, or by any combination of these. (2003-403, s. 18.)

§ 160A-516. Issuance of bonds.

(a) The commission shall have power to issue bonds from time to time for any of its corporate purposes including the payment of principal and interest upon any advances for surveys and plans for redevelopment projects. The commission shall also have power to issue refunding bonds for the purpose of paying or retiring or in exchange for bonds previously issued by it. The commission may issue such types of bonds as it may determine, including (without limiting the generality of the foregoing) bonds on which the principal and interest are payable:

(1) Exclusively from the income, proceeds, and revenues of the redevelopment project financed with the proceeds of such bonds; or

(2) Exclusively from the income, proceeds, and revenues of any of its redevelopment projects whether or not they are financed in whole or in part with the proceeds of such bonds; provided, that any such bonds may be additionally secured by a pledge of any loan, grant or contributions, or parts thereof, from the federal government or other source, or a mortgage of any redevelopment project or projects of the commission.

(b) Neither the commissioners of a commission nor any person executing the bonds shall be liable personally on the bonds by reason of the issuance of the bonds. The bonds and other obligations of the commission (and the bonds and obligations shall so state on their face) shall not be a debt of the municipality, the county, or the State and neither the municipality, the county, nor the State shall be liable on the bonds, nor in any event shall the bonds or obligations be payable out of any funds or properties other than those of the commission acquired for the purpose of this Article. The bonds shall not constitute an indebtedness of the municipality within the meaning of any constitutional or statutory debt limitation or restriction. Bonds of a commission are declared to be issued for an essential public and governmental purpose and to be public instrumentalities. The bonds are exempt from all State, county, and municipal taxation or assessment, direct or indirect, general or special, whether imposed for the purpose of general revenue or otherwise, excluding inheritance and gift taxes, income taxes on the gain from the transfer of the bonds and notes, and franchise taxes. The interest on the bonds is not subject to taxation as income. Bonds may be issued by a commission under this Article notwithstanding any debt or other limitation prescribed in any statute. This Article without reference to other statutes of the State shall constitute full and complete authority for the authorization and issuance of bonds by the commission under this Article and this authorization and issuance shall not be subject to any conditions, restrictions, or limitations imposed by any other statute whether general, special, or local, except as provided in subsection (d) of this section.

(c) Bonds of the commission shall be authorized by its resolution and may be issued in one or more series and shall bear such date or dates, be payable upon demand or mature at such time or times, bear interest at such rate or rates, be in such denomination or denominations, be in such form either coupon or registered, carry such conversion or registration privileges, have such rank or priority, be executed in such manner, be payable in such medium of payment, at such place or places, and be subject to such terms of redemption (with or without premium) as such resolution, its trust indenture or mortgage may provide.

(d) Bonds shall be sold by the redevelopment commission at either public or private sale upon such terms and in such manner, consistent with the provisions hereof, as the redevelopment commission may determine. Prior to the public sale of bonds hereunder, the redevelopment commission shall first cause a notice of the sale of the bonds to be published at least once at least 10 days before the date fixed for the receipt of bids for the bonds (i) in a newspaper having the largest or next largest circulation in the redevelopment commission's area of operation and (ii) in a publication that carries advertisements for the sale of State and municipal bonds published in the City of New York in the State of New York; provided, however, that in its discretion the redevelopment commission may cause any such notice of sale in the New York publication to be published as part of a consolidated notice of sale offering for sale the obligations of other public agencies in addition to the redevelopment commission's bonds, and provided, further, that any bonds may be sold by the redevelopment commission at private sale upon such terms and conditions as are mutually agreed upon between the commission and the purchaser. No bonds issued pursuant to this Article shall be sold at less than par and accrued interest. The provisions of the Local Government Finance Act shall not be applicable with respect to bonds sold or issued under this Article.

(e) In case any of the commissioners or officers of the commission whose signatures appear on any bonds or coupons shall cease to be such commissioners or officers before the delivery of such bonds, such signatures shall, nevertheless, be valid and sufficient for all purposes, the same as if such commissioners or officers had remained in office until such delivery. Any provisions of any law to the contrary notwithstanding, any bonds issued pursuant to this Article shall be fully negotiable.

(f) In any suit, action or proceedings involving the validity or enforceability of any bond of the commission or the security therefor, any such bond reciting in substance that it has been issued by the commission to aid in financing a redevelopment project, as herein defined, shall be conclusively deemed to have been issued for such purpose and such project shall be conclusively deemed to have been planned, located and carried out in accordance with the purposes and provisions of this Article.

(g) Bonds (including, without limitation, interim and long-term notes) may be issued or sold under this Article at private sale upon such terms and conditions as may be negotiated and mutually agreed upon by the commission and the purchaser (who may be the government or other public or private lender or purchaser). (1951, c. 1095, s. 13; 1961, c. 837, s. 10; 1971, c. 87, s. 3; 1973, c. 426, s. 75; 1981, c. 907, ss. 3, 4; 1995, c. 46, s. 20.)

## § 160A-517. Powers in connection with issuance of bonds.

(a) In connection with the issuance of bonds or the incurring of obligations and in order to secure the payment of such bonds or obligations, the commission, in addition to its other powers, shall have power:

(1) To pledge all or any part of its gross or net rents, fees or revenues to which its right then exists or may thereafter come into existence;

(2) To mortgage all or any part of its real or personal property, then owned or thereafter acquired;

(3) To covenant against pledging all or any part of its rents, fees and revenues, or against mortgaging all or any part of its real or personal property, to which its right or title then exists or may thereafter come into existence or against permitting or suffering any lien on such revenues or property; to covenant with respect to limitations on its right to sell, lease or otherwise dispose of any redevelopment project or any part thereof; and to covenant as to what other, or additional debts or obligations may be incurred by it;

(4) To covenant as to the bonds to be issued and as to the issuance of such bonds in escrow or otherwise, and as to the use and disposition of the proceeds thereof; to provide for the replacement of lost, destroyed or mutilated bonds, to covenant against extending the time for the payment of its bonds or interest thereon; and to covenant for the redemption of the bonds and to provide the terms and conditions thereof;

(5) To covenant (subject to the limitations contained in this Article) as to the amount of revenues to be raised each year or other period of time by rents, fees and other revenues, and as to the use and disposition to be made thereof; to create or to authorize the creation of special funds for moneys held for operating costs, debt service, reserves, or other purposes, and to covenant as to the use and disposition of the moneys held in such funds;

(6) To prescribe the procedure, if any, by which the terms of any contract with bondholders may be amended or abrogated, the amount of bonds the

holders of which must consent thereto and the manner in which such consent may be given;

(7) To covenant as to the use, maintenance and replacement of any of or all of its real or personal property, the insurance to be carried thereon and the use and disposition of insurance moneys, and to warrant its title to such property;

(8) To covenant as to the rights, liabilities, powers and duties arising upon the breach by it of any covenants, conditions or obligations; and to covenant and prescribe as to events of default and terms and conditions upon which any or all of its bonds or obligations shall become or may be declared due before maturity and as to the terms and conditions upon which such declaration and its consequences may be waived;

(9) To vest in any obligees of the commissions the right to enforce the payment of the bonds or any covenants securing or relating to the bonds; to vest in any obligee or obligees holding a specified amount in bonds the right, in the event of a default to take possession of and use, operate and manage any redevelopment project or any part thereof, title to which is in the commission, or any funds connected therewith, and to collect the rents and revenues arising therefrom and to dispose of such moneys in accordance with the agreement with such obligees; to provide for the powers and duties of such obligees and to limit the liabilities thereof, and to provide the terms and conditions upon which such obligees may enforce any covenant or rights securing or relating to the bonds; and

(10) To exercise all or any part or combination of the powers herein granted; to make such covenants (other than and in addition to the covenants herein expressly authorized) and to do any and all such acts and things as may be necessary or convenient or desirable in order to secure its bonds, or, in the absolute discretion of said commission, as will tend to make the bonds more marketable notwithstanding that such covenants, acts or things may not be enumerated herein.

(b) The commission shall have power by its resolution, trust indenture, mortgage lease or other contract to confer upon any obligee holding or representing a specified amount in bonds, the right (in addition to all rights that may otherwise be conferred), upon the happening of an event of default as defined in such resolution or instrument, by suit, action or proceeding in any court of competent jurisdiction:

(1) To cause possession of any redevelopment project or any part thereof title to which is in the commission, to be surrendered to any such obligee;

(2) To obtain the appointment of a receiver of any redevelopment project of said commission or any part thereof, title to which is in the commission and of the rents and profits therefrom. If such receiver be appointed, he may enter and take possession of, carry out, operate and maintain such project or any part therefrom and collect and receive all fees, rents, revenues, or other charges thereafter arising therefrom, and shall keep such moneys in a separate account or accounts and apply the same in accordance with the obligations of said commission as the court shall direct; and

(3) To require said commission and the commissioners, officers, agents and employees thereof to account as if it and they were the trustees of an express trust. (1951, c. 1095, s. 14; 1973, c. 426, s. 75.)

## § 160A-518. Right of obligee.

An obligee of the commission shall have the right in addition to all other rights which may be conferred on such obligee, subject only to any contractual restrictions binding upon such obligee:

(1) By mandamus, suit, action or proceeding at law or in equity to compel said commission and the commissioners, officers, agents or employees thereof to perform each and every term, provision and covenant contained in any contract of said commission with or for the benefit of such obligee, and to require the carrying out of any or all such covenants and agreements of said commission and the fulfillment of all duties imposed upon said commission by this Article; and

(2) By suit, action or proceeding in equity, to enjoin any acts or things which may be unlawful, or the violation of any of the rights of such obligee of said commission. (1951, c. 1095, s. 15; 1973, c. 426, s. 75.)

## § 160A-519. Cooperation by public bodies.

(a) For the purpose of aiding and cooperating in the planning, undertaking or carrying out of a redevelopment project located within the area in which it is authorized to act, any public body may, upon such terms, with or without consideration, as it may determine:

(1) Dedicate, sell, convey or lease any of its interest in any property, or grant easements, licenses or any other rights or privileges therein to a commission;

(2) Cause parks, playgrounds, recreational, community, educational, water, sewer or drainage facilities, or any other works which it is otherwise empowered to undertake, to be furnished in connection with a redevelopment project;

(3) Furnish, dedicate, close, vacate, pave, install, grade, regrade, plan or replan streets, roads,

sidewalks, ways or other places, which it is otherwise empowered to undertake;

(4) Plan or replan, zone or rezone any part of the redevelopment;

(5) Cause administrative and other services to be furnished to the commission of the character which the public body is otherwise empowered to undertake or furnish for the same or other purposes;

(6) Incur the entire expense of any public improvements made by such public body in exercising the powers granted in this section;

(7) Do any and all things necessary or convenient to aid and cooperate in the planning or carrying out of a redevelopment plan.

(b) Any sale, conveyance, or agreement provided for in this section may be made by a public body without public notice, advertisement or public bidding. (1951, c. 1095, s. 16; 1973, c. 426, s. 75.)

## § 160A-520. Grant of funds by community.

Any municipality located within the area of operation of a commission may appropriate funds to a commission for the purpose of aiding such commission in carrying out any of its powers and functions under this Article. To obtain funds for this purpose, the municipality may levy taxes and may in the manner prescribed by law issue and sell its bonds. (1951, c. 1095, s. 17; 1973, c. 426, s. 75.)

## § 160A-521. Records and reports.

(a) The books and records of a commission shall at all times be open and subject to inspection by the public.

(b) A copy of all bylaws and rules and regulations and amendments thereto adopted by it, from time to time, shall be filed with the city clerk and shall be open for public inspection.

(c) At least once each year a report of its activities for the preceding year and such other reports as may be required shall be made. Copies of such reports shall be filed with the mayor and governing body of the municipality. (1951, c. 1095, s. 18; 1973, c. 426, s. 75.)

## § 160A-522. Title of purchaser.

Any instrument executed by a commission and purporting to convey any right, title or interest in any property under this Article shall be conclusive evidence of compliance with the provisions of this Article insofar as title or other interest of any bona fide purchasers, lessees or transferees of such property is concerned. (1951, c. 1095, s. 19; 1973, c. 426, s. 75.)

## § 160A-523. Preparation of general plan by local governing body.

The governing body of any municipality or county, which is not otherwise authorized to create a planning commission with power to prepare a general plan for the development of the community, is hereby authorized and empowered to prepare such a general plan prior to the initiation and carrying out of a redevelopment project under this Article. (1951, c. 1095, s. 20; 1973, c. 426, s. 75.)

## § 160A-524. Inconsistent provisions.

Insofar as the provisions of this Article are inconsistent with the provisions of any other law, the provisions of this Article shall be controlling. (1951, c. 1095, s. 22; 1955, c. 1349; 1957, c. 502, s. 4; 1973, c. 426, s. 75.)

## § 160A-525. Certain actions and proceedings validated.

All proceedings, resolutions, ordinances, motions, notices, findings, determinations, and other actions of redevelopment commissions, incorporated cities and towns, governing bodies, and planning boards and commissions, had and taken prior to January 1, 1965, pursuant to or purporting to comply with the Urban Redevelopment Law (G.S. 160A-500 to 160A-526) and incident to the creation and organization of redevelopment commissions and appointment of members thereof, designation of redevelopment and project areas, findings and determinations respecting conditions in redevelopment and project areas, preparation, development, review, processing and approval of urban redevelopment projects and plans, including redevelopment plans, calling and holding of public hearings, and the time and manner of giving and publishing notices thereof, are hereby in all respects legalized, ratified, approved, validated and confirmed, and all such actions are declared to be valid and lawfully authorized; provided, however, that no such action shall be legalized, ratified, approved, validated or confirmed, under this section if they appertain to any redevelopment or project area, the acquisition or taking of any property in any such area, any urban redevelopment project or any redevelopment plan respecting which any decree or judgment has been rendered by the Supreme Court of North Carolina prior to May 25, 1965. (1963, c. 194; 1965, c. 680; 1973, c. 426, s. 75.)

## § 160A-526. Contracts and agreements validated.

All contracts or agreements of redevelopment commissions heretofore entered into with the federal government or its agencies, and with municipalities or others relating to financial assistance for redevelopment projects in which it was required that loans or advances shall bear an interest rate in excess of six per centum (6%) per annum, or in which a municipality or others had agreed to pay funds equal to the interest in excess of six per centum (6%) per annum are hereby validated, ratified, confirmed, approved and declared legal with respect to the payment of interest in excess of six per centum (6%), and all things done or performed in reference thereto. The redevelopment commissions are hereby authorized to assume the full obligation of the municipalities under the contracts or agreements with reference to interest in excess of six per centum (6%), and to reimburse any municipality which has made any interest payment under such contracts or agreements. (1971, c. 87, s. 4; 1973, c. 426, s. 75.)

**§§ 160A-527 through 160A-534. Reserved for future codification purposes.**

# Statutory Limitations on Local Governments

Fair Housing Act.
G.S. Chapter 41A.
State Fair Housing Act.

### § 41A-1. Title.
This Chapter shall be known and may be cited as the State Fair Housing Act. (1983, c. 522, s. 1.)

### § 41A-2. Purpose.
The purpose of this Chapter is to provide fair housing throughout the State of North Carolina. (1983, c. 522, s. 1.)

### § 41A-3. Definitions.
For the purposes of this Chapter, the following definitions apply:

(1) The "Commission" means the North Carolina Human Relations Commission;

(1a) "Covered multifamily dwellings" means:

    a. A building, including all units and common use areas, in which there are four or more units if the building has one or more elevators; or

    b. Ground floor units and ground floor common use areas in a building with four or more units.

(1b) "Familial status" means one or more persons who have not attained the age of 18 years being domiciled with:

    a. A parent or another person having legal custody of the person or persons; or

    b. The designee of the parent or other person having custody, provided the designee has the written permission of the parent or other person.

The protections against discrimination on the basis of familial status shall apply to any person who is pregnant or is in the process of securing legal custody of any person who has not attained the age of 18 years.

(2) "Family" includes a single individual;

(3) "Financial institution" means any banking corporation or trust company, savings and loan association, credit union, insurance company, or related corporation, partnership, foundation, or other institution engaged primarily in lending or investing funds;

(3a) "Handicapping condition" means (i) a physical or mental impairment which substantially limits one or more of a person's major life activities, (ii) a record of having such an impairment, or (iii) being regarded as having such an impairment. Handicapping condition does not include current, illegal use of or addiction to a controlled substance as defined in 21 U.S.C. § 802, the Controlled Substances Act. The protections against discrimination on the basis of handicapping condition shall apply to a buyer or renter of a dwelling, a person residing in or intending to reside in the dwelling after it is sold, rented, or made available, or any person associated with the buyer or renter.

(4) "Housing accommodation" means any improved or unimproved real property, or part thereof, which is used or occupied, or is intended, arranged, or designed to be used or occupied, as the home or residence of one or more individuals;

(5) "Person" means any individual, association, corporation, political subdivision, partnership, labor union, legal representative, mutual company, joint stock company, trust, trustee in bankruptcy, unincorporated organization, or other legal or commercial entity, the State, or governmental entity or agency;

(6) "Real estate broker or salesman" means a person, whether licensed or not, who, for or with the expectation of receiving a consideration, lists, sells, purchases, exchanges, rents, or leases real property, or who negotiates or attempts to negotiate any of these activities, or who holds himself out as engaged in these activities, or who negotiates or attempts to negotiate a loan secured or to be secured by mortgage or other encumbrance upon real property, or who is engaged in the business of listing real property in a publication; or a person employed by or acting on behalf of any of these persons;

(7) "Real estate transaction" means the sale, exchange, rental, or lease of real property;

(8) "Real property" means a building, structure, real estate, land, tenement, leasehold, interest in real estate cooperatives, condominium, and hereditament, corporeal and incorporeal, or any

interest therein. (1983, c. 522, s. 1; 1989, c. 507, s. 1; 1989 (Reg. Sess., 1990), c. 979, s. 1(1).)

## § 41A-4. Unlawful discriminatory housing practices.

(a) It is an unlawful discriminatory housing practice for any person in a real estate transaction, because of race, color, religion, sex, national origin, handicapping condition, or familial status to:

(1) Refuse to engage in a real estate transaction;

(2) Discriminate against a person in the terms, conditions, or privileges of a real estate transaction or in the furnishing of facilities or services in connection therewith;

(2a) Refuse to permit, at the expense of a handicapped person, reasonable modifications of existing premises occupied or to be occupied by the person if the modifications are necessary to the handicapped person's full enjoyment of the premises; except that, in the case of a rental unit, the landlord may, where it is reasonable to do so, condition permission for modifications on agreement by the renter to restore the interior of the premises to the condition that existed before the modifications, reasonable wear and tear excepted;

(2b) Refuse to make reasonable accommodations in rules, policies, practices, or services, when these accommodations may be necessary to a handicapped person's equal use and enjoyment of a dwelling;

(2c) Fail to design and construct covered multifamily dwellings available for first occupancy after March 13, 1991, so that:

    a. The dwellings have at least one building entrance on an accessible route, unless it is impractical to do so because of terrain or unusual site characteristics; or

    b. With respect to dwellings with a building entrance on an accessible route:

       1. The public and common use portions are readily accessible to and usable by handicapped persons;

       2. There is an accessible route into and through all dwellings and units;

       3. All doors designed to allow passage into, within, and through these dwellings and individual units are wide enough for wheelchairs;

       4. Light switches, electrical switches, electrical outlets, thermostats, and other environmental controls are in accessible locations;

       5. Bathroom walls are reinforced to allow later installation of grab bars; and

       6. Kitchens and bathrooms have space for an individual in a wheelchair to maneuver;

(3) Refuse to receive or fail to transmit a bona fide offer to engage in a real estate transaction;

(4) Refuse to negotiate for a real estate transaction;

(5) Represent to a person that real property is not available for inspection, sale, rental, or lease when in fact it is so available, or fail to bring a property listing to his attention, or refuse to permit him to inspect real property;

(6) Make, print, circulate, post, or mail or cause to be so published a statement, advertisement, or sign, or use a form or application for a real estate transaction, or make a record or inquiry in connection with a prospective real estate transaction, which indicates directly or indirectly, an intent to make a limitation, specification, or discrimination with respect thereto;

(7) Offer, solicit, accept, use, or retain a listing of real property with the understanding that any person may be discriminated against in a real estate transaction or in the furnishing of facilities or services in connection therewith; or

(8) Otherwise make unavailable or deny housing.

(b) Repealed by Session Laws 1989, c. 507, s. 2.

(b1) It is an unlawful discriminatory housing practice for any person or other entity whose business includes engaging in residential real estate related transactions to discriminate against any person in making available such a transaction, or in the terms and conditions of such a transaction, because of race, color, religion, sex, national origin, handicapping condition, or familial status. As used in this subsection, "residential real estate related transaction" means:

(1) The making or purchasing of loans or providing financial assistance (i) for purchasing, constructing, improving, repairing, or maintaining a dwelling, or (ii) where the security is residential real estate; or

(2) The selling, brokering, or appraising of residential real estate. The provisions of this subsection shall not prohibit any financial institution from using a loan application which inquires into a person's financial and dependent obligations or from basing its actions on the income or financial abilities of any person.

(c) It is an unlawful discriminatory housing practice for a person to induce or attempt to induce another to enter into a real estate transaction from which such person may profit:

(1) By representing that a change has occurred, or may or will occur in the composition of the residents of the block, neighborhood, or area in which the real property is located with respect to race, color, religion, sex, national origin,

handicapping condition, or familial status of the owners or occupants; or

(2) By representing that a change has resulted, or may or will result in the lowering of property values, an increase in criminal or antisocial behavior, or a decline in the quality of schools in the block, neighborhood, or area in which the real property is located.

(d) It is an unlawful discriminatory housing practice to deny any person who is otherwise qualified by State law access to or membership or participation in any real estate brokers' organization, multiple listing service, or other service, organization, or facility relating to the business of engaging in real estate transactions, or to discriminate in the terms or conditions of such access, membership, or participation because of race, color, religion, sex, national origin, handicapping condition, or familial status.

(e) It is an unlawful discriminatory housing practice to coerce, intimidate, threaten, or interfere with any person in the exercise or enjoyment of, on account of having exercised or enjoyed, or on account of having aided or encouraged any other person in the exercise or enjoyment of any right granted or protected by this Chapter. (1983, c. 522, s. 1; 1989, c. 507, s. 2; 1989 (Reg. Sess., 1990), c. 979, s. 3.)

## § 41A-5. Proof of violation.

(a) It is a violation of this Chapter if:

(1) A person by his act or failure to act intends to discriminate against a person. A person intends to discriminate if, in committing an unlawful discriminatory housing practice described in G.S. 41A-4 he was motivated in full, or in any part at all, by race, color, religion, sex, national origin, handicapping condition, or familial status. An intent to discriminate may be established by direct or circumstantial evidence; or

(2) A person's act or failure to act has the effect, regardless of intent, of discriminating, as set forth in G.S. 41A-4, against a person of a particular race, color, religion, sex, national origin, handicapping condition, or familial status. However, it is not a violation of this Chapter if a person whose action or inaction has an unintended discriminatory effect, proves that his action or inaction was motivated and justified by business necessity.

(b) It shall be no defense to a violation of this Chapter that the violation was requested, sought, or otherwise procured by another person. (1983, c. 522, s. 1; 1987, c. 603, s. 1; 1989, c. 507, s. 3.)

## § 41A-6. Exemptions.

(a) The provisions of G.S. 41A-4, except for subdivision (a)(6), do not apply to the following:

(1) The rental of a housing accommodation in a building which contains housing accommodations for not more than four families living independently of each other, if the lessor or a member of his family resides in one of the housing accommodations;

(2) The rental of a room or rooms in a private house, not a boarding house, if the lessor or a member of his family resides in the house;

(3) Religious institutions or organizations or charitable or educational organizations operated, supervised, or controlled by religious institutions or organizations which give preference to members of the same religion in a real estate transaction, as long as membership in such religion is not restricted by race, color, sex, national origin, handicapping condition, or familial status;

(4) Private clubs, not in fact open to the public, which incident to their primary purpose or purposes provide lodging, which they own or operate for other than a commercial purpose, to their members or give preference to their members;

(5) With respect to discrimination based on sex, the rental or leasing of housing accommodations in single-sex dormitory property; and

(6) Repealed by Session Laws 1989 (Reg. Sess., 1990), c. 979, s. 4.

(7) The sale, rental, exchange, or lease of commercial real estate. For the purposes of this Chapter, commercial real estate means real property which is not intended for residential use.

(b) No provision of this Chapter requires that a dwelling be made available to a person whose tenancy would constitute a direct threat to the health or safety of other persons or whose tenancy would result in substantial physical damage to the property of others.

(c) No provision of this Chapter limits the applicability of any reasonable local or State restrictions regarding the maximum number of occupants permitted to occupy a dwelling unit.

(d) Nothing in this Chapter shall be deemed to nullify any provisions of the North Carolina Building Code applicable to the construction of residential housing for the handicapped.

(e) No provision of this Chapter regarding familial status applies with respect to housing for older persons. "Housing for older persons" means housing:

(1) Provided under any State or federal program specifically designed and operated to assist elderly persons as defined in the program;

(2) Intended for and solely occupied by person 62 years or older. Housing satisfies the requirements of this subdivision even though there are persons residing in such housing on September 13, 1988, who are under 62 years of age, provided that all

new occupants after September 13, 1988, are 62 years or older; or

(3) Intended for and operated for occupancy by at least one person 55 years of age or older per unit as shown by such factors as (i) the existence of significant facilities and services specifically designed to meet the physical and social needs of older persons or, if this is not practicable, that the housing provides important housing opportunities for older persons, (ii) at least eighty percent (80%) of the units are occupied by at least one person 55 years of age or older per unit; and (iii) the publication of and adherence to policies and procedures which demonstrate an intent by the owner or manager to provide housing for persons 55 years or older. Housing satisfies the requirements of this subdivision even though on September 13, 1988, under eighty percent (80%) of the units in the housing facility are occupied by at least one person 55 years or older per unit, provided that eighty percent (80%) of the units that are occupied by new tenants after September 13, 1988, are occupied by at least one person 55 years or older per unit until such time as eighty percent (80%) of all the units in the housing facility are occupied by at least one person 55 years or older. Housing facilities newly constructed for first occupancy after March 12, 1989, shall satisfy the requirements of this subdivision if (i) when twenty-five percent (25%) of the units are occupied, eighty percent (80%) of the occupied units are occupied by at least one person 55 years or older, and thereafter (ii) eighty percent (80%) of all newly occupied units are occupied by at least one person 55 years or older until such time as eighty percent (80%) of all the units in the housing facility are occupied by at least one person 55 years of age or older.

Housing satisfies the requirements of subdivisions (2) and (3) of this subsection even though there are units occupied by employees of the housing facility who are under the minimum age or family members of the employees residing in the same unit who are under the minimum age, provided the employees perform substantial duties directly related to the management of the housing. (1983, c. 522, s. 1; 1985, c. 371, ss. 1, 2; 1989, c. 507, s. 4, c. 721, s. 1; 1989 (Reg. Sess., 1990), c. 979, s. 4.)

## § 41A-7. Enforcement.

(a) Any person who claims to have been injured by an unlawful discriminatory housing practice or who reasonably believes that he will be irrevocably injured by an unlawful discriminatory housing practice may file a complaint with the North Carolina Human Relations Commission. A fair housing enforcement organization, as defined in

regulations adopted under 42 U.S.C. § 3602 (1968), may file a complaint with the Commission on behalf of a person who claims to have been injured by or reasonably believes he will be irrevocably injured by an unlawful discriminatory housing practice. Complaints shall be in writing, shall state the facts upon which the allegation of an unlawful discriminatory housing practice is based, and shall contain such other information and be in such form as the Commission requires. Commission employees shall assist complainants in reducing complaints to writing and shall assist in setting forth the information in the complaint as may be required by the Commission. Within 10 days after receipt of the complaint, the Director of the Commission shall serve on the respondent a copy of the complaint and a notice advising the respondent of his procedural rights and obligations under this Chapter. Within 10 days after receipt of the complaint, the Director of the Commission shall serve on the complainant a notice acknowledging the filing of the complaint and informing the complainant of his time limits and choice of forums under this Chapter.

No complaint may be filed with the Commission under this section during any period in which the Commission is not certified by the Secretary of the United States Department of Housing and Urban Development in accordance with 42 U.S.C. § 3610(f) to have jurisdiction over the subject matter of the complaint. Provided, however, that during any such period in which the Commission is not certified, any person who claims to have been injured by an unlawful discriminatory practice or who reasonably believes that he will be irrevocably injured by an unlawful discriminatory housing practice may bring a civil action directly in superior court in accordance with the provisions of subsection (j) of this section, except that any such civil action shall be commenced within one year after the occurrence or termination of the alleged unlawful discriminatory housing practice.

(b) A complaint under subsection (a) shall be filed within one year after the alleged unlawful discriminatory housing practice occurred. A respondent may file an answer to the complaint against him within 10 days after receiving a copy of the complaint. With the leave of the Commission, which shall be granted whenever it would be reasonable and fair to do so, the complaint and the answer may be amended at any time. Complaints and answers shall be verified. The Commission shall make final administrative disposition of a complaint within one year of the date the complaint is filed, unless it is impracticable to do so. If the Commission is unable to do so, it shall notify the complainant and respondent, in writing, of the reasons for not doing so.

(c) Whenever another agency of the State or any other unit of government of the State has jurisdiction over the subject matter of any complaint filed under this section, and such agency or unit of government has legal authority equivalent to or greater than the authority under this Chapter to investigate or act upon the complaint, the Commission shall be divested of jurisdiction over such complaint. The Commission shall, within 30 days, notify the agency or unit of government of the apparent unlawful discriminatory housing practice, and request that the complaint be investigated in accordance with such authority.

(d) Complaints may be resolved at any time by informal conference, conciliation, or persuasion. Nothing said or done in the course of such informal procedure may be made public by the Commission or used as evidence in a subsequent proceeding under this Chapter without the written consent of the person concerned.

(e) Within 30 days after the filing of the complaint, the Commission shall commence an investigation of the complaint to ascertain the facts relating to the alleged unlawful discriminatory housing practice. If the complaint is not resolved before the investigation is complete, upon completion of the investigation, the Commission shall determine whether or not there are reasonable grounds to believe that an unlawful discriminatory housing practice has occurred. The Commission shall make a determination within 90 days after the filing of the complaint. If the Commission is unable to complete the investigation and issue a determination within 90 days after the filing of the complaint, the Commission shall notify the complainant and respondent in writing of the reasons for not doing so. If the Commission concludes at any time following the filing of a complaint under this section that prompt judicial action is necessary to carry out the purposes of this Chapter, the Commission may commence a civil action for, and the court may grant, appropriate temporary or preliminary relief pending final disposition of the complaint. Any temporary restraining order or other order granting preliminary or temporary relief shall be issued in accordance with G.S. 1A-1, et seq., Rules of Civil Procedure. The commencement of a civil action under this subsection does not affect the continuation of the Commission's investigation or the initiation of a separate civil action pursuant to other subsections of this section.

(f) If the Commission finds no reasonable ground to believe that an unlawful discriminatory housing practice has occurred or is about to occur it shall dismiss the complaint and issue to the complainant a right-to-sue letter which will enable him to bring a civil action in superior court in accordance with the provisions of subsection (j) of this section.

(g) If the Commission finds reasonable grounds to believe that an unlawful discriminatory housing practice has occurred or is about to occur it shall proceed to try to eliminate or correct the discriminatory housing practice by informal conference, conciliation, or persuasion. Each conciliation agreement arising out of conciliation efforts by the Commission, whether reached before or after the Commission makes a determination of the complaint pursuant to subsection (e), shall be:

(1) An agreement between the respondent and the complainant and shall be subject to the approval of the Commission. The Commission may also be a party to such conciliation agreements; and

(2) Made public unless the complainant and respondent otherwise agree, and the Commission determines that disclosure is not required to further the purposes of this Chapter.

(h) If the Commission is unable to resolve the alleged unlawful discriminatory housing practice it shall notify the parties in writing that conciliation efforts have failed.

(i) A complainant may make a written request to the Commission for a right-to-sue letter:

(1) Within 10 days following the receipt of a notice of conciliation failure; or

(2) After 130 days following the filing of a complaint, if the Commission has not issued a notice of conciliation failure.

Upon receipt of a timely request, the Commission shall issue to the complainant a right-to-sue letter which will enable him to bring a civil action in superior court in accordance with the provisions of subsection (j) of this section.

(j) A civil action brought by a complainant pursuant to subsections (f) or (i) of this section shall be commenced within one year after the right-to-sue letter is issued. The court may grant relief, as it deems appropriate, including any permanent or temporary injunction, temporary restraining order, or other order, and may award to the plaintiff, actual and punitive damages, and may award court costs, and reasonable attorney's fees to the prevailing party. Provided, however, that a prevailing respondent may be awarded court costs and reasonable attorney's fees only upon a showing that the case is frivolous, unreasonable, or without foundation.

(k) After the Commission has issued a notice of conciliation failure pursuant to subsection (h) of this section, if the complainant does not request a right-to-sue letter pursuant to subsection (i) of this section, the complainant, the respondent, or the Commission may elect to have the claims and issues asserted in the reasonable grounds determination decided in a civil action commenced and maintained by the Commission.

(1) An election for a civil action under this subsection shall be made no later than 20 days after an electing complainant or respondent receives the notice of conciliation failure, or if the Commission makes the election, not more than 20 days after the notice of conciliation failure is issued. A complainant or respondent who makes an election for a civil action pursuant to this subsection shall give notice to the Commission. If the Commission makes an election, it shall notify all complainants and respondents of the election.

(2) If an election is made under this subsection, no later than 60 days after the election is made the Commission shall commence a civil action in superior court in its own name on behalf of the complainant. In such an action, the Commission shall be represented by an attorney employed by the Commission, and G.S. 114-2 shall not apply.

In a civil action brought under this subsection, the court may grant relief as it deems appropriate, including any permanent or temporary injunction, temporary restraining order, or other equitable relief and may award to any person aggrieved by an unlawful discriminatory housing practice compensatory and punitive damages. Parties to a civil action brought pursuant to this Chapter shall have the right to a jury trial as provided for by the North Carolina Rules of Civil Procedure.

(l) After the Commission has issued a notice of conciliation failure pursuant to subsection (h) of this section, if the complainant does not request a right-to-sue letter pursuant to subsection (i) of this section, and if an election for a civil action is not made pursuant to subsection (k) of this section, the Commission shall apply to the Director of the Office of Administrative Hearings for the designation of an administrative law judge to preside at a hearing of the case. Upon receipt of the application, the Director of the Office of Administrative Hearings shall, without undue delay, assign an administrative law judge to hear the case.

    (1) All hearings shall be conducted pursuant to the provisions of Article 3A of Chapter 150B of the General Statutes, except that the case in support of the complaint shall be presented at the hearing by the Commission's attorney or agent, and G.S.114-2 shall not apply. The parties to the complaint shall otherwise be given an opportunity to participate in the hearing as provided in G.S. 150B-40(a).

    (2) The administrative law judge assigned to hear a case pursuant to this subsection shall sit in place of the Commission and shall have the authority of a presiding officer in a contested case under Article 3A of Chapter 150B of the General Statutes. The administrative law judge shall make a proposal for decision, which shall contain proposed findings of fact, proposed conclusions of law, and proposed relief, if appropriate. The Commission may make its final decision only after carefully reviewing and considering the administrative law judge's proposal for decision, and after a copy of that proposal for decision is served on the parties and an opportunity is given each party to file exceptions and proposed findings of fact and to present oral and written arguments to the Commission.

    (3) The Commission's final decision may be made by a panel consisting of three Commission members appointed by the chairperson of the Commission. If the Commission, in its final decision, finds that a respondent has violated or is about to violate this Chapter, it may order such relief as may be appropriate, including payment to the complainant by the respondent of compensatory damages and injunctive or other equitable relief. The Commission's order may also assess a civil penalty against the respondent:

        a. In an amount not exceeding ten thousand dollars ($10,000) if the respondent has not been adjudged to have committed any prior unlawful discriminatory housing practices;

        b. In an amount not exceeding twenty-five thousand dollars ($25,000) if the respondent has been adjudged to have committed one other unlawful discriminatory housing practice during the five-year period ending on the date of the filing of the complaint; or

        c. In an amount not exceeding fifty thousand dollars ($50,000) if the respondent has been adjudged to have committed two or more unlawful discriminatory housing practices during the seven-year period ending on the date of the filing of the complaint.

If the acts constituting the unlawful discriminatory housing practice that is the object of the complaint are committed by the same natural person who has been previously adjudged to have committed acts constituting an unlawful discriminatory housing practice, then the civil penalties set forth in sub-subdivisions b and c of this subsection may be imposed without regard to the period of time within which any subsequent discriminatory housing practice occurred.

The clear proceeds of civil penalties assessed pursuant to this subdivision shall be remitted to the Civil Penalty and Forfeiture Fund in accordance with G.S. 115C-457.2.

(m) Any person aggrieved by the final agency decision following a hearing may petition for judicial review in accordance with the provisions of G.S. 150B-43 through G.S. 150B-52. The court in a review proceeding may:

    (1) Affirm, modify, or reverse the Commission's decision in accordance with G.S. 150B-51;

    (2) Remand the case to the Commission for further proceedings;

    (3) Grant to any party such temporary relief, restraining order, or other order as it deems appropriate; or

    (4) Issue an order to enforce the Commission's order to the extent that the order is affirmed or modified.

(n) If, within 30 days after service on the parties of the Commission's decision and order following a hearing, no party has petitioned for judicial review, the Commission or the person entitled to relief may file with the clerk of superior court in the county where the unlawful discriminatory housing practice occurred, or in the county where the real property is located, a certified copy of the Commission's final order. Upon such a filing, the clerk of the court shall enter an order enforcing the Commission's final order. (1983, c. 522, s. 1; 1985, c. 371, ss. 3-5; 1987, c. 603, ss. 2-4; 1989, c. 721, s. 2; 1989 (Reg. Sess., 1990), c. 979, ss. 1(2), 5, 6; 1998-215, s. 1; 2003-136, s. 1.)

### § 41A-8. Investigation; subpoenas.

(a) In conducting an investigation, the Commission shall have access at all reasonable times to premises, records, documents, individuals, and other evidence or possible sources of evidence and may examine, record, and copy such materials and take and record the testimony or statements of such persons as are reasonably necessary for the furtherance of the investigation: Provided, however, that the Commission first complies with the provisions of the Fourth Amendment to the United States Constitution relating to unreasonable searches and seizures.

(b) The Commission may issue subpoenas to compel access to or the production of such materials, or the appearance of such persons, and may issue interrogatories to a respondent, to the same extent and subject to the same limitations as would apply if the subpoenas or interrogatories were issued or served in aid of a civil action in the general court of justice.

(c) Upon written application to the Commission, a respondent shall be entitled to the issuance of a reasonable number of subpoenas subject to the same limitations as subpoenas issued by the Commission. Subpoenas issued at the request of a respondent shall show on their face the name and address of such respondent and shall state that they were issued at his request.

(d) In case of contumacy or refusal to obey a subpoena, the Commission or the respondent may petition for its enforcement in the superior court for the district in which the person to whom the subpoena was addressed resides, was served, or transacts business. (1983, c. 522, s. 1; 1989 (Reg. Sess., 1990), c. 979, s. 1(3).)

### § 41A-9: Repealed by Session Laws 1989, c. 721, s. 3.

### § 41A-10. Venue.

All civil actions shall be commenced in the county where the alleged unlawful discriminatory housing practice occurred, or in the county where the real property is located. (1983, c. 522, s. 1.)

# Housing for Handicapped Persons Statutes

G.S. Chapter 168.
Handicapped Persons.
Article 1.
Rights.

### § 168-1. Purpose and definition.

The State shall encourage and enable handicapped persons to participate fully in the social and economic life of the State and to engage in remunerative employment. The definition of "handicapped persons" shall include those individuals with physical, mental and visual disabilities. For the purposes of this Article the definition of "visually impaired" in G.S. 111-11 shall apply. (1973, c. 493, s. 1; 2000-121, s. 33.)

### § 168-2. Right of access to and use of public places.

Handicapped persons have the same right as the able-bodied to the full and free use of the streets, highways, sidewalks, walkways, public buildings, public facilities, and all other buildings and facilities, both publicly and privately owned, which serve the public. The Department of Health and Human Services shall develop, print, and promote the publication ACCESS NORTH CAROLINA. It shall make copies of the publication available to the Department of Commerce for its use in Welcome Centers and other appropriate Department of Commerce offices. The Department of Commerce shall promote ACCESS NORTH CAROLINA in its publications (including providing a toll-free telephone line and an address for requesting copies of the publication) and provide technical assistance to the Department of Health and Human Services on travel attractions to be included in ACCESS NORTH CAROLINA. The Department of Commerce shall forward all requests for mailing ACCESS NORTH CAROLINA to the Department of Health and Human Services. (1973, c. 493, s. 1; 1991, c. 672, s. 4; c. 726, s. 23; 1991 (Reg. Sess., 1992), c. 959, ss. 84, 85; 1997-443, s. 11A.118(a).)

### § 168-3. Right to use of public conveyances, accommodations, etc.

The handicapped and physically disabled are entitled to accommodations, advantages, facilities, and privileges of all common carriers, airplanes, motor vehicles, railroad trains, motor buses, streetcars, boats, or any other public conveyances or modes of transportation; hotels, lodging places, places of public accommodation, amusement or resort to which the general public is invited, subject only to the conditions and limitations established by law and applicable alike to all persons. (1973, c. 493, s. 1.)

**§§ 168-4 through 168-4.1: Repealed by Session Laws 1985, c. 514, s. 1.**

### § 168-4.2. May be accompanied by service animal.

Every mobility impaired person, as defined in this section, visually impaired person, as broadly defined to include visual disability, or hearing impaired person, as defined in G.S. 8B-1(2), has the right to be accompanied by an assistance dog especially trained for the purpose of providing assistance to a person with the same impairing condition as the person wishing to be accompanied, in any of the places listed in G.S. 168-3, and has the right to keep the assistance dog on any premises the person leases, rents, or uses. The person qualifies for these rights upon the showing of a tag, issued by the Department of Health and Human Services, pursuant to G.S. 168-4.3, stamped "NORTH CAROLINA ASSISTANCE DOG PERMANENT REGISTRATION" and stamped with a registration number, or upon a showing that the dog is being trained or has been trained as an assistance dog. An assistance dog may accompany a person in any of the places listed in G.S. 168-3 but may not occupy a seat in any of these places. The trainer of the assistance dog may be accompanied by the dog during training sessions in any of the places listed in G.S. 168-3.

A mobility impaired person is a person with a physiological deficiency, regardless of its cause, nature, or extent, that renders the individual unable to move about without the aid of crutches, a wheelchair, or other form of support, or that limits the person's functional ability to ambulate, climb, descend, sit, rise, or perform any other related function. (1985, c. 514, s. 1; 1987, c. 401, s. 1; 1995, c. 276, s. 1; 1997-443, s. 11A.118(a).)

### § 168-4.3. Training and registration of service animal.

The Department of Health and Human Services, shall adopt rules for the registration of assistance dogs and shall issue registrations to a visually impaired person, a hearing impaired person, or a mobility impaired person who makes application for registration of a dog that serves as an assistance dog. The rules adopted regarding registration shall require that the dog be trained as an assistance dog by an appropriate agency, and that the certification and registration be permanent for the particular dog and need not be renewed while that particular dog serves the person applying for registration as an assistance dog. No fee may be charged the person for the application, registration, tag, or replacement in the event the original is lost. The Department of Health and Human Services may, by rule, issue a certification or accept the certification issued by the appropriate training facilities. (1985, c. 514, s. 1; 1987, c. 401, s. 2; 1997-443, s. 11A.118(a).)

### § 168-4.4. Responsibility for service animal.

The visually impaired person, hearing impaired person, or mobility impaired person who is accompanied by an assistance dog may not be required to pay any extra compensation for the dog. The person has all the responsibilities and liabilities placed on any person by any applicable law when that person owns or uses any dog, including liability for any damage done by the dog. (1985, c. 514, s. 1.)

### § 168-4.5. Penalty.

It is unlawful to disguise a dog as an assistance dog, or to deprive a visually impaired person, a hearing impaired person, or a mobility impaired person of any rights granted the person pursuant to G.S. 168-4.2 through G.S. 168-4.4, or of any rights or privileges granted the general public with respect to being accompanied by dogs, or to charge any fee for the use of the assistance dog. Violation of this section shall be a Class 3 misdemeanor. (1985, c. 514, s. 1; 1987, c. 401, s. 3; 1993, c. 539, s. 1120; 1994, Ex. Sess., c. 24, s. 14(c).)

### § 168-4.6. Donation of dogs for training.

Dogs impounded by a local dog warden that are not redeemed shall be donated to a nonprofit agency engaged in the training of assistance dogs, upon the agency's request. (1985, c. 514, s.1.)

### § 168-5. Traffic and other rights of persons using certain canes.

The driver of a vehicle approaching a visually impaired pedestrian who is carrying a cane predominantly white or silver in color (with or without a red tip) or using a guide dog shall take all necessary precautions to avoid injury to such pedestrian. (1973, c. 493, s. 1; 2000-121, s. 34.)

### § 168-6. Repealed by Session Laws 1985, c. 571, s. 3.

### §§ 168-7 through 168-7.1: Repealed by Session Laws 1985, c. 514, s. 1.

### § 168-8. Right to habilation and rehabilitation services.

Handicapped persons shall be entitled to such habilation and rehabilitation services as available and needed for the development or restoration of their capabilities to the fullest extent possible. Such services shall include, but not be limited to, education, training, treatment and other services to provide for adequate food, clothing, housing and transportation during the course of education, training and treatment. Handicapped persons shall be entitled to these rights subject only to the conditions and limitations established by law and applicable alike to all persons. (1973, c. 493, s. 1.)

## § 168.9. Right to housing.

Each handicapped citizen shall have the same right as any other citizen to live and reside in residential communities, homes, and group homes, and no person or group of persons, including governmental bodies or political subdivisions of the State, shall be permitted, or have the authority, to prevent any handicapped citizen, on the basis of his or her handicap, from living and residing in residential communities, homes, and group homes on the same basis and conditions as any other citizen. Nothing herein shall be construed to conflict with provisions of Chapter 122C of the General Statutes. (1975, c. 635; 1985, c. 589, s. 61.)

## § 168-10. Eliminate discrimination in treatment of handicapped and disabled.

Each handicapped person shall have the same consideration as any other person for individual accident and health insurance coverage, and no insurer, service corporation, multiple employer welfare arrangement, or health maintenance organization subject to Chapter 58 of the General Statutes solely on the basis of the person's handicap, shall deny such coverage or benefits. The availability of coverage or benefits shall not be denied solely because of the handicap; however, any such insurer may charge the appropriate premiums or fees for the risk insured on the same basis and conditions as insurance issued to other persons, in accordance with actuarial and underwriting principles and other coverage provisions prescribed in Chapter 58 of the General Statutes. No insurer, service corporation, multiple employer welfare arrangement, or health maintenance organization subject to Chapter 58 of the General Statutes shall be prohibited from excluding by waiver or otherwise, any preexisting conditions from coverage as prescribed in G.S. 58-51-15(a)(2)b. (1977, c. 894, ss. 1, 2; 1991, c. 720, s. 80; 1999-219, s. 3.1.)

## § 168-11. Reserved for future codification purposes.

## § 168-12. Reserved for future codification purposes.

## § 168-13. Reserved for future codification purposes.

## Article 2.
## Vocational Rehabilitation.

## § 168-14. Vocational rehabilitation services for deaf persons.

The Department of Health and Human Services shall promote the employment of deaf persons in this State. The Department shall assist deaf persons whose disability limits employment opportunities in obtaining gainful employment commensurate with their abilities and in maintaining such employment. The Department, in furtherance of these objectives, shall maintain statistics regarding trades and occupations in which deaf persons are employed.

The Department shall attempt to employ deaf persons in its vocational rehabilitation services for deaf persons and shall have at least one deaf person so employed. (1975, c. 412, s. 2; 1997-443, s. 11A.118(a).)

## §§ 168-15 through 168-19. Reserved for future codification purposes.

## Article 3.
## Family Care Homes.

## § 168-20. Public policy.

The General Assembly has declared in Article 1 of this Chapter that it is the public policy of this State to provide handicapped persons with the opportunity to live in a normal residential environment. (1981, c. 565, s. 1.)

## § 168-21. Definitions.

As used in this Article:

(1) "Family care home" means a home with support and supervisory personnel that provides room and board, personal care and habilitation services in a family environment for not more than six resident handicapped persons.

(2) "Handicapped person" means a person with a temporary or permanent physical, emotional, or mental disability including but not limited to mental retardation, cerebral palsy, epilepsy, autism, hearing and sight impairments, emotional disturbances and orthopedic impairments but not including mentally ill persons who are dangerous to others as defined in G.S. 122C-3(11)b. (1981, c. 565, s. 1; 1985, c. 589, s. 62; 1995, c. 535, s. 36; 2002-159, s. 24.)

## § 168-22. Family care home; zoning and other purposes.

(a) A family care home shall be deemed a residential use of property for zoning purposes and shall be a permissible use in all residential districts of all political subdivisions. No political subdivision may require that a family care home, its owner, or operator obtain, because of the use, a conditional use permit, special use permit, special exception or variance from any such zoning ordinance or plan; provided, however, that a political subdivision may prohibit a family care home from being located within a one-half mile radius of an existing family care home.

(b) A family care home shall be deemed a residential use of property for the purposes of determining charges or assessments imposed by political subdivisions or businesses for water, sewer, power, telephone service, cable television, garbage and trash collection, repairs or improvements to roads, streets, and sidewalks, and other services, utilities, and improvements. (1981, c. 565, s. 1; 1993 (Reg. Sess., 1994), c. 619, s. 1; 1999-219, s. 3.2.)

### § 168-23. Certain private agreements void.

Any restriction, reservation, condition, exception, or covenant in any subdivision plan, deed, or other instrument of or pertaining to the transfer, sale, lease, or use of property which would permit residential use of property but prohibit the use of such property as a family care home shall, to the extent of such prohibition, be void as against public policy and shall be given no legal or equitable force or effect. (1981, c. 565, s. 1.)

# Other Important Statutes— North Carolina Housing Finance Agency

Housing Finance Agency.
G.S. Chapter 122A.
North Carolina Housing Finance Agency.

### § 122A-1. Short title.

This Chapter shall be known and may be cited as the "North Carolina Housing Finance Agency Act." (1969, c. 1235, s. 1; 1973, c. 1296, s. 1.)

### § 122A-2. Legislative findings and purposes.

The General Assembly hereby finds and declares that as a result of the spread of slum conditions and blight to formerly sound urban and rural neighborhoods and as a result of actions involving highways, public facilities and urban renewal activities there exists in the State of North Carolina a serious shortage of decent, safe and sanitary residential housing available at low prices or rentals to persons and families of lower income. This shortage is severe in certain urban areas of the State, is especially critical in the rural areas, and is inimical to the health, safety, welfare and prosperity of all residents of the State and to the sound growth of North Carolina communities.

The General Assembly hereby finds and declares further that private enterprise and investment have not been able to produce, without assistance, the needed construction of decent, safe and sanitary residential housing at low prices or rentals which persons and families of lower income can afford, or to achieve the urgently needed rehabilitation of much of the present lower income housing. It is imperative that the supply of residential housing for persons and families of lower income affected by the spread of slum conditions and blight and for persons and families of lower income displaced by public actions or natural disaster be increased; and that private enterprise and investment be encouraged to sponsor, build and rehabilitate residential housing for such persons and families, to help prevent the recurrence of slum conditions and blight and assist in their permanent elimination throughout North Carolina.

The General Assembly hereby finds and declares further that the purposes of this Chapter are to provide financing for residential housing construction, new or rehabilitated, for sale or rental to persons and families of lower income.

The General Assembly hereby finds and declares further that in accomplishing this purpose, the North Carolina Housing Finance Agency, a public agency and an instrumentality of the State, is acting in all respects for the benefit of the people of the State in the performance of essential public functions and serves a public purpose in improving and otherwise promoting their health, welfare and prosperity, and that the North Carolina Housing Finance Agency, is empowered to act on behalf of the State of North Carolina and its people in serving this public purpose for the benefit of the general public.

The General Assembly hereby further finds and declares that it shall be the policy of said Agency, whenever feasible, to give first priority in its programs to assisting persons and families of lower income in the purchase and rehabilitation of residential housing, and to undertake its programs in the areas where the greatest housing need exists, and to give priority to projects and individual units which conform to sound principles and practices of comprehensive land use and environmental planning, regional development planning and transportation planning as established by units of local government and regional organizations having jurisdiction over the area within which such projects and units are to be located if such government agencies exist in an area under consideration. However, no area of need shall be penalized because government planning agencies do not exist in such areas.

The General Assembly hereby also further finds and declares that private enterprise and investment have not been able to provide, without assistance, the needed installation of energy saving materials in owner occupied residences of persons and families of lower income. It is imperative for the health, safety and welfare of these persons and the general public that their residences be suitably heated at affordable cost in order to provide decent housing; and that the consumption of nonrenewable sources of energy be reduced. Therefore, the General Assembly finds that one of the purposes of this Chapter is to assist persons and families of lower income to obtain loans for the purpose of heating their homes at affordable cost and at the same time to significantly reduce the amount of consumption of nonrenewable sources of energy. (1969, c. 1235, s. 2; 1973, c. 1296, s. 2; 1977, c. 1083, s. 1.)

### § 122A-3. Definitions.

The following words and terms, unless the context clearly indicates a different meaning, shall have the following respective meanings:

(1) "Bonds" or "notes" mean the bonds or the bond anticipation notes or construction loan notes authorized to be issued by the Agency under this Chapter;

(2) "Agency" means the North Carolina Housing Finance Agency created by this Chapter;

(3) Repealed by Session Laws 1973, c. 1296, s. 5;

(4) Repealed by Session Laws 1973, c. 1296, s. 6;

(5) "Governmental agency" means any department, division, public agency, political subdivision or other public instrumentality of the State, the federal government, any other State or public agency, or any two or more thereof;

(6) Repealed by Session Laws 1973, c. 1296, s. 8;

(7) Repealed by Session Laws 1973, c. 1296, s. 9;

(8) "Mortgage" or "mortgage loan" means a mortgage loan for residential housing, including, without limitation, a mortgage loan to finance, either temporarily or permanently, the construction, rehabilitation, improvement, or acquisition and rehabilitation or improvement of residential housing and a mortgage loan insured or guaranteed by the United States or an instrumentality thereof or for which there is a commitment by the United States or an instrumentality thereof to insure such a mortgage;

(9) Repealed by Session Laws 1973, c. 1296, s. 11;

(10) "Obligations" means any bonds or bond anticipation notes authorized to be issued by the Agency under the provisions of this Chapter;

(11) "Persons and families of lower income" means persons and families deemed by the Agency to require such assistance as is made available by this Chapter on account of insufficient personal or family income, taking into consideration, without limitation, (i) the amount of the total income of such persons and families available for housing needs, (ii) the size of the family, (iii) the cost and condition of housing facilities available, (iv) the eligibility of such persons and families for federal housing assistance of any type predicated upon a lower income basis and (v) the ability of such persons and families to compete successfully in the normal housing market and to pay the amounts at which private enterprise is providing decent, safe and sanitary housing and deemed by the Agency therefore to be eligible to occupy residential housing financed wholly or in part, with mortgages, or with other public or private assistance;

(12) "Residential housing" means a specific work or improvement undertaken primarily to provide dwelling accommodations for persons and families of lower income, including the rehabilitation of buildings and improvements, and such other nonhousing facilities as may be incidental or appurtenant thereto;

(13) "State" means the State of North Carolina;

(14) "Federally insured securities" means an evidence of indebtedness secured by a first mortgage lien on residential housing for persons of lower income and insured or guaranteed as to repayment of principal and interest by the United States or any agency or instrumentality thereof; and

(15) "Mortgage lenders" means any bank or trust company, savings bank, national banking association, savings and loan association, or building and loan association, life insurance company, mortgage banking company, the federal government and any other financial institution authorized to transact business in the State;

(16) "Energy conservation loan" means a loan obtained from a mortgage lender for the purpose of satisfying an existing obligation of a borrower who is the resident owner of a single family dwelling or of "residential housing." The existing obligation of the owner in an "energy conservation loan" must have been incurred to pay for the purchase of materials or the installation of materials, or both, which results in a significant decrease in the amount of consumption of nonrenewable sources of energy in order to provide or maintain a comfortable level of room temperatures in his residence during the winter. "Energy conservation loan" does not include a loan obtained to refinance an existing loan agreement unless payment or collection of the original loan was guaranteed by the agency.

(17) "Rehabilitation" means the renovation or improvement of residential housing by the owner of said residential housing. (1969, c. 1235, s. 3; 1973, c. 1296, ss. 3-6, 8-14, 16, 17; 1975, c. 19, s. 42; 1977, c. 1083, s. 2; 1979, 2nd Sess., c. 1238, s. 1; 1981, c. 344, s. 1; 1983, c. 148, s. 1.)

## § 122A-4. North Carolina Housing Finance Agency.

(a) There is hereby created a body politic and corporate to be known as "North Carolina Housing Finance Agency" which shall be constituted a public agency and an instrumentality of the State for the performance of essential public functions.

(b) The Agency shall be governed by a board of directors composed of 13 members. The directors of the Agency shall be residents of the State and shall not hold other public office.

(c) The General Assembly shall appoint eight directors, four upon the recommendation of the Speaker of the House of Representatives (at least one of whom shall have had experience with a mortgage-servicing institution and one of whom shall be experienced as a licensed real estate broker), and four upon the recommendation of the President Pro Tempore of the Senate (at least one of whom shall be experienced with a savings and loan institution and one of whom shall be experienced in home building). Appointments by the General Assembly shall be made in accordance with G.S. 120-121, and vacancies in those appointments shall be filled in accordance with G.S. 120-122. Notwithstanding any other provision of law, the terms of the four noncategorical appointments by the General Assembly shall expire on June 30, 1983. Subsequent noncategorical appointments shall be for terms of two years each. The terms of the initial categorical appointees by the General Assembly upon the recommendation of the Speaker shall expire on June 30, 1983; the terms of subsequent appointees shall be two years. The term of one of the initial categorical appointees by the General Assembly upon the recommendation of the President of the Senate shall expire on June 30, 1983, and the other on June 30, 1985; the terms of subsequent appointees shall be four years.

(d) The Governor shall appoint four of the directors of the Agency; one of such appointees shall be experienced in community planning, one shall be experienced in subsidized housing management, one shall be experienced as a specialist in public housing policy, and one shall be experienced in the manufactured housing industry. The four appointees of the Governor shall be appointed for staggered four-year terms, two being appointed initially for three years and two for four years, and shall continue in office until their successors are duly appointed and qualified. Any person appointed to fill a vacancy shall serve only for the unexpired term.

(e) Any member of the board of directors shall be eligible for reappointment. The 12 members of the board shall then elect a thirteenth member to the board by simple majority vote. Each member of the board of directors may be removed by the Governor for misfeasance, malfeasance or neglect of duty after reasonable notice and a public hearing, unless the same are in writing expressly waived. Each member of the board of directors before entering upon his duties shall take an oath of office to administer the duties of his office faithfully and impartially, and a record of such oath shall be filed in the office of the Secretary of State.

(f) The Governor shall designate from among the members of the Board a chairman and a vice-chairman. The terms of the chairman and vice-chairman shall extend to the earlier of either two years or the date of expiration of their then current terms as members of the Board of Directors of the Agency. The Agency shall exercise all of its prescribed statutory powers independently of any principal State Department except as described in this Chapter. The Executive Director of the Agency shall be appointed by the Board of Directors, subject to approval by the Governor. All staff and employees of the Agency shall be appointed by the Executive Director, subject to approval by the Board of Directors; shall be eligible for participation in the State Employees' Retirement System; and shall be exempt from the provisions of the State Personnel Act. All employees other than the Executive Director shall be compensated in accordance with the salary schedules adopted pursuant to the State Personnel Act. The salary of the Executive Director shall be fixed by the General Assembly in the Current Operations Appropriations Act. The salary of the Executive Director and all staff and employees of the Agency shall not be subject to any limitations imposed pursuant to any salary schedule adopted pursuant to the terms of the State Personnel Act. The Board of Directors shall, subject to the approval of the Governor, elect and prescribe the duties of any other officers it finds necessary or advisable, and the General Assembly shall fix the compensation of these officers in the Current Operations Appropriations Act. The books and records of the Agency shall be maintained by the Agency and shall be subject to periodic review and audit by the State.

No part of the revenues or assets of the Agency shall inure to the benefit of or be distributable to its members or officers or other private persons. The members of the Agency shall receive no compensation for their services but shall be entitled to receive, from funds of the Agency, for attendance at meetings of the Agency or any committee thereof and for other services for the Agency reimbursement for such actual expenses as may be incurred for travel and subsistence in the performance of official duties and such per diem as is allowed by law for members of other State boards, commissions and committees.

The Executive Director shall administer, manage and direct the affairs and business of the Agency, subject to the policies, control and direction of the members of the Agency Board of Directors. The Secretary of the Agency shall keep a record of the proceedings of the Agency and shall be custodian of all books, documents and papers filed with the Agency, the minute book or journal of the Agency and its official seal. The Secretary may have copies made of all minutes and other records and documents of the Agency and may give certificates under the official seal of the Agency to the effect that such copies are true copies, and all persons dealing with the Agency may rely upon such certificates. Seven members of the Board of Directors of the Agency shall constitute a quorum and the affirmative vote of a majority of the members present at a meeting of the Board of Directors duly called and held shall be necessary for any action taken by the Board of Directors of the Agency, except adjournment; provided, however, that the Board of Directors may appoint an executive committee to act in behalf of said Board during the period between regular meetings of said Board, and said committee shall have full power to act upon the vote of a majority of its members. No vacancy in the membership of the Agency shall impair the rights of a quorum to exercise all the rights and to perform all the duties of the Agency. (1969, c. 1235, s. 4; 1973, c. 476, s. 128; c. 1262, ss. 51, 86; c. 1296, ss. 18-20; 1975, c. 19, s. 43; 1977, c. 673, s. 4; c. 771, s. 4; 1981, c. 895, s. 2; 1981 (Reg. Sess., 1982), c. 1191, s. 32; 1983, c. 148, s. 4; c. 717, ss. 36-37; 1985, c. 479, s. 222; 1987, c. 305, s. 3; 1991 (Reg. Sess., 1992), c. 1039, s. 26; 1995, c. 490, s. 24.)

## § 122A-5. General powers.

The Agency shall have all of the powers necessary or convenient to carry out and effectuate the purposes and provisions of this Chapter, including, but without limiting the generality of the foregoing, the power:

(1) To participate in any federally assisted lease program for housing for persons of lower income under any federal legislation, including, without limitation, section 8 of the National Housing Act; provided, however, that such participation may take place only upon the request and approval of the governing body of the county, city or town in which any such project is to be located;

(2) To make or participate in the making of mortgage loans to sponsors of residential housing; provided, however, that such loans shall be made only upon the determination by the Agency that mortgage loans are not otherwise available wholly or in part from private lenders upon reasonably equivalent terms and conditions;

(3) To purchase or participate in the purchase and enter into commitments by itself or together with others for

    a. The purchase of mortgage loans made by mortgage lenders to sponsors of residential housing or to persons of lower income for residential housing where the Agency has given its approval prior to the initial making of the mortgage loan; provided, however, that any such purchase shall be made only upon the determination by the Agency that mortgage loans were, at the time the approval was given, not otherwise available, wholly or in part, from private lenders upon reasonably equivalent terms and conditions, or

    b. The purchase of mortgage loans made by mortgage lenders without such prior approval to sponsors of housing for persons and families of any income or to persons of any income for housing upon such terms and conditions requiring the proceeds thereof to be used by such mortgage lenders for the making of new mortgage loans to sponsors of residential housing or to persons of lower income for residential housing as the Agency may prescribe by its rules and regulations; provided, however, that (i) any such purchase of existing mortgage loans shall be made only upon the determination by the Agency that such new mortgage loans are not otherwise available from private lenders upon reasonably equivalent terms and conditions, and (ii) the Agency shall purchase mortgage loans made to sponsors of housing for persons and families not of lower income or to persons not of lower income for housing only upon the determination by the Agency that mortgage loans made to sponsors of residential housing or to persons of lower income for residential housing are not available for purchase by the Agency upon reasonable terms and conditions;

(4) Repealed by Session Laws 1973, c. 1296, s. 24;

(4a) To make loans to mortgage lenders on terms and conditions requiring the proceeds thereof to be used by such mortgage lenders to originate new mortgage loans to (i) sponsors of residential housing for persons and families of lower income and persons and families of moderate income and (ii) persons and families of lower income and persons and families of moderate income for residential housing. The loans to mortgage lenders and the loans to be made by such mortgage lenders shall be made on such applicable terms and conditions as are set forth in rules and regulations of the Agency; Provided, however, that loans shall be made by such mortgage lenders only upon the determination by the Agency that such financing is not otherwise available, wholly or in part, from private lenders upon reasonably equivalent terms and conditions;

(5) To collect and pay reasonable fees and charges in connection with making, purchasing and servicing its loans, notes, bonds, commitments and other evidences of indebtedness;

(6) To acquire on a temporary basis real property, or an interest therein, in its own name, by purchase, transfer or foreclosure, where such acquisition is necessary or appropriate to protect any loan in which the Agency has an interest and to sell, transfer and convey any such property to a buyer and, in the event such sale, transfer or conveyance cannot be effected with reasonable promptness or at a reasonable price, to rent or lease such property to a tenant pending such sale, transfer or conveyance;

(7) To sell, at public or private sale, all or any part of any mortgage or other instrument or document securing a loan of any type permitted by this Chapter;

(8) To procure insurance against any loss in connection with its operations in such amounts, and from such insurers, as it may deem necessary or desirable;

(9) To consent, whenever it deems it necessary or desirable in the fulfillment of its corporate purposes, to the modification of the rate of interest, time of payment of any installment of principal or interest, or any other terms, of any mortgage loan, mortgage loan commitment, contract or agreement of any kind to which the Agency is a party;

(10) To borrow money as herein provided to carry out and effectuate its corporate purposes and to issue its obligation as evidence of any such borrowing;

(11) To include in any borrowing such amounts as may be deemed necessary by the Agency to pay financing charges, interest on the obligations for a period not exceeding two years from their date, consultant, advisory and legal fees and such other expenses as are necessary or incident to such borrowing;

(12) To make and publish rules and regulations respecting its lending programs and such other rules and regulations as are necessary to effectuate its corporate purposes;

(13) To provide technical and advisory services to sponsors, builders and developers of residential housing and to residents thereof;

(14) To promote research and development in scientific methods of constructing low-cost residential housing of high durability;

(15) To service or contract for the servicing of mortgage loans and to make and execute agreements, contracts and other instruments necessary or convenient in the exercise of the powers and functions of the Agency under this Chapter, including contracts with any person, firm, corporation, governmental agency or other entity, and each and any North Carolina governmental agency is hereby authorized to enter into contracts and otherwise cooperate with the Agency to facilitate the purposes of this Chapter;

(16) To receive, administer and comply with the conditions and requirements respecting any appropriation or any gift, grant or donation of any property or money, including the proceeds of general obligation bonds of the State;

(17) To sue and be sued in its own name, plead and be impleaded;

(18) To establish and maintain an office for the transaction of its business in the City of Raleigh and at such place or places as the board of directors deems advisable or necessary in carrying out the purposes of this Chapter; provided,

however, that the Agency shall comply with the provisions of Articles 6 and 7 of Chapter 146 of the General Statutes governing the acquisition of office space;

(19) To adopt an official seal and alter the same at pleasure;

(20) To adopt bylaws for the regulation of its affairs and the conduct of its business and to prescribe rules, regulations and policies in connection with the performance of its functions and duties;

(21) To employ fiscal consultants, engineers, attorneys, real estate counselors, appraisers and such other consultants and employees as may be required in the judgment of the Agency and to fix and pay their compensation from funds available to the Agency therefor;

(22) To purchase or to participate in the purchase and enter into commitments by itself or together with others for the purchase of federally insured securities; provided, however, that the Agency shall first determine that the proceeds of such securities will be utilized for the purpose of making new mortgage loans to sponsors of residential housing or to persons of lower income for residential housing, all as specified in regulations to be adopted by the Agency;

(23) To provide, or contract for the providing of, management and counseling services whenever, in the judgment of the Agency, no other satisfactory low-income housing counseling service is available for occupants of rental projects for persons of lower income or for prospective homeowners of lower income; provided, however, that no such program shall be undertaken until the Agency shall have made a study of its feasibility and shall have determined that the undertaking of such program will not adversely affect other programs of the Agency;

(24) To advise the Governor regarding the coordination of public and private low- and moderate-income housing programs; and

(25) To participate in and administer federal housing programs, including housing rehabilitation, construction of new housing, assistance to the homeless, and home ownership assistance. (1969, c.1235, s. 5; 1973, c. 1296, ss. 21-24, 27, 29, 35, 36, 40-43; 1975, c. 616, ss. 1, 2; 1981, c. 895, s. 3; 1983, c. 148, s. 2; 1993, c. 321, s. 305(b).)

## § 122A-5.1. Rules and regulations governing Agency activity.

(a) The Agency shall from time to time adopt, modify or repeal rules and regulations governing the purchase of federally insured securities by the Agency and the purchase and sale of mortgage loans and the application of the proceeds thereof, including rules and regulations as to any or all of the following:

(1) Procedures for the submission of requests or the invitation of proposals for the purchase and sale of mortgage loans or for the purchase of federally insured securities;

(2) Limitations or restrictions as to the number of family units, location or other qualifications or characteristics of residences to be financed by mortgage loans and requirements as to the income limits of persons and families of lower income occupying such residences;

(3) Restrictions as to the interest rates on mortgage loans or the return which may be realized by mortgage lenders on any mortgage loans or on the sale of federally insured securities to the Agency;

(4) Requirements as to commitments by mortgage lenders with respect to the use of the proceeds of sale of any federally insured securities;

(5) Schedules of any fees and charges necessary to provide for expenses and reserves of the Agency; and

(6) Any other matters related to the duties and the exercise of the powers of the Agency to purchase and sell mortgage loans, or to purchase federally insured securities.

Such rules and regulations shall be designed to effectuate the general purposes of this Chapter and the following specific objectives: (i) the construction of decent, safe and sanitary residential housing at low prices or rentals which persons and families of lower income can afford; (ii) the rehabilitation of present lower-income housing; (iii) increasing the supply of residential housing for persons and families of lower income affected by the spread of slum conditions and blight and for persons and families of lower income displaced by public action or natural disaster; (iv) the encouraging of private enterprise and investment to sponsor, build and rehabilitate residential housing for such persons and families to prevent the recurrence of slum conditions and blight and assist in their permanent elimination throughout the State; and (v) the restriction of the financial return and benefit to that necessary to protect against the realization by mortgage lenders of an excessive financial return or benefit as determined by prevailing market conditions.

(b) The interest rate or rates and other terms of federally insured securities or mortgage loans purchased from the proceeds of any issue of bonds of the Agency shall be at least sufficient to assure the payment of said bonds and the interest thereon as the same become due from the amounts received by the Agency in repayment of such federally insured securities or such loans and interest thereon.

(c) The Agency shall require as a condition of the purchase of federally insured securities from a mortgage lender and the purchase or the making of a commitment

to purchase mortgage loans from a mortgage lender where the Agency has not given its approval prior to the initial making of the mortgage loan that such mortgage lender shall on or prior to the one-hundred-eightieth day (or such earlier day as may be prescribed by rules and regulations of the Agency) following the receipt of the sale proceeds have entered into written commitments to make, and shall thereafter proceed as promptly as practicable to make from such sale proceeds, new mortgage loans with respect to residential housing in the State having a stated maturity of not less than 20 years from the date thereof in an aggregate principal amount equal to the amount of such sale proceeds. The Agency shall not purchase nor make commitment to purchase mortgage loans, federally insured securities or other obligations from a mortgage lender from which it has previously purchased federally insured securities or mortgage loans initially made without such prior approval unless said mortgage lender has either made or entered into written commitments to make such new mortgage loans. (1973, c. 1296, s. 44; 1975, c. 616, s. 3.)

## § 122A-5.2. Mortgage insurance authority.

(a) The Agency may upon application of a proposed mortgagee insure and make advance commitments to insure payments required by a loan for residential housing for persons of lower income upon such terms and conditions as the Agency may prescribe. Mortgage loans insured by the Agency under this Chapter may provide financing for related ancillary facilities to the extent permitted by applicable Agency regulations. Mortgage loans insured by the Agency under this Chapter shall be secured by a first mortgage.

The aggregate principal amount of all mortgages so insured by the Agency under this Chapter and outstanding at any one time shall not exceed 10 times the average annual balance for the preceding calendar year of funds on deposit in the housing mortgage insurance fund, the creation of which is hereby authorized. The aggregate amount of principal obligations of all mortgages so insured shall not be deemed to constitute a debt, liability or obligation of the State or of any political subdivision thereof or a pledge of the faith and credit of the State or of any such political subdivision, but shall be payable solely from moneys on deposit to the credit of the housing mortgage insurance fund. Any contract of insurance executed by the Agency under this section shall be conclusive evidence of eligibility for such mortgage insurance and the validity of any contract of insurance so executed or of an advance commitment to issue such shall be incontestable in the hands of a mortgagee from the date of execution of such contract or commitment, except for fraud or misrepresentation on the part of such mortgagee and, as to commitments to insure, noncompliance with the terms of the advance commitment or Agency regulations in force at the time of issuance of the advance commitment.

(b) For mortgage payments to be eligible for insurance under the provisions of this Chapter, the underlying mortgage loan shall:

(1) Be one which is made and held by a mortgagee approved by the Agency as responsible and able to service the mortgage properly;

(2) Not exceed (i) ninety percent (90%) of the estimated cost of the proposed housing if owned or to be owned by a profit-making sponsor or (ii) one hundred percent (100%) of the estimated cost of such proposed housing if owned or to be owned by a nonprofit housing sponsor or, if owned by a person or family of lower income, in the case of a single family dwelling or condominium;

(3) Have a maturity satisfactory to the Agency but in no case longer than eighty percent (80%) of the Corporation's [Agency's] estimate of the remaining useful life of said housing or 40 years from the date of the issuance of insurance, whichever is earlier;

(4) Contain amortization provisions satisfactory to the Agency requiring periodic payments by the mortgagor not in excess of his ability to pay as determined by the Agency;

(5) Be in such form and contain such terms and provisions with respect to maturity, property insurance, repairs, alterations, payment of taxes and assessments, default reserves, delinquency charges, default remedies, anticipation of maturity, additional and secondary liens, equitable and legal redemption rights, prepayment privileges and other matters as the Agency may prescribe.

(c) All applications for mortgage insurance shall be forwarded, together with an application fee prescribed by the Agency, to the executive director of the Agency. The Agency shall cause an investigation of the proposed housing to be made, review the application and the report of the investigation, and approve or deny the application. No application shall be approved unless the Agency finds that it is consistent with the purposes of this Chapter and further finds that the financing plan for the proposed housing is sound. The Agency shall notify the applicant and the proposed lender of its decision. Any such approval shall be conditioned upon payment to the Agency, within such reasonable time and after notification of approval as may be specified by the Agency, of the commitment fee prescribed by the Agency.

(d) The Agency shall fix mortgage insurance premiums for the insurance of mortgage payments under the provision of this Chapter. Such premiums shall be computed as a percentage of the principal of the mortgage outstanding at the beginning of each mortgage year, but shall not be more than one half of one percent (1/2 of 1%) per year of such principal amount. The amount of premium need not be uniform for all insured loans. Such premiums shall be payable by mortgagors or mortgagees in such manner as prescribed by the Agency.

(e) In the event of default by the mortgagor, the mortgagee shall notify the Agency both of the default and the mortgagee's proposed course of action. When it appears feasible, the Agency may for a temporary period upon default or threatened default by the mortgagor authorize mortgage payments to be made by the Agency to the mortgagee which payments shall be repaid under such conditions as the Agency may prescribe. The Agency may also agree to revised terms of financing when such appear prudent. The mortgagee shall be entitled to receive the benefits of the insurance provided herein upon:

(1) Any sale of the mortgaged property by court order in foreclosure or a sale with the consent of the Agency by the mortgagor or a subsequent owner of the property or by the mortgagee after foreclosure or acquisition by deed in lieu of foreclosure, provided all claims of the mortgagee against the mortgagor or others arising from the mortgage, foreclosure, or any deficiency judgment shall be assigned to the Agency without recourse except such claims as may have been released with the consent of the Agency; or

(2) The expiration of six months after the mortgagee has taken title to the mortgaged property under judgment of strict foreclosure, foreclosure by sale or other judicial sale, or under a deed in lieu of foreclosure if during such period the mortgagee has made a bona fide attempt to sell the property, and thereafter conveys the property to the Agency with an assignment, without recourse, to the Agency of all claims of the mortgagee against the mortgagor or others arising out of the mortgage foreclosure, or deficiency judgment; or

(3) The acceptance by the Agency of title to the property or an assignment of the mortgage, without recourse to the Agency, in the event the Agency determines it imprudent to proceed under (1) or (2) above.

Upon the occurrence of either (1), (2) or (3) hereof, the obligation of the mortgagee to pay premium charges for insurance shall cease, and the Agency shall, within 30 days thereafter, pay to the mortgagee ninety-eight percent (98%) of the sum of (i) the then unpaid principal balance of the insured indebtedness, (ii) the unpaid interest to the date of conveyance or assignment to the Agency, as the case may be, (iii) the amount of all payments made by the mortgagee for which it has not been reimbursed for taxes, insurance, assessments and mortgage insurance premiums, and (iv) such other necessary fees, costs or expenses of the mortgagee as may be approved by the Agency.

(f) Upon request of the mortgagee, the Agency may at any time, under such terms and conditions as it may prescribe, consent to the release of the mortgagor from his liability or consent to the release of parts of the property from the lien of the mortgage, or approve a substitute mortgagor or sale of the property or part thereof.

(g) No claim for the benefit of the insurance provided in this Chapter shall be accepted by the Agency except within one year after any sale or acquisition of title of the mortgaged premises described in subdivisions (1) or (2) of subsection (e) of this section.

(h) There shall be paid into the housing mortgage insurance fund (i) all premiums received by the Agency for the granting of such mortgage insurance, (ii) any moneys or other assets received by the Agency as a result of default or delinquency on mortgage loans insured by the Agency, including any proceeds from the sale or lease of real property, (iii) any moneys appropriated and made available by the State for the purpose of such fund. (1973, c. 1296, s. 45.)

### § 122A-5.3. Energy conservation loan authority.

(a) The Agency may guarantee the payment or collection of energy conservation loans pursuant to and in accordance with the provisions of this Chapter when the Agency has given its approval prior to the initial making of the loan; provided that any such guarantee shall be made only upon determination by the Agency that energy conservation loans were at the time of approval not otherwise available from private lenders upon reasonably equivalent terms and conditions; and provided further, no single guarantee of payment or collection shall exceed the sum of twelve hundred dollars ($1200) and no person or family of lower income shall be entitled to more than one loan guarantee.

(b) At no time may the Agency have outstanding loan guarantees in which the liability of the Agency exceeds 15 times any amounts remaining unspent from the specific funds appropriated by the General Assembly for the energy conservation loan guarantee program plus any specific grants or donations for this purpose; but the Agency is authorized to expend any unspent amounts from these sources to satisfy its liabilities under the loan guarantee program; provided no other assets of the Agency shall be obligated or expended in satisfaction of its energy conservation loan guarantee liability.

(c) The Agency shall from time to time adopt, modify, or repeal rules and regulations governing the guaranteeing of energy conservation loans including rules and regulations as to any or all of the following:

(1) Procedures for the submission and approval of requests to guarantee energy conservation loans including advance commitments by the Agency to guarantee loans;

(2) Limitations and restrictions on the number of family units, location or other qualifications or characteristics of residences in regard to which energy conservation work is performed to qualify for a loan guarantee;

(3) Restrictions as to interest rates on energy conservation loans or the return which may be realized by mortgage lenders on energy conservation loans guaranteed by the Agency;

(4) Schedules of any fees and charges necessary to provide for the administrative expenses of the Agency allocable to the administration of the energy conservation loan guarantee program;

(5) Procedures regarding the servicing of energy conservation loan guarantees including procedures for honoring defaults and procedures to be implemented to enforce the obligations of the borrowers to repay guaranteed energy conservation loans;

(6) Any other matters related to the duties and the exercise of the power of the Agency with respect to the energy conservation loan guarantee program deemed necessary to effectuate the purposes of this act. (1977, c. 1083, s. 3.)

### § 122A-5.4. Housing for persons and families of moderate income.

(a) The General Assembly hereby finds and determines that there is a serious shortage of decent, safe and sanitary housing which persons and families of moderate income in the State can afford; that it is in the best interests of the State to encourage home ownership by persons and families of moderate income; that the assistance provided by this section will enable persons and families of moderate income to acquire existing decent, safe and sanitary housing without undue financial hardship and will encourage private enterprise to sponsor, build and rehabilitate additional housing for such persons and families; and that the Agency in providing such assistance is promoting the health, welfare and prosperity of all citizens of the State and is serving a public purpose for the benefit of the general public.

(b) The terms "persons and families of lower income" and "persons of lower income" wherever they appear in this Chapter, except where they appear in G.S. 122A-2 and 122A-3(11), shall be deemed to include "persons and families of moderate income" as defined in clause (c) of this section.

(c) "Persons and families of moderate income" means persons and families deemed by the Agency to require the assistance made available by this Chapter on account of insufficient personal or family income taking into consideration, without limitation, (i) the amount of the total income of such persons and families available for housing needs, (ii) the size of the family, (iii) the cost and condition of housing facilities available and (iv) the eligibility of such persons and families for federal housing assistance of any type predicated upon a moderate or low and moderate income basis. (1979, c. 810.)

## § 122A-5.5. Rehabilitation Loan Authority.

(a) In order to effectuate the authority of the Agency to participate in commitments to purchase and to purchase mortgage loans for the rehabilitation of existing residential housing the Agency is hereby empowered to adopt, modify or repeal rules and regulations governing the making or participation in the making of mortgage loans and the purchase or participation in commitments for the purchase of mortgage loans for the rehabilitation of existing residential housing.

(b) The rules and regulations of the Agency adopted pursuant to this section shall provide at a minimum that:

(1) Rehabilitation mortgage loans shall be for the purpose of owner-financed improvements to or renovation of residential housing;

(2) Requirements for eligibility for rehabilitation mortgage loans shall be consistent with all applicable federal laws and regulations governing bonds for rehabilitation mortgage loans in order to insure that such bonds are exempt from taxation. (1981, c. 344, s. 2.)

## § 122A-5.6. Terms and conditions of loans to and by mortgage lenders.

(a) The Agency shall from time to time adopt, modify, amend or repeal rules and regulations governing the making of loans to mortgage lenders and the application of the proceeds thereof. These rules and regulations shall be designed to effectuate the general purposes of this Chapter and the following specific objectives: (i) the construction and rehabilitation of decent, safe and sanitary residential housing available to persons and families of lower income and persons and families of moderate income at prices or rentals that they can afford; (ii) the encouragement of private enterprise and investment to sponsor, build and rehabilitate residential housing for persons and families of lower income and persons and families of moderate income; and (iii) the restriction of the financial return and benefit to the mortgage lenders from such loans to an amount that is necessary to induce their participation and that is not excessive as determined by prevailing market conditions.

(b) Notwithstanding any other provision of this section, the interest rate or rates and other terms of the loans to mortgage lenders made from the proceeds of any issue of bonds of the Agency shall provide that the amounts received by the Agency in repayment of the loans and interest thereon shall be at least sufficient to assure the payment of the principal of and the interest on the bonds as they become due.

(c) The Agency shall enter into a written agreement with each mortgage lender that shall require as a condition of each loan to such mortgage lender that the mortgage lender shall originate new mortgage loans within a reasonable period of time as determined by the Agency's rules and regulations and that such new mortgage loans shall have such stated maturities as determined by the Agency's rules and regulations.

(d) The loans to mortgage lenders shall be general obligations of the respective mortgage lenders owing them. The Agency shall require that such loans shall be additionally secured as to payment of both principal and interest by a pledge and lien upon collateral security. The collateral security itself shall be in such amount as the Agency determines will assure the payment of the principal of and the interest on the bonds as they become due. Collateral security shall be deemed to be sufficient if the principal of and the interest on the collateral security, when due, will be sufficient to pay the principal of and the interest on the bonds. The collateral security shall consist of any of the following items: (i) direct obligations of, or obligations guaranteed by, the State or the United States of America; (ii) bonds, debentures, notes or other evidences of indebtedness, satisfactory to the Agency, issued by any of the following federal agencies: Bank for Cooperatives, Federal Intermediate Credit Bank, Federal Home Loan Bank System, Export-Import Bank of Washington, Federal Land Banks, Fannie Mae or the Government National Mortgage Association; (iii) direct obligations of or obligations guaranteed by the State; (iv) mortgages insured or guaranteed by the United States of America or an instrumentality of it as to payment of principal and interest; (v) any other mortgages secured by real estate on which there is located a residential structure, the collateral value of which shall be determined by the regulations issued from time to time by the Agency; (vi) obligations of Federal Home Loan Banks; (vii) certificates of deposit of banks or trust companies, including the trustee, organized under the laws of the United States or any state, which have a combined capital and surplus of at least fifteen million dollars ($15,000,000); (viii) Bankers Acceptances; and (ix) commercial paper that has been classified for rating purposes by Dun & Bradstreet, Inc., as Prime-1 or by Standard & Poor's Corp. as A-1.

(e) The Agency may require as a condition of any loan to a mortgage lender such representations and warranties that it determines to be necessary to secure such loans and to carry out the purposes of this section. (1983, c. 148, s. 3; 2001-487, s. 14(i).)

## § 122A-5.7. Homeownership Assistance Fund authorized; authority.

The North Carolina Housing Finance Agency is authorized to establish a Homeownership Assistance Fund (hereinafter referred to as "the Fund") to assist families of low and moderate income in the purchase of affordable residential housing. To achieve this purpose, the Agency may use the Fund to provide additional security for eligible loans, to subsidize down payments, principal payments and interest payments, and to provide any type of mortgage assistance the Agency deems necessary. The Fund shall operate as a revolving fund. The Agency shall adopt rules for the operation and use of the Fund. These funds shall be used for people who otherwise would be unable to receive subsidized loans from the Housing Finance Agency. (1983, c. 923, s. 203.)

## § 122A-5.8. Distressed multi-family residential rental housing provisions.

(a) The General Assembly hereby finds and determines that a serious shortage of decent, safe and sanitary multi-family residential rental housing which persons and families of low and moderate income in the State can afford continues to exist; that it is in the best interests of the State to continue to promote and maintain the viability of such housing and to encourage private enterprise to sponsor, build and rehabilitate additional multi-family residential rental housing for such low and moderate income persons and families; that certain multi-family residential rental housing projects financed by the Agency are currently experiencing financial difficulties due to low occupancy levels; that measures to facilitate higher occupancy levels by extending occupancy on a temporary basis to those with incomes in excess of required low and moderate levels will help to maintain certain multi-family residential rental housing for persons and families of low and moderate income to prevent foreclosure and the use of such facilities without regard to income limitations; and that the Agency in providing such temporary assistance is promoting the health, welfare and property of all citizens of the State and is serving a public purpose for the benefit of the general public.

(b) "Distressed rental housing project" means any multi-family residential rental housing project heretofore or hereafter financed by the Agency that, as determined by resolution of the Board of Directors of the Agency, has an occupancy level below that required for sustaining operation and as a result thereof needs to increase its occupancy levels in order to avoid foreclosure and the subsequent use of such facilities without regard to the Agency's income limitations. In determining the foregoing, the Board of Directors of the Agency shall take into consideration (1) occupancy rates of the project, (2) market conditions affecting the project, (3) costs of operation of the project, (4) debt service for the project, (5) management of the project and such other factors as the Board of Directors may deem relevant.

(c) The Board of Directors of the Agency may determine, by resolution, to permit not in excess of ten percent (10%) of the rental units in any distressed rental housing project to be rented to persons or families without regard to income until the project's occupancy levels, in the judgment of the Agency, will sustain operations at a level sufficient to prevent delinquency or default.

(d) The Board of Directors may also determine, by resolution, to permit additional rental units at any such distressed rental housing project, to be rented to persons or families without regard to income, subject to the restriction contained in subsection (c) of this section, provided that: (1) the units therein that have been available for rental without regard to income have been available for a period of time not less than three months, (2) the Agency has determined that permitting additional units, in excess of ten percent (10%), to be rented without regard to income is necessary in order for such distressed rental housing project to avoid foreclosure, and (3) the total number of housing units at any distressed rental housing project rented without regard to income shall not exceed fifteen percent (15%) of the total number of units therein.

(e) Once a distressed rental housing project attains sustaining occupancy at a level satisfactory to the Agency, the Agency will thereafter require the owners of such distressed rental housing project to rent only to persons and families of low and moderate income and will require that any units that were leased without regard to income limitations pursuant to the provisions of this section will next be leased, when such units become vacant, only to persons and families whose incomes fall within the then current Agency income limitations. (1987, c. 305, s. 1; 1989, c. 454, ss. 1-3; 1989, c. 454, s. 3.)

## § 122A-5.9. Formation of subsidiary corporations to own and operate housing projects.

(a) The Agency may acquire, by purchase or otherwise, construct, acquire, develop, own, repair, maintain, improve, rehabilitate, renovate, furnish, equip, operate, and manage residential rental housing projects to rent to persons and families of lower and moderate income.

(b) The Agency may form a nonprofit corporation or corporations under the laws of this State which may acquire, construct, develop, repair, improve, rehabilitate, renovate, furnish, equip, operate and manage residential rental housing projects for persons and families of lower and moderate income. All of the stock of a nonprofit corporation formed by the Agency shall be owned by the Agency and its Board of Directors shall be elected or appointed by the Agency.

(c) No statutory provisions with respect to the acquisition, operation or disposition of property by other public bodies shall be applicable to the Agency or to any nonprofit corporation formed pursuant to this section. (1987, c. 305, s. 2.)

## § 122A-5.10. Housing Coordination and Policy Council; creation; duties.

(a) There is created the Housing Coordination and Policy Council in the Office of the Governor. The Housing Coordination and Policy Council shall have the following functions and duties:

(1) To advise the Governor regarding the coordination of various public and private low- and moderate-income housing programs;

(2) To advise the Governor in the preparation of an overall, comprehensive State housing plan with specific recommendations to address identified areas of need, which report shall be presented to the General Assembly;

(3) To advise the Governor with respect to the best use of housing resources; and

(4) To advise the Governor regarding any other matter relating to housing the Governor may refer to it.

(b) Nothing herein shall abrogate the existing statutory responsibility of any other agency to develop housing plans and policies relating to specific housing programs. (1993, c. 321, s. 305(d).)

## § 122A-5.11. Council membership; compensation; procedures.

(a) The Housing Coordination and Policy Council shall consist of 15 representatives, as follows:

(1) One member of the N.C. Housing Partnership who is experienced with housing programs for low-income persons, as designated by the chair.

(2) One member of the Community Development Council who is experienced with federal, State, and local housing programs, as designated by the chair.

(3) One member of the N.C. Housing Finance Agency Board of Directors who is experienced with real estate finance and development, as designated by the chair.

(4) One member of the Weatherization Policy Advisory Council who is experienced with community weatherization programs, as designated by the chair.

(5) One member of the Governor's Advocacy Council for Persons with Disabilities who is familiar with the housing needs of the disabled.

(6) The executive director of the Commission of Indian Affairs, or a designee familiar with Indian housing programs.

(7) The Assistant Secretary of Community Development and Housing, or a designee familiar with housing programs related to community development and housing functions.

(8) The director of the Division of Aging, or a designee familiar with the housing programs of the Division.

(9) The executive director of the N.C. Housing Finance Agency, or a designee familiar with the housing programs of the Agency.

(10) The director of the Division of Mental Health, or a designee familiar with housing for those with mental disabilities.

(11) The executive director of the N.C. Human Relations Commission, or a designee familiar with federal and State fair housing laws.

(12) The head of the AIDS Care Branch, or a designee familiar with the housing programs of the Division of Adult Health Promotion.

(13) The director of the Office of Economic Opportunity, or a designee familiar with programs for the homeless.

(14) Two members of nonprofit organizations who are experienced with housing advocacy for low-income persons and State and federal housing programs.

(b) All members except those serving ex officio shall be appointed by the Governor. The Governor shall designate one member of the Council to serve as Chair.

(c) The initial members of the Council other than those serving ex officio shall be appointed to serve for terms of four years and until their successors are appointed and qualified. Any appointment to fill a vacancy created by resignation, dismissal, death, or disability of a member shall be for the balance of the term.

(d) Members of the Council may receive per diem and necessary travel and subsistence expenses in accordance with the provisions of G.S. 138-5.

(e) A majority of the Council shall constitute a quorum for the transaction of business.

(f) All clerical and other services required by the Council shall be supplied by the Housing Finance Agency. (1993, c. 321, s. 305(d); 1995, c. 263, s. 1.)

## § 122A-5.12. Council meetings; report.

(a) The Housing Coordination and Policy Council shall meet at least quarterly and may hold special meetings at any time and place within the State at the call of the Chair or upon written request of a majority of the members.

(b) The Council shall assist in the preparation and filing of an annual written report which contains a review of work completed, a review of ongoing activities, and housing policy recommendations. This report shall be filed with the General Assembly and the Governor by May 1. (1993, c. 321, s. 305(d).)

## § 122A-5.13. Adult Care Home, Group Home, and Nursing Home Fire Protection Fund authorized; authority.

(a) The North Carolina Housing Finance Agency shall establish an Adult Care Home, Group Home, and Nursing Home Fire Protection Fund (hereinafter "Fire Protection Fund") to assist owners of adult care homes, group homes for developmentally disabled adults, and nursing homes with the purchase and installation of fire protection systems and emergency generators in existing and new adult care homes, group homes for developmentally disabled adults, and nursing homes. The Fire Protection Fund shall be a revolving fund.

(b) The Agency, in consultation with the Department of Health and Human Services, shall adopt rules for the management and use of the Fire Protection Fund. These rules at a minimum shall provide for the following:

(1) Financial incentives for owners of facilities who utilize Fire Protection Fund monies to install sprinkler systems instead of smoke detection equipment.

(2) Maximum loan amounts of one dollar and seventy-five cents ($1.75) per square foot for advanced smoke detectors and digital communication equipment, three dollars and seventy-five cents ($3.75) per square foot for residential sprinkler systems, and six dollars ($6.00) per square foot for institutional sprinkler systems.

(3) Interest rates from three percent (3%) to six percent (6%) for a period not to exceed 20 years for sprinkler systems and 10 years for smoke detection systems.

(4) Documentary verification that owners of facilities obtain fire protection systems and emergency generators at a reasonable cost.

(5) Acceleration of a loan when statutory fire protection requirements are not met by the facility for which the loan was made.

(6) Loan approval priority criteria that considers the frailty level of residents at a facility.

(7) Loan origination and servicing fees.

(c) Proceeds from the Fire Protection Fund, not to exceed ten thousand dollars ($10,000) annually, may be used to provide staff support to the North Carolina Housing Finance Agency for loan processing under this section and to the Department of Health and Human Services for review and approval of fire protection plans and inspection of fire protection systems. (1996, 2nd Ex. Sess., c. 18, s. 24.26B(a); 1997-443, s. 11A.118(a); 1999-237, s. 11.17; 2000-67, s. 11.10.)

### § 122A-6. Credit of State not pledged.

Obligations issued under the provisions of this Chapter shall not be deemed to constitute a debt, liability or obligation of the State or of any political subdivision thereof or a pledge of the faith and credit of the State or of any such political subdivision, but shall be payable solely from the revenues or assets of the Agency. Each obligation issued under this Chapter shall contain on the face thereof a statement to the effect that the Agency shall not be obligated to pay the same nor the interest thereon except from the revenues or assets pledged therefor and that neither the faith and credit nor the taxing power of the State or of any political subdivision thereof is pledged

to the payment of the principal of or the interest on such obligation.

Expenses incurred by the Agency in carrying out the provisions of this Chapter may be made payable from funds provided pursuant to this Chapter and no liability shall be incurred by the Agency hereunder beyond the extent to which moneys shall have been so provided. Provided the provisions of this section do not apply to the liability of the Agency with respect to energy conservation loan guarantees. (1969, c. 1235, s. 6; 1973, c. 1296, s. 46; 1977, c. 1083, s. 4.)

### § 122A-6.1. Credit of State not pledged to satisfy liabilities under energy conservation loan guarantees.

Energy conservation loan guarantees issued under the provisions of this Chapter shall not be deemed to constitute a debt, liability, obligation of the State or of any political subdivision thereof, or a pledge of the faith and credit of the State or of any political subdivision thereof, but shall be payable solely from any unspent specific appropriations by the General Assembly for the energy conservation loan guarantee program and any donations and grants for this specific purpose. Each guarantee issued by the Agency shall contain on its face a statement to the effect that the Agency shall not be obligated to pay the same nor the interest thereon except from the unspent specific appropriations by the General Assembly for the energy conservation loan guarantee program and any specific donations and grants for this purpose, and that neither the faith and credit nor the taxing power of the State or of any political subdivision thereof is pledged to the payment of the principal of or the interest on such guarantees.

Provided any recoveries from the borrower or others which ultimately reduce the amounts paid out by the Agency in satisfaction of its liabilities under the energy conservation loan guarantee program shall be deemed unspent appropriations, donations or grants. (1977, c. 1083, s. 5.)

### § 122A-7. Repealed by Session Laws 1973, c. 1296, s. 47.

### § 122A-8. Bonds and notes.

The Agency is hereby authorized to provide for the issuance, at one time or from time to time, of bonds and notes of the Agency to carry out and effectuate its corporate purposes. The Agency also is hereby authorized to provide for the issuance, at one time or from time to time of (i) bond anticipation notes in anticipation of the issuance of such bonds and (ii) construction loan notes to finance the making or purchase of mortgage loans to sponsors of residential housing for the construction, rehabilitation or improvement of residential housing. The total amount of bonds, bond anticipation notes, and construction loan notes outstanding at any one time shall not exceed three billion dollars ($3,000,000,000) excluding therefrom any bond anticipation notes for the payment of which bonds have been issued. The principal of and the interest on such bonds or notes shall be payable solely from the funds herein provided for such payment. Any such notes may be made payable from the proceeds of bonds or renewal notes or, in the event bond or renewal note proceeds are not available, such notes may be paid from any available revenues or assets of the Agency. The bonds or notes of each issue shall be dated and may be made redeemable before maturity at the option of the Agency at such price or prices and under such terms and conditions as may be determined by the Agency. Any such bonds or notes shall bear interest at such rate or rates as may be determined by the Local Government Commission of North Carolina with the approval of the Agency. Notes shall mature at such time or times not exceeding 10 years from their date or dates and bonds shall mature at such time or times not exceeding 43 years from their date or dates, as may be determined by the Agency. The Agency shall determine the form and manner of execution of the bonds or notes, including any interest coupons to be attached thereto, and shall fix the denomination or denominations and the place or places of payment of principal and interest, which may be any bank or trust company within or without the State. In case any officer whose signature or a facsimile of whose signature shall appear on any bonds or notes or coupons attached thereto shall cease to be such officer before the delivery thereof, such signature or such facsimile shall nevertheless be valid and sufficient for all purposes the same as if he had remained in office until such delivery. The Agency may also provide for the authentication of the bonds or notes by a trustee or fiscal agent. The bonds or notes may be issued in coupon or in registered form, or both, as the Agency may determine, and provision may be made for the registration of any coupon bonds or notes as to principal alone and also as to both principal and interest, and for the reconversion into coupon bonds or notes of any bonds or notes registered as to both principal and interest, and for the interchange of registered and coupon bonds or notes. Upon the filing with the Local Government Commission of North Carolina of a resolution of the Agency requesting that its bonds and notes be sold, such bonds or notes may be sold in such manner, either at public or private sale, and for such price as the Commission shall determine to be for the best interest of the Agency and best effectuate the purposes of this Chapter, as long as the sale is approved by the Agency.

The proceeds of any bonds or notes shall be used solely for the purposes for which issued and shall be disbursed in such manner and under such restrictions, if any, as the Agency may provide in the resolution authorizing the issuance of such bonds or notes or in the trust agreement hereinafter mentioned securing the same.

Prior to the preparation of definitive bonds, the Agency may, under like restrictions, issue interim receipts or temporary bonds, with or without coupons, exchangeable for definitive bonds when such bonds shall have been executed and are available for delivery. The Agency may also provide for the replacement of any bonds or notes which shall become mutilated or shall be destroyed or lost.

Bonds or notes may be issued under the provisions of this Chapter without obtaining, except as otherwise expressly provided in this Chapter, the consent of any department, division, commission, board, body, bureau or agency of the State, and without any other proceedings or the happening of any conditions or things other than those proceedings, conditions or things which are specifically required by this Chapter and the provisions of the resolution authorizing the issuance of such bonds or notes or the trust agreement securing the same. (1969, c. 1235, s. 8; 1973, c. 1296, s. 48; 1979, c. 844; 1979, 2nd Sess., c. 1238, s. 2; 1981, c. 343; 1983 (Reg. Sess., 1984), c. 1062, s. 2; 1985, c. 769, s. 2; 1997-13, s. 1; 2001-185, s. 1.)

## § 122A-8.1. Powers of the State Treasurer.

Notwithstanding any other provisions of this act, the State Treasurer shall have the exclusive power to issue bonds and notes authorized under the act upon request of the Agency and with the approval of the Local Government Commission.

The State Treasurer in his sole discretion shall determine the interest rates, maturities, and other terms and conditions of the bonds and notes authorized by this act.

The North Carolina Housing Finance Agency shall determine when a bond issue is indicated. The Agency shall cooperate with the State Treasurer in structuring any bond issue in general, and also in soliciting proposals from financial consultants, underwriters, and bond attorneys.

The State Treasurer shall have the exclusive power to employ and designate the financial consultants, underwriters, and bond attorneys to be associated with the bond issue; provided, at least annually, the Treasurer shall seek the written recommendations of the Housing Finance Agency; and, subsequent to each bond issue, the Treasurer shall conduct a formal performance evaluation of the financial consultants, underwriters and bond attorneys which shall be open to public inspection.

The Director of the Budget shall provide to the State Treasurer the funds necessary to defray the costs incurred in performing the fiscal functions reserved to the Treasurer under this act from the funds allocated to the Agency pursuant to the 1975 Session Laws. Prior to taking any action under this paragraph, the Director of the Budget may consult with the Advisory Budget Commission.

Nothing in this act is intended to abrogate or diminish the inherent power of the State Treasurer to negotiate the terms and conditions of the bonds and notes, and to issue the bonds and notes authorized by General Statutes Chapter 122A. (1977, c. 673, s. 5; 1983, c. 717, s. 38; 1985, c. 723, s. 5; 1985 (Reg. Sess., 1986), c. 955, ss. 41, 42.)

## § 122A-9. Trust agreement or resolution.

In the discretion of the Agency any obligations issued under the provisions of this Chapter may be secured by a trust agreement by and between the Agency and a corporate trustee, which may be any trust company or bank having the powers of a trust company within or without the State. Such trust agreement or the resolution providing for the issuance of such obligations may pledge or assign all or any part of the revenues or assets of the Agency, including, without limitation, mortgage loans, mortgage loan commitments, contracts, agreements and other security or investment obligations, the fees or charges made or received by the Agency, the moneys received in payment of loans and interest thereon and any other moneys received or to be received by the Agency. Such trust agreement or resolution may contain such provisions for protecting and enforcing the rights and remedies of the holders of any such obligations as may be reasonable and proper and not in violation of law, including covenants setting forth the duties of the Agency in relation to the purposes to which obligation proceeds may be applied, the disposition or pledging of the revenues or assets of the Agency, the terms and conditions for the issuance of additional obligations, and the custody, safeguarding and application of all moneys. It shall be lawful for any bank or trust company incorporated under the laws of the State which may act as depositary of the proceeds of obligations, revenues or other money hereunder to furnish such indemnifying bonds or to pledge such securities as may be required by the Agency. Any such trust agreement or resolution may set forth the rights and remedies of the holders of any obligations and of the trustee, and may restrict the individual right of action by any such holders. In addition to the foregoing, any such trust agreement or resolution may contain such other provisions as the Agency may deem reasonable and proper for the security of the holders of any obligations. All expenses incurred in carrying out the provisions of such trust agreement or resolution may be paid from the revenues or assets pledged or assigned to the payment of the principal of and the interest on obligations or from any other funds available to the Agency. (1969, c. 1235, s. 9; 1973, c. 1296, s. 49.)

## § 122A-10. Validity of any pledge.

The pledge of any assets or revenues of the Agency to the payment of the principal of or the interest on any obligations of the Agency shall be valid and binding from the time when the pledge is made and any such assets or revenues shall immediately be subject to the lien of such pledge without any physical delivery thereof or further act, and the lien of any such pledge shall be valid and binding as against all parties having claims of any kind in tort, contract or otherwise against the Agency, irrespective of whether such parties have notice thereof. Nothing herein shall be construed to prohibit the Agency from selling any assets subject to any such pledge except to the extent that any such sale may be restricted by the trust agreement or resolution providing for the issuance of such obligations. (1969, c. 1235, s. 10; 1973, c. 1296, s. 50.)

## § 122A-11. Trust funds.

Notwithstanding any other provisions of law to the contrary, all moneys received pursuant to the authority of this Chapter shall be deemed to be trust funds to be held and applied solely as provided in this Chapter. The resolution authorizing any obligations or the trust agreement securing the same may provide that any of such moneys may be temporarily invested pending the disbursement thereof and shall provide that any officer with whom, or any bank or trust company with which, such moneys shall be deposited shall act as trustee of such moneys and shall hold and apply the same for the purposes hereof, subject to such regulations as this Chapter and such resolution or trust agreement may provide.

Any moneys received pursuant to the authority of this Chapter and any other moneys available to the Agency for investment may be invested:

(1) As provided in G.S. 159-30, except that for purposes of G.S. 159-30(b) the Agency may deposit moneys at interest in banks or trust companies outside as well as in this State, as long as any moneys at deposit outside this State are collateralized to the same extent and manner as if at deposit in this State;

(2) In evidences of ownership of, or fractional undivided interests in, future interest and principal payments on either direct obligations of the United States government or obligations the principal of and the interest on which are guaranteed by the United States government, which obligations are held by a bank or trust company organized and existing under the laws of the United States of America or any state in the capacity of custodian;

(3) In obligations which are collateralized by mortgage pass-through securities guaranteed by the Government National Mortgage Association, the Federal Home Loan Mortgage Corporation, or Fannie Mae;

(4) In a trust certificate or similar instrument evidencing an equity investment in a trust or other similar arrangement which is formed for the purpose of issuing obligations which are collateralized by mortgage pass-through or participation certificates guaranteed by the Government National Mortgage Association, the Federal Home Loan Mortgage Corporation or Fannie Mae; and

(5) In repurchase agreements with respect to (i) direct obligations of the United States government,

(ii) obligations the principal of and the interest on which are guaranteed by the United States government, or (iii) obligations described in G.S.159-30(c)(2), (3), (6), or (7), if all of the following conditions are met:

a. The repurchase agreement is entered into with an institution whose ability to pay its unsecured long-term obligations (including, if the institution is an insurance company, its claims paying ability) is rated in one of the two highest ratings categories by a nationally recognized securities rating agency. If the term of the repurchase agreement is for a period of one year or less, however, the repurchase agreement may be entered into with an institution that does not have such a long-term rating if its ability to pay its unsecured short-term obligations is rated in one of the two highest ratings categories by a nationally recognized securities rating agency. If the institution with which the agreement is to be entered does not meet the ratings requirement of this subparagraph, the repurchase agreement may nevertheless be entered into with the institution if the obligations of the institution under the repurchase agreement are fully guaranteed by another institution that does meet the ratings requirement of this subparagraph.

b. The repurchase agreement provides that it shall be terminated, without penalty, if the institution with which the repurchase agreement is entered or by whom the institution's obligations are guaranteed fails to maintain (i) in the event that the repurchase agreement was entered into in reliance upon the rating of the institution's long-term obligations, a rating of its long-term obligations in one of the three highest ratings categories by at least one nationally recognized securities rating agency, or (ii) in the event that the repurchase agreement was entered into in reliance upon the rating of the institution's short-term obligations, a rating of its short-term obligations in one of the two highest ratings categories by at least one nationally recognized securities rating agency. The repurchase agreement does not have to be terminated, however, if a new guarantor meeting the rating requirement set forth in subparagraph a. as the requirement necessary for the Agency to enter the repurchase agreement agrees to fully guarantee the obligations of the institution under the repurchase agreement.

c. The obligations that are subject to the repurchase agreement are delivered (in physical or in book entry form) to the Agency, or any financial institution serving either as trustee for obligations issued by the Agency or as fiscal agent for the Agency or the State Treasurer or are supported by a safekeeping receipt issued by a depository satisfactory to the Agency. The repurchase agreement must provide that the value of the underlying obligations shall be maintained at a current market value, calculated at least daily, of not less than one hundred percent (100%) of the repurchase price. The financial institution serving either as trustee or as fiscal agent for the Agency holding the obligations subject to the repurchase agreement hereunder or the depository issuing the safekeeping receipt shall not be the provider of the repurchase agreement.

d. A valid and perfected first security interest in the obligations which are the subject of the repurchase agreement has been granted to the Agency or its assignee or book entry procedures, conforming, to the extent practicable, with federal regulations and satisfactory to the agency have been established for the benefit of the Agency or its assignee.

e. The securities are free and clear of any adverse third-party claims.

f. The repurchase agreement is in a form satisfactory to the Agency. (1969, c. 1235, s. 11; 1973, c. 1296, s. 51; 1985, c. 479, s. 149(b); 1985 (Reg. Sess., 1986), c. 1014, s. 185; 1997-13, s. 2; 2001-181, s. 1.)

## § 122A-12. Remedies.

Any holder of obligations issued under the provisions of this Chapter or any coupons appertaining thereto, and the trustee under any trust agreement or resolution authorizing the issuance of such obligations, except to the extent the rights herein given may be restricted by such trust agreement or resolution, may, either at law or in equity, by suit, action, mandamus or other proceeding, protect and enforce any and all rights under the laws of the State or granted hereunder or under such trust agreement or resolution, or under any other contract executed by the Agency pursuant to this Chapter, and may enforce and compel the performance of all duties required by this Chapter or by such trust agreement or resolution to be performed by the Agency or by any officer thereof. (1969, c. 1235, s. 12; 1973, c. 1296, s. 52.)

## § 122A-13. Negotiable instruments.

Notwithstanding any of the foregoing provisions of this Chapter or any recitals in any obligations issued under the provisions of this Chapter, all such obligations and interest coupons appertaining thereto shall be and are hereby made negotiable instruments under the laws of this State, subject only to any applicable provisions for registration. (1969, c. 1235, s. 13.)

## § 122A-14. Obligations eligible for investment.

Obligations issued under the provisions of this Chapter are hereby made securities in which all public officers and public bodies of the State and its political subdivisions, all insurance companies, trust companies, banking associations, investment companies, executors, administrators, trustees and other fiduciaries may properly and legally invest funds, including capital in their control or belonging to them. Such obligations are hereby made securities which may properly and legally be deposited with and received by any State or municipal officer or any agency or political subdivision of the State for any purpose for which the deposit of bonds, notes or obligations of the State is now or may hereafter be authorized by law. (1969, c. 1235, s. 14.)

## § 122A-15. Refunding obligations.

The Agency is hereby authorized to provide for the issuance of refunding obligations for the purpose of refunding any obligations then outstanding which shall have been issued under the provisions of this Chapter, including the payment of any redemption premium thereon and any interest accrued or to accrue to the date of redemption of such obligations and, if deemed advisable by the Agency, for any corporate purpose of the Agency. The issuance of such obligations, the maturities and other details thereof, the rights of the holders thereof, and the rights, duties and obligations of the Agency in respect of the same shall be governed by the provisions of this Chapter which relate to the issuance of obligations, insofar as such provisions may be appropriate therefor.

Refunding obligations may be sold or exchanged for outstanding obligations issued under this Chapter and, if sold, the proceeds thereof may be applied, in addition to any other authorized purposes, to the purchase, redemption or payment of such outstanding obligations. Pending the application of the proceeds of any such refunding obligations, with any other available funds, to the payment of the principal, accrued interest and any redemption premium on the obligations being refunded, and, if so provided or permitted in the resolution authorizing the issuance of such refunding obligations or in the trust agreement securing the same, to the payment of any interest on such refunding obligations and any expenses in connection with such refunding, such proceeds may be invested in direct obligations of, or obligations the

principal of and the interest on which are unconditionally guaranteed by, the United States of America which shall mature or which shall be subject to redemption by the holders thereof, at the option of such holders, not later than the respective dates when the proceeds, together with the interest accruing thereon, will be required for the purposes intended. (1965, c. 1235, s. 15; 1973, c. 1296, s. 55.)

## § 122A-16. Oversight by committees of General Assembly; annual reports.

The Finance Committee of the House of Representatives and the Finance Committee of the Senate shall exercise continuing oversight of the Agency in order to assure that the Agency is effectively fulfilling its statutory purpose; provided, however, that nothing in this Chapter shall be construed as required by the Agency to receive legislative approval for the exercise of any of the powers granted by this Chapter. The Agency shall, promptly following the close of each fiscal year, submit an annual report of its activities for the preceding year to the Governor, the Office of State Budget and Management, State Auditor, the aforementioned committees of the General Assembly, the Advisory Budget Commission and the Local Government Commission. Each such report shall set forth a complete operating and financial statement of the Agency during such year. The Agency shall cause an audit of its books and accounts to be made at least once in each year by an independent certified public accountant and the cost thereof may be paid from any available moneys of the Agency. The Agency shall on January 1 and July 1 of each year submit a written report of its activities to the Joint Legislative Commission on Governmental Operations. The Agency shall also at the end of each fiscal year submit a written report of its budget expenditures by line item to the Joint Legislative Commission on Governmental Operations. (1969, c. 1235, s. 16; 1973, c. 1296, s. 56; 1977, c. 673, s. 3; c. 771, s. 4; 1981, c. 895, s. 4; 1981 (Reg. Sess., 1982), c. 1191, s. 34; 1983 (Reg. Sess., 1984), c. 1034, s. 134; 2000-140, s. 93.1(a); 2001-424, s. 12.2(b).)

## § 122A-17. Officers not liable.

No member or other officer of the Agency shall be subject to any personal liability or accountability by reason of his execution of any obligations or the issuance thereof. (1969, c. 1235, s. 17; 1973, c. 1296, s. 57.)

## § 122A-18. Authorization to accept appropriated moneys.

The Agency is authorized to accept such moneys as may be appropriated from time to time by the General Assembly for effectuating its corporate purposes including, without limitation, the payment of the initial expenses of administration and operation and the establishment of a reserve or contingency fund to be available for the payment of the principal of and the interest on any bonds or notes of the Agency. (1969, c. 1235, s. 18; 1973, c. 1296, s. 58.)

## § 122A-19. Tax exemption.

The exercise of the powers granted by this Chapter will be in all respects for the benefit of the people of the State, for their well-being and prosperity and for the improvement of their social and economic conditions, and the Agency shall not be required to pay any tax or assessment on any property owned by the Agency under the provisions of this Chapter or upon the income therefrom.

Any obligations issued by the Agency under the provisions of this Chapter shall at all times be free from taxation by the State or any local unit or political subdivision or other instrumentality of the State, excepting inheritance or gift taxes, income taxes on the gain from the transfer of the obligations, and franchise taxes. The interest on the obligations is not subject to taxation as income. (1969, c. 1235, s. 19; 1973, c. 1296, s. 59; 1995, c. 46, s. 10.)

## § 122A-20. Conflict of interest.

If any member, officer or employee of the Agency shall be interested either directly or indirectly, or shall be an officer or employee of or have an ownership interest in any firm or corporation interested directly or indirectly in any contract with the Agency, including any loan to any sponsor, builder or developer, such interest shall be disclosed to the Agency and shall be set forth in the minutes of the Agency, and the member, officer or employee having such interest therein shall not participate on behalf of the Agency in the authorization of any such contract. (1969, c. 1235, s. 20; 1973, c. 1296, s. 60.)

## § 122A-21. Additional method.

The foregoing sections of this Chapter shall be deemed to provide an additional and alternative method for the doing of the things authorized thereby and shall be regarded as supplemental and additional to powers conferred by other laws, and shall not be regarded as in derogation of any powers now existing; provided, however, that the issuance of bonds or notes under the provisions of this Chapter need not comply with the requirements of any other law applicable to the issuance of bonds or notes. (1969, c. 1235, s. 21.)

## § 122A-22. Chapter liberally construed.

This Chapter, being necessary for the prosperity of the State and its inhabitants, shall be liberally construed to effect the purposes thereof. (1969, c. 1235, s. 22.)

## § 122A-23. Inconsistent laws inapplicable.

Insofar as the provisions of this Chapter are inconsistent with the provisions of any general or special laws, or parts thereof, the provisions of this Chapter shall be controlling. (1969, c. 1235, s. 24.)

# Other Important Statutes— North Carolina Housing Trust

North Carolina Housing Trust.
G.S. Chapter 122E.
North Carolina Housing Trust and Oil Overcharge Act.

## § 122E-1. Short title.

This Chapter shall be known and may be cited as the "North Carolina Housing Trust and Oil Overcharge Act." (1987, c. 841, s. 1.)

## § 122E-2. Definitions.

As used in this Chapter:

(1) The term "substandard unit" means a housing unit which, by reason of dilapidation, deterioration, age or obsolescence, inadequate provision for ventilation, light, air, sanitation, or open spaces, high density of population and overcrowding, unsanitary or unsafe conditions, or the existence of conditions which endanger life or property by fire and other causes, or any combination of such factors, is conducive to ill health, transmission of disease, or has an adverse effect upon the public health, safety, morals or welfare of its inhabitants.

(2) The term "Partnership" means the North Carolina Housing Partnership.

(3) The term "Agency" means the North Carolina Housing Finance agency.

(4) The term "Fund" means the North Carolina Housing Trust Fund.

(5) The term "Treasurer" means the North Carolina State Treasurer.

(6) The term "affordable housing unit" means a unit for which an occupant is paying no more than thirty percent (30%) of gross monthly household income for rent and utilities.

(7) The term "Stripper Well Litigation Funds" means funds received by North Carolina, and all interest and other income generated by such funds, pursuant to the Settlement Agreement that was approved by Order of the Court, dated July 7, 1986, in In re: The Department of Energy Stripper Well Exemption Litigation M.D.L. No. 378 (D. Kan.).

(8) The term "Diamond Shamrock Litigation Funds" means funds received by North Carolina, and all interest and other income generated by such funds, pursuant to the Order of the Court, dated June 6, 1986, in Diamond Shamrock Refining and Marketing Co. v. Standard Oil Co., Civil Action No. C2-84-1432 (S.D. Ohio). (1987, c. 841, s. 1.)

## § 122E-3. North Carolina Housing Trust Fund.

(a) There is established a North Carolina Housing Trust Fund, separate and distinct from the General Fund.

(b) The Fund shall consist of monies received under this act and any other sources of revenue, public or private, dedicated for inclusion in the Fund.

(c) The State Treasurer shall serve as trustee for the Fund. The Treasurer shall invest the North Carolina Housing Trust Fund revenues he receives as provided in G.S. 147-69.2(b). The Treasurer shall provide the Agency with quarterly and annual reports of Fund revenues and interest earnings. (1987, c. 841, s. 1.)

## § 122E-4. North Carolina Housing Partnership created; compensation; organization.

(a) The North Carolina Housing Partnership is hereby created within the North Carolina Housing Finance Agency to establish policy, promulgate rules and regulations, and oversee the operation of the Fund. The Partnership shall be constituted to coordinate private enterprise and investment with public efforts to address the serious shortage of decent, safe, and affordable housing for low and moderate income citizens of this State.

(b) The Partnership shall consist of 13 members as follows:

(1) The Executive Director of the North Carolina Housing Finance Agency shall serve ex officio;

(2) The Secretary of the Department of Commerce or his designee shall serve ex officio;

(3) The State Treasurer or his designee shall serve ex officio;

(4) In accordance with G.S. 120-121, five members shall be appointed by the General Assembly upon the recommendation of the President Pro Tempore of the Senate, provided that one member shall be a representative of the homebuilding industry, one member shall be a low income housing advocate, and one member shall be a representative of the League of Municipalities;

(5) In accordance with G.S. 120-121, five members shall be appointed by the General Assembly upon the recommendation of the Speaker of the House of Representatives, provided that one member shall be a representative of the real estate lending industry; one member shall be a representative of a non-profit housing development corporation; and one member shall be a resident of low income housing.

The members of the Partnership shall elect one of their members to serve as Chairman for a term of one year. Seven members of the Partnership shall constitute a quorum. All members shall have the right to vote on all issues before the Partnership.

(c) Members of the Partnership shall serve for three year terms. Initial terms shall begin on September 1, 1987. Appointed members shall serve until their successors are appointed and qualify.

(d) Vacancies in the offices of any appointed members shall be filled in accordance with G.S. 120-122 for the remainder of the unexpired term. No vacant office shall be included in the determination of a quorum. No vacancy in office shall impair the rights of the members to exercise all rights and conduct the official business of the Partnership.

(e) Members of the Partnership shall receive as compensation for each day spent on work for the Partnership such actual expenses as may be incurred for such travel and subsistence in the performance of official duties and such per diem as is allowed by law for other such State boards and commissions. Members shall not receive a salary for the performance of their duties as members.

(f) The Partnership shall have the following powers and duties:

(1) To promulgate rules and regulations governing all policy matters relating to the implementation of all programs for uses of the Fund and the Partnership's oversight of the Agency's administration of the Fund.

(2) To promote the development of a coordinated State low income housing plan.

(3) To obtain necessary information from other State agencies concerning housing; and

(4) To allocate monies contained in the Fund.

(g) The Partnership may appoint an Executive Director. The Executive Director shall be empowered to employ such additional professional and clerical assistance as the Partnership may deem necessary to administer the provisions of this Chapter. All employees of the Partnership, other than the Executive Director, shall be compensated in accordance with the salary schedules adopted pursuant to the State Personnel Act. The Partnership and the Agency may enter into agreements for the use of Agency staff to assist the Partnership and the provision of administrative support for the Partnership by the Agency.

(h) The Partnership shall meet quarterly and can meet more regularly upon the call of the Chairman or upon written request of four members.

(i) Members of the Partnership may not receive any direct benefit from, or participate in, the programs of the Fund Members of the Partnership may be employed by, or serve as a board member of, a nonprofit entity participating in a program of the Fund if the member discloses the employment or the membership in the minutes of the Partnership and does not vote on any matter pertaining to the entity's participation. This policy applies to:

(1) Individual members of the Partnership;

(2) Businesses, corporations, or partnerships owned in whole or in part by members of the Partnership; and

(3) The immediate family members of the members of the Partnership. (1987, c. 841, s. 1; 1989, c. 727, s. 223(c); c. 751, ss. 7(12), 9(c); c. 754, s. 53; 1991 (Reg. Sess., 1992), c. 959, s. 31; 1995, c. 490, s. 25.)

## § 122E-5. Administration.

(a) The North Carolina Housing Finance Agency shall administer the Fund in accordance with the policies, rules and regulations promulgated by the Partnership.

(b) The Agency's responsibilities shall include:

(1) The Management of the overall program for the use of the fund;

(2) Development of program design in accordance with policies established by the Partnership;

(3) Development and management of a selection system in accordance with policies established by the Partnership;

(4) Provision of technical assistance to prospective applicants; and

(5) Monitoring of projects to ensure compliance with applicable State and federal laws and regulations and relevant court decisions.

(6) The Agency shall promulgate rules and regulations governing the administration of the Fund and its overall program for use of the Fund in accordance with the policies, rules and regulations promulgated by the Partnership.

(c) In administering the Fund, the Agency shall maintain a separate account for and shall keep separate records regarding the principal and expenditures made from the Stripper Well Litigation funds and the Diamond Shamrock Litigation funds in order to assure the proper expenditure and reporting of these funds to the respective courts and to the United States Department of Energy.

(d) The Agency shall file all required reports with the appropriate courts in the Stripper Well Litigation and in the Diamond Shamrock Litigation, and otherwise shall fully comply with all relevant court orders. The Agency also shall file the report of planned expenditures which is required under Paragraph II. B. 3. f. iv of the Final Settlement Agreement in the Stripper Well Litigation prior to its first expenditure of Stripper Well Litigation Funds. (1987, c. 841, s. 1.)

## § 122E-6. Uses of funds.

Funds from the Fund shall be used to increase the supply of decent, affordable and energy-efficient housing for low, very low, and moderate income residents of the State as defined in G.S. 122E-2. Such funds shall be used to finance, in whole or in part, projects and activities eligible under this section. The Agency shall make available loans, grants, interest reduction payments, or other comparable forms of assistance to eligible applicants. Provided, however, that with regard to those funds of the Fund which are Stripper Well Litigation Funds or Diamond Shamrock Funds, grants shall be from both the principal and income generated by the principal of such Funds so that all such Funds will be expended within a reasonable period of time. Provided, further, that with regard to that portion of the Fund which is derived from the appropriation of State funds, the amount of grants to be made in any fiscal year shall be limited to the amount of income generated by the principal of that portion of the Fund.

(a) Beneficiaries.

(1) The Partnership shall ensure that the Agency's program for uses of monies from the Fund directly benefit low, very low and moderate income persons and families as set forth in subsections (2), (3), and (4) below.

(2) The Partnership shall ensure that at least thirty percent (30%) of the total funds from the Fund eligible for expenditure by the Agency in any fiscal year directly benefit persons and families whose incomes do not exceed thirty percent (30%) of the median family income for the local area, with adjustments for family size, according to the latest figures available from the U.S. Department of Housing and Urban Development.

(3) The Partnership shall be authorized to allocate up to thirty percent (30%) of the total funds from the Fund for the benefit of persons and families whose incomes do not exceed fifty percent (50%) of the median family income for the local area, with adjustments for family size, according to the latest figures available from the U.S. Department of Housing and Urban Development; provided, however, these funds may also be directed for the benefit of the persons and families defined in subsection (2).

(4) The Partnership shall ensure that no more than forty percent (40%) of the total funds from the fund eligible for expenditure by the Agency in any fiscal year directly benefit persons and families whose incomes do not exceed eighty percent (80%) of the median family income for the local area, with adjustments for family size, according to the latest figures available from the U.S. Department of Housing and Urban Development.

(b) Eligible Projects.

(1) An eligible project consists of one or more residential buildings containing similarly constructed units, the site on which the building(s)

is located and any functionally related facilities. Multiple buildings may constitute a project only if bounded together as a result of proximate location, or common ownership and financing.

(2) Projects which provide for the construction or rehabilitation of rental projects must contain contractual guarantees to ensure that at least twenty percent (20%) of the units are occupied by persons and families defined in G.S. 122E-6(a) (2) and (3) for a period of time following the award of grants or loan funds from the Fund, said period to be not less than 10 years, and shall be established by the rules and regulations promulgated by the Partnership and are affordable housing units as defined in G.S. 122E-2(9) [G.S. 122E-2(6)].

(c) Eligible Uses for State Appropriated Funds. Eligible activities include, but are not limited to the following:

(1) Rehabilitation, including weatherization, of sub-standard housing units;

(2) Assistance for costs of necessary studies, surveys, plans and permits, engineering, legal and architectural and other technical services;

(3) New construction, including costs of land acquisition and site preparation;

(4) Assistance for the construction or rehabilitation of shelters for the homeless;

(5) Assistance in the development of manufactured housing sites which constitute eligible projects as defined in subsection (b) of this section. The Agency may contract with outside organizations to provide such assistance; and

(6) Such other programs which increase the supply of decent and affordable housing for low, very low, and moderate income persons which the Partnership shall deem appropriate to meet the purposes stated in this section.

(d) Eligible Uses for Stripper Well Litigation Funds and Diamond Shamrock Litigation Funds.

(1) Eligible uses for the Stripper Well Litigation funds shall be those uses permitted under Paragraph II.B.3.f.ii. of the Settlement Agreement that was approved by Order of the Court, dated July 7, 1986, including, but not limited to, those residential energy-related uses which are identified in Exhibit J to said Settlement Agreement.

(2) Eligible uses for the Diamond Shamrock Litigation funds shall be those uses permitted under Exhibit B to the Order of the Court, dated June 6, 1986, including but no [not] limited to those residential energy-related uses which are identified in Attachment C to Exhibit B to said Order. (1987, c. 841, s. 1.)

## § 122E-7. Eligible applicants.

Eligible applicants shall include units of State and local governments including municipal corporations, for profit and nonprofit housing developers. Provided, however, that the Partnership's rules and regulations shall ensure an equitable distribution of Fund funds based upon population and low and moderate income housing needs across the State. (1987, c. 841, s. 1.)

## § 122E-8. Allocation of funds.

(a) Monies within the Fund shall be allocated to eligible applicants under this Chapter by the Agency, in accordance with funding cycles established at least annually. The Partnership shall establish rules and regulations with full public input, including at least one public hearing for which adequate notice is provided in a timely manner. These rules and regulations shall establish general policies governing the eligibility of applicants, application procedures, project eligibility requirements, and the criteria and standards for awarding grants and loans. Such rules and regulations shall be adopted within 270 days from the effective date of this Chapter.

(b) The Agency shall promulgate rules and regulations governing the review of applications for assistance and the awarding of grants or loans under this Chapter in accordance with the rules and regulations adopted pursuant to subsection (a) above. The rules and regulations shall provide that if an application is rejected, the Agency shall detail in writing the reasons for the rejection.

(c) The Agency shall give priority to applications providing for:

(1) The improvement of existing housing stock which is affordable for low and very low income families;

(2) The construction of housing units for very low income families; and

(3) The leveraging of Fund monies by combination with other private or governmental loan grant or bond financing programs.

(d) The Agency shall also give priority to applications which include provisions such as:

(1) Interest rates and loan terms more favorable than those conventionally offered;

(2) Developer contributions to project costs;

(3) Local government contributions to project costs, including infrastructure improvements, contributions of publicly owned land for housing development, and the provision of funds for such services as child care and job training;

(4) Coordination with other housing and/or infrastructure investments in the community;

(5) Provision of housing to the disabled, single parent households, or rurally isolated households; or

(6) Provision of housing to persons whose current housing fails to meet basic standards of health and

safety and who have little prospect of improving the condition of their housing except by residing in an eligible project receiving assistance under this Chapter. (1987, c. 841, s. 1; 1997-506, s. 44.)

## § 122E-9. Displacement.

In establishing criteria for G.S. 122E-8(a), the Agency shall give special attention to designing protections to provide that any lawful occupants who live in a project as defined in G.S. 122E-6(b) prior to rehabilitation or demolition shall not be displaced as a result of such activity, other than temporarily, in which case suitable relocation arrangements shall be provided. The Agency shall promulgate rules concerning acquisition of property and relocation. (1987, c. 841, s. 1.)

# Index

www.ingramcontent.com/pod-product-compliance
Lightning Source LLC
Chambersburg PA
CBHW081436270326
41932CB00019B/3221